Praise for The Space of t

'One of the most pressing questions of our time is the impact of social media on our life-world and our sense of self. This book by Nick Couldry provides the most subtle, far-reaching and theoretically balanced answer to that question yet. In an admirable mixture of sociological observations, philosophical reflections and political considerations, the author succeeds in describing the devastating effects and the small potentials that the internet brings with it in terms of political life and human interaction.'
Axel Honneth, Jack B. Weinstein Professor of the Humanities,
Columbia University

'Nick Couldry's *The Space of the World* is a truly astonishing book. His analysis digs much deeper than the design of the digital platform industry; he relates the problems of a toxic digital world to the commercialization of public space and climate change. This first part of a monumental trilogy opens much-needed vistas into the future of humanity, way beyond the digital domain. Indeed, if humans aspire to a future on this planet, that future needs humanizing: solidarity, connectedness, communal rationality.'
José van Dijck, Professor of Media and Digital Society at
Utrecht University and author of *The Culture of Connectivity* and
The Platform Society

'Nick Couldry writes with urgency, clarity, purpose and deep feeling about what we have lost in ceding our digital spaces to large platform companies – and what we can get back, for ourselves and for humanity, by choosing another path. As we stand on the precipice of a new digital era, Couldry is issuing a visionary call to reconsider our design choices of the last few decades and redesign social media from the ground up.'
Eli Pariser, Co-Director, New_ Public

'Humanity is what exists in the spaces that neither capitalism nor computers knows how to define. As always, Nick Couldry brings a unique and necessary rigour to our shared quest for a more humane, intuitive and resonance-based approach to designing a digital society from the bottom up.'
Douglas Rushkoff, author of *Team Human* and *Survival of the Richest*

'Technologies are made by humans, yet not always humane. Couldry takes a deep dive into how capitalist norms render social justice an afterthought, and how this impacts our technologies and our futures. A much-needed manifesto for our civic future.'

Zizi Papacharissi, author of *After Democracy:*
Imagining our Political Future

'Couldry makes a clear and unambiguous argument for how Big Tech has taken over the digital "space of the world" and contributed to the multiple crises the world is now facing. But, rather than wallowing in despair, he invites us to take the first steps towards a different solidaristic future in the hope that these will resonate far and wide and build action for social change. Pragmatic and hopeful, Couldry encourages us to see that another world is not only possible but has already begun to be built.'

Natalie Fenton, Goldsmiths, University of London, and author of
Democratic Delusions

The Space of the World

To Louise

THE SPACE OF THE WORLD

Can Human Solidarity Survive
Social Media and What If It Can't?

Nick Couldry

polity

First published in 2025 by Polity Press

Polity Press
65 Bridge Street
Cambridge CB2 1UR, UK

Polity Press
111 River Street
Hoboken, NJ 07030, USA

ISBN-13: 978-1-5095-5472-0
ISBN-13: 978-1-5095-5473-7(pb)

A catalogue record for this book is available from the British Library.

Library of Congress Control Number: 2024934002

Typeset in 11.5 on 14pt Adobe Garamond
by Fakenham Prepress Solutions, Fakenham, Norfolk NR21 8NL
Printed and bound in Great Britain by CPI Group (UK) Ltd, Croydon

For further information on Polity, visit our website:
politybooks.com

Contents

Figures

Preface to Humanising the Future *Trilogy*

It has become a cliché to say we live in an age of multiple and seemingly permanent crises.

A crisis of global and local inequality, as the violent legacies of capitalism and colonialism pile up, and the challenge of redressing them becomes ever more urgent. A crisis of human recognition, as a century or more of attempts to rebalance injustices in human relations (between men and women, between ethnicities, between sexualities, between bodies of different abilities) is being challenged, retrenched and even reversed. And the all-encompassing crisis of climate change, which brings the threat of planetary catastrophe ever closer.

All these crises demand a fundamental reordering of what and why we think and write. The climate crisis does this most drastically, because it threatens the terrestrial horizon in which every other human struggle must play out. It not only requires us to adjust our actions, but also, in the words of climate scientist Mike Hulme, 'to rethink and renegotiate our wider social goals about how and why we live on this planet'.[1] For me, as someone who does social theory, not climate science, it raises the further question of how well human beings are placed to reorganise their lives, collaboratively or not, as the climate crisis will without doubt require.

I hope over three books to reconsider the terrain of social life from the perspective of this last issue, a question that might seem to one side of the climate emergency but is, in fact, closely implicated with our capacities for responding to it.

In this, the first book, I will ask: is human solidarity possible in a world of continuous digital connection and commercially managed platforms for conducting social life, and what if it isn't? (It is clear that we won't address the climate emergency without more solidarity between us.)

In the second book, to be called *Corporatising the Mind*, I will investigate the impact on human beings' self-understanding of recent perspectives on the brain and human intelligence, above all the idea (or myth) of artificial intelligence: what harm does that myth do to longer-established ideas of human reflection and reason? (Unless human beings respect their capacities for intelligent reflexive action, they may not be motivated to face the problem of climate change at all.)

In the third book, I hope to explore what role art and human creativity, and more broadly imagination, can still play in broadening and deepening humans' understanding of themselves in these extreme times, and as a result how they can contribute in unexpected and positive ways to our adequacy as a species in the face of the climate emergency.

I have called this projected trilogy *Humanising the Future*. The reason is simple. Unless we find positive answers to the three problems investigated in these books – the problem of a toxic digital world, the problem of a discounted view of human rationality and the problem of sustaining imaginative freedom – there is unlikely to be a future for humans.

I use the word 'human' here with caution. For there will be no succeeding in any of these struggles unless human beings reassess fundamentally who and what they are, and, just as important, what they have been and have done. There can be no question of retreating back into inherited views of humanity's supposed great past achievements. On the contrary, it is a matter, as Joanna Zylinska has well said, of finding 'ways of becoming better in the world'.[2]

But, equally, there is no future in abandoning our responsibilities and history as a species, in pursuit of speculations about the posthuman, let alone the post-planetary. It is a matter then of redefining what 'humanising' means, while protecting our better possibilities from ever-expanding forces of extraction and domination.

That at least is the hope on which this project rests.

Nick Couldry
Islip, UK
March 2024

PART 1

Introduction: What Have We Done?

'The natural state of the world is not connected.' (Andrew Bosworth, Facebook executive, 2016)[1]

'Connected lives become selectively, variably and sometimes acutely vulnerable lives.' (Onora O'Neill, philosopher, 1996)[2]

Between two and three decades ago, humanity made a huge mistake. The mistake was to delegate to businesses, whose overriding goal is profit and value extraction, the construction and management of the spaces where our social life unfolds. We handed over to businesses the design of our social world. This is something we should never have done.

By spaces, I don't mean buildings, town squares or street plans.[3] I mean the highly artificial spaces, built through computer software and hardware, that today, in effect, regulate what interactions count as social and how meaning circulates through those interactions – to whom, in what sequence, over what distance and at what speed. We call those spaces 'platforms'.

Platforms help us manage our relations with a much larger space that is also artificial: the space of *almost all possible* information and inter-action spaces that is the internet. Huge hope was placed on the internet as a realm of infinite human connection. But the way we chose to bring that space into everyday focus contained a fatal flaw.

We handed over to businesses decisions that, until thirty years ago, no business would ever have dreamed of taking: decisions about the design of social life itself. Their decisions proved reckless, and today we suffer the consequences. Just consider a sample of the internet- and social media-related problems troubling policymakers today, as evidenced by media stories in the UK and elsewhere from the past three years.

Eight-year-old Lalani Walton from Texas and nine-year-old Arriani Arroya from Wisconsin died from the effects of daring 'challenges'

3

that they learned about on TikTok.[4] In the UK, press speculated that twelve-year-old Archie Battersbee had died after taking a similar TikTok challenge; however, the inquest found persistent bullying on WhatsApp as the cause.[5] UK teachers and police expressed concern about how far-right-wing extremists are increasingly using social media to groom young children, mainly boys, for participation in their activities, while journalists based in Ireland and the US expressed concerns at how Facebook and Instagram are becoming markets for child trafficking.[6] The US state of New Mexico is suing Meta for being 'prime locations' for sexual predators to target children.[7] In China, under pressure from the government, TenCent limited the hours children spend playing games on its platform.[8] As to adults, the UK's Financial Conduct Authority recently concluded that Facebook and Instagram are serving as 'gateways' for financial fraudsters to reach innocent people.[9] Indeed Meta has been cited as the location of more than half the digital payment scams and two-thirds of online shopping scams in the UK.[10]

I could go on . . . But in case it merely seems that pre-existing social problems are moving online, consider problems of a different sort.

Supporters of defeated ex-President Bolsonaro who plotted to storm Brazil's capital in January 2023 used WhatsApp, Telegram and other platforms to help them broadcast live video of the coup attempt.[11] In the migrant crisis affecting Europe, the Middle East and North Africa, social media platforms such as Facebook and Twitter have been amplifiers of racist abuse linked to subsequent physical attacks.[12] In Kenya, Facebook faced calls in 2022 to be banned for failing to censor hate speech that fuelled ethnical conflict, with TikTok being similarly criticised.[13] In South Asia, anti-caste abuse has exploded in recent years in part because, according to one Dalit activist, 'physical distance is no longer a barrier to these abusers', when they can use Facebook and other social media with inadequate moderation processes.[14] Frances Haugen, an ex-Instagram employee, in autumn 2021 testified to the US Congress on Instagram's role in stimulating membership of extremist groups that promoted hate speech against Myanmar's Muslim Rohingya minority, including through its own recommendation tools.[15] In 2022 researchers in the journal *Nature* reported evidence of growing polarisation around climate change issues among people of all ages on social media.[16]

This second set of examples makes clear that something about social media is shaping how politics unfolds today. Sadly both types of problem I have outlined are becoming familiar: they have featured in countless critiques of how our digital platforms extract data for profit. But there is something connecting all these cases that has been less noticed. It has to do with space.

Over the past three decades, humanity devised an infinitely large, information-saturated, social space in which today almost everyone lives and interacts. I will call this space the *space of the world*. Beyond all the details and policy dilemmas associated with digital platforms, it is *this* that needs to be examined, and, I'll argue, fundamentally redesigned. The term 'space of the world' refers both to the toxic social world invented for us by Big Tech and to the less toxic social world that we might recover if we take action to correct for Big Tech's errors. Quite simply, we built the wrong space of the world and now we need to build a better one.

I say '*humanity* devised', but in reality it was some very specific elites, almost all in rich countries. If we want to challenge the current space of the world, that will mean confronting those elites' power head-on. Note: I am *not* saying the trends underlying the stories just told have social media as their sole cause.[17] Far from it. But, as later chapters show, social media – the space for interaction that social media distinctively make possible – is a key factor that amplifies and extends underlying social concerns; indeed, given the overwhelming circum-stantial evidence, it would be strange not to consider social media as a causal factor.

Commercial platforms don't want to hear this, because it goes to the core of how they make money. It is not something many academic and tech commentators want to talk about, because they, like most of us, have had to adapt to 'platform society',[18] whatever their misgivings. Indeed, today's space of the world is a deeply inconvenient problem for *any of us* to confront, given how much of our everyday life has moved online, and particularly onto social media platforms. But we must face directly how we got things so wrong, and talk openly about what we can do to correct it. That means identifying the underlying problem: the space of the world that resulted from commercial and policy decisions taken up to three decades ago.

Social Engineering by Default

It might seem extraordinary that such a wide set of problems – from adolescent mental health to the growth of financial fraud, from polarised political conflict to the unnecessarily fractious debate about the climate emergency – should have one factor in common, a factor that results from decisions humans made just a few years back. But the fact that we recklessly damaged and then failed to repair our space of the world is itself a measure of how strangely our relations with technology evolved in the past three decades.

The Problem With Our Space of the World

For sure, the problem is not exactly with online space, but with the *social space* that results when we spend so much time online, including on what we call 'social' media. We urgently need to understand this social space better. And that's not easy, because the sorts of changes under way are not ones we are used to thinking about. They are changes that pass by unnoticed unless we ask some seemingly abstract questions about the digital spaces in which we now spend so much of our time.

What we're concerned with here involves what we might call for convenience *information space*, rather than the physical spaces where people live (their homes, streets, playgrounds and so on). *Those* physical spaces are not filling up with evil in new ways, at least not directly; nor are traditional, old-style media becoming noticeably more toxic than in the past. No, the change is happening somewhere else.

Throughout history, the information spaces that we access (via messages or newspapers or, now, our social media newsfeeds) have been part of how we live. When our information spaces take on new dimensions, then the overall space where we live (the social world we inhabit) is changed too. Changes in information space are hardly new: information space has changed every time new information technologies have been introduced (from newspapers to the novel, from the telegraph to television), enabling people to communicate with each other over ever-longer distances. But in the past thirty years our information space has changed in truly unprecedented ways.

6

Today our expanded information space includes almost everyone and gives them access to unimaginably large amounts of content. It has become massively faster: sitting on one side of the planet, I can point to an image or article, so you see it the next moment on the other side of the planet. And it operates in a massively more dynamic way: in principle, everyone, wherever they are, can not only receive, but also upload, information so that it becomes accessible by anyone anywhere; the receivers too can comment and recommend things, wherever they are. When our power is cut or for other reasons we lose online access, we suddenly realise the importance of that expanded information space in our lives.

And there's one final change that's even more striking: information space's new designability and controllability. We enter today's massively fast, global and everywhere-accessible information space through access-points (platforms like Facebook or WeChat, YouTube or TikTok) that do not exist naturally, but have been designed, very largely, by commercial corporations, to meet *their* needs, which are not necessarily ours. Their needs include managing and nudging how we move around in their platforms, tracking and storing everything we do there, and in these ways serving a larger goal (again, theirs not ours), which is to generate as much economic value as possible from our engagement with the platform.

Bring all that together and you have a completely unprecedented change, not just in information space, but in the whole social world we inhabit. And this is the most shocking thing: in past eras, new technologies circulated information across space, and, of course, that had consequences, but there remained plenty of spaces – real social spaces – where the information that technologies circulated *didn't reach*, where the influence and imperatives of business *were absent*. This changed when we started carrying connected computer devices with us wherever we went and allowed commercial forces to manage those devices, their connections, and the infrastructures that supported those connections.

At that point, mere information space began to overlay ever more intensively two other types of space: the physical space where our bodies move and the social space comprised by our everyday social interactions (whether in physical or information space). Today information space saturates our physical spaces and our social spaces to such a degree that all now seem indistinguishable. The result is a social *world* so different from that of previous eras that we need a special term to help us think about it: the space of the world. We need a social theory that investigates that space's implications for social life on the broadest scale. This book develops that theory.

It is not that earlier eras didn't, implicitly, have their own 'space of the world'. They did, as we realise when we think about how the circulation of information in society changed in the era of the printing press. But in those earlier eras, the space of social life, as expanded by circulating information, did not need a name, because no one imagined anyone controlling or managing it. We are, after all, talking about something mind-bogglingly large: the space of *almost all possible* spaces in which human beings and their communications interact. But today we do need a new term – the 'space of the world' – to name this previously taken-for-granted background feature of human existence. Why? Because now it is designable, and quite possibly for the worse. This transformation is, I will argue, at the root of all the problems listed at the start of the chapter, and many more. Which is why we can only address those problems if we have a language to describe that transformation.

Today's transformed space of the world brings with it an important new type of institutional power. Around three decades ago vast numbers of people started connecting to each other by email, listserv and by viewing each other's webpages. Around two decades ago we started connecting to each other also through a more limited number of online platforms and access-points (Facebook, Twitter, Instagram, WhatsApp, Telegram, WeChat and more recently TikTok, plus all their related message services). When all that happened, an extraordinary new type of power devolved to the people and corporations who design those access-points, whether search engines, platforms or apps. The power literally to design the space in which our social lives play out: the power to design the space of the world.

Why do I say the space *of the world*, not the space of social media? Because vast numbers of us, across the world, are living much of what's important and trivial in our lives with social media, through social media, in social media. Social media platforms, for many purposes, have *become* our world and, even more important, the world where we expect each other to be.

The parents of Lalani Walton maybe didn't know much about TikTok, but their daughter's use of it had devastating impacts on their lives all the same. When 3 billion of the planet's inhabitants use Facebook but just a few of its inhabitants use a GoPro camera to broadcast their atrocities live via a feature of Facebook or Instagram, as did the Christchurch mosque mass murderer in March 2018 and the killer in Louisville, Kentucky in April 2023,[19] social space gets corrupted for all of us. Corrupted not exactly through the intention of those platforms' designers, but as a direct result of something Meta executives *did* design: their platform's functions, the way they interface with the rest of the internet and the business model that drives all that. How prophetic today sound the words at the start of the chapter from philosopher Onora O'Neill, written at the dawn of the internet age: 'connected lives become . . . *vulnerable* lives'.

The error of allowing commercial forces to design the basic conditions under which we socially interact goes wider than the much-debated problems of social media. Search engines enable us to find whatever is out there in the almost infinite space of the internet, but Google, the developer of the world's leading search engine, also operates only to suit its commercial goals.[20] And that's potentially a problem for how we come to know the social and economic world today. A problem that extends to Baidu, Google's equivalent search engine in China, and to other apps such as Naver in South Korea[21] that in some countries are more important search portals than Google. It applies to countless other forms of search, embedded inside platforms, that shape how platforms present some things for our attention and not others. And it applies in some form to the large-scale AI that drives ChatGPT, Bard, and all the other 'conversational' forms of search that have recently become popular. In all these ways, we have become used to a world that, on every scale and for every purpose, is searchable (that's good!), but on terms that corporations set (that's much less obviously good).

The issues with AI-driven information/knowledge and with social media platforms are two versions of the same underlying problem: that we have delegated the design of our world, our space of the world, to businesses whose goal is profit and not good social design. As if *anyone* knows how to design social space for everyone! But note this book will be about the specific problems of social media and the searchable internet, rather than advanced AI: the problems with so-called 'generative' AI are only just, as I write, emerging fully and will be addressed in the second book of the trilogy. Social media and the 'traditional' searchable internet already give us more than enough to think about.

My core argument will be that, while the internet does have huge potential for good, and while it cannot be uninvented, the way we chose two to three decades ago to bring the internet into focus – via commercially managed platforms, portals, apps and search engines – was deeply problematic. Instead of managing and controlling the risks that inevitably flowed when we created a space to connect up every item of information and every person on the planet, the online gateways (platforms) that got built targeted profit instead. While the worse problems here derive from social media platforms, the workings of commercial search engines are problematic too. In both cases, we have failed to grasp the negative social consequences of generating profit directly *from* social life itself and its design, indeed of the idea that any organisation should be allowed to *design* the space of the world, the space where we all live.

The Link to the Climate Emergency

This book risks expanding to cover the entire history of humanity's interactions in digital space. But, to keep the story within limits, I'll emphasise one risk in particular: the danger that today's space of the world makes it ever less likely that human beings will find the political and social solidarity they need to confront their major challenges.

This might seem like a problem only for those who care about politics, which not everyone does. But, whether politics interests them or not, most people care about the biggest challenge to humanity of all, the climate emergency. Addressing climate change will require a huge transformation in how we live – at the level of governments, businesses, markets, cities and small communities. It is impossible to imagine such change happening without some coordination, which need not be imposed top-down, and might develop more effectively at the level of networks and local communities. Communities will need to change how they live, both to avert the ultimate climate catastrophe and to adapt to the forms of climate change that, because of historic carbon emissions, are already guaranteed.[22] But how will that happen?

Such coordination is inconceivable without a growth in solidarity: a practical sense that all of us have a stake in working with, or alongside, the people around us and the people within reach of us, towards the common goal of averting catastrophic climate change. But what if today's space of the world undermines such solidarity? What if, by building it, we have created a trap entirely of our own making, over and above the largely self-inflicted trap of climate change? As Naomi Klein has recently written with the toxic culture of social media in mind:

> it's the scramble for separateness that is richly rewarded and encouraged in our zero-sum economy, while the urge to act in solidarity and mutual aid with others is discounted and disappeared, when not being actively punished. This *bias against solidarity* is particularly dangerous in our present moment.[23]

So, while other books focus on what to do directly about climate change, this book focuses on a related, but so far neglected, question: how do we escape from the trap into which our new, toxic space of the world is driving us – a slow-moving social emergency that, unless we act urgently, will make it ever harder for us to act together, as we must?

We really need to start caring about our space of the world. People are starting finally to realise this. In January 2024 the World Economic Forum published its annual Global Risks Report. While the long-term risks were dominated by the climate emergency, the 'short-term' risks converged on the social emergency generated by our digital space of the world: 'misinformation and disinformation', 'societal polarisation' and 'cyber insecurity'.[24] The space of the world starts to seem less abstract after all.

Why Digital Space Matters

I hope I have convinced you that digital space matters. But it remains really hard to think about. Digital space is the container where everything else we are interested in goes on. It's much easier to think about the contents that fill this space – such as the scandals we are from time to time exercised about – than about the space itself (the larger container). Yet we must do, if it's the overall space of social media, and even the internet itself, that is the problem, and especially if it's the very idea of allowing business to manage the whole space of possible human connections that is the deepest problem.

Spatial terms are flexible. Sometimes they refer to bounded spaces, like a bar, public square or apartment; sometimes they refer to the larger space that contains all those specific spaces; and sometimes they refer, as with our ideas of public space and the public sphere, to the accumulating consequences of what we do to each other in space. All those types of space (at least their digital analogues) will be important in this book, because the space of the world is the larger space of human interaction and information flows that results from the online circulation of digital information, the creation of social media platforms and the expansion of the internet more generally. It contains everything we are doing online and all the consequences those things have for the social worlds in which we live. All of this makes up our life-space today, our distinctive space of the world.

I already noted that the information spaces generated by communications technologies have been changing throughout history, and this is not the first such change to generate cries of alarm. Often that alarm was found to have exaggerated what had changed or to have misunderstood the deeper transformations in human life that were under way through the medium of technology.[25] When in the eighteenth century the novel and newspaper became popular, some feared that culture was becoming cruder, less educated, more commercially driven.[26] And when the first telephone (what we now, dismissively, call a 'landline') became a feature of everyday life in the early twentieth century, upper-class people were alarmed that anyone might phone them up at any time! But subsequent history proved both fears wrong: the spatial and cultural consequences of technology proved more subtle and less absolute than had been feared.[27] People used the telephone to talk mainly with the same people (friends and family) they had talked to before, just as in the eighteenth century novels and newspapers widened people's perspective on how the rest of society lived, but didn't fundamentally change the types of interactions people had or the strangers they encountered daily.

Should we dismiss today's concerns about social media and the internet as just growing pains, another example of what sociologists once famously called 'moral panic'?[28] The answer is no. Those historical changes certainly introduced a new medium of information circulation – the stories about the world contained within the covers of a novel or a newspaper, the talk between two physically separated people contained in the duration of a phone call – but it turned out that they didn't change fundamentally who was connected, and how. But the changes to information space of the past thirty years have been more fundamental.

Those recent changes have often been compared not with a single new technology, but with the advent of a whole new era, such as the era of print.[29] They have involved two things that were absolutely new. First, the increasing saturation of physical and social space everywhere with new types of information flows: content circulated not just by media institutions but by all of us.[30] Second, the design of new ways of interacting with this vast information universe and, through it, with everyone else (interactive platforms, apps, search engines). In a long-term historical perspective, these changes certainly justify comparison with the impact of printing.

But then there's a third change that perhaps uniquely characterises our recent period: the design of the overall space in which those first two transformations play out. In recent decades, for the first time in history, human beings started designing, even if haphazardly, something which never before could be designed: the space, potentially, of *all possible* spaces where people live and interact, and how information and communication circulate between those spaces. Think of the infrastructure of wireless connection that links our smart phones, think of the design of digital platforms which shapes what we can and can't do on them every day. No king or emperor ever had an analogous control over the space of all possible spaces of human interaction, the space of the world. But now businesses have acquired exactly this sort of power, and they exercise it largely for profit.

So far debate on this huge and unprecedented social transformation has tended to focus on specific doubts and worries, rather than the whole picture. When people are asked about the net gains and benefits from social media – let alone from social media, the internet and mobile phones taken together – they are, not surprisingly, unsure.[31] No way are most of us going to say *all that* is bad. Indeed, isolating exactly where, amid a mass of technological changes, is the source of what's going wrong is a topic on which academics, inevitably, disagree, as we'll see in Chapter 3.

But instinctive approval of the digital world in general comes with some very significant doubts. A substantial majority in nineteen rich countries believe the internet and social media have 'made people more vulnerable to misinformation' and 'made people more divided in their political opinions', while in three rich countries (France, the Netherlands, and the USA) a majority think social media is negative for democracy itself.[32]

Social media and the internet are not like new shows on Netflix or new political parties: specific cultural products that, in the end, you can take a view on, or simply ignore. Social media and the internet *are* the tools through which we live our lives today, whatever our views and tastes, and almost wherever we are. And yet the companies who run them are comprised of small managing elites (the top engineers and financial executives at Meta, the lead management of Google, the designers of the TikTok algorithm). Elites that are generally white, male and wealthy.[33]

How could such small elites possibly have acquired such vast influence over the world? Why would we ever have given such influence to small groups of individuals? One reason is that no one quite realised it was influence on that scale that was being handed over. Social media platforms were built, and then people started using them, until almost everyone was on them. Initially many people liked them, and when problems emerged, it was assumed these were specific problems that would find specific solutions. The much larger problems that emerged later were, at first, dismissed as unintended side-effects of something that itself was an automatic good (more connection). Perhaps this explains the blandness with which Mark Zuckerberg, after a period of growing unease about Facebook's impacts, announced in early 2018 a rebalancing of its News Feed 'away from the most important thing Facebook can do – help us connect with each other': 'we feel', he said, 'a responsibility to make sure our services *aren't just fun to use,* but also good for people's well being'.[34]

But the wider social wreckage generated by platforms like Facebook had not yet come into view, perhaps because no one imagined they were delegating to a small group of techies the design of something as large as the space of the world. How could they have imagined this? Until three decades ago, the space of the world was not there for *anyone* to design. Until then, everyday space was far less saturated with information space than it is today, and no one had anything like overall control over how we accessed our various information spaces. Yes, television channels were powerful, but that old form of media power pales into insignificance when compared to the transformative power of today's social media platforms.

What marks out the social worries listed earlier? No one is making the naive claim that fraudsters, right-wing extremists, sexual predators or political extremists, or even misinformation, are somehow new, let alone caused entirely by social media platforms and the structure of the internet. Of course not. What is new in each example is that people, young and old, are living more and more of their lives in online spaces that expose them to specific bad people and bad things more regularly and more intensively than ever before, in ways that escape normal social monitoring (whether by parents, teachers or people in their community), and under conditions that are unwittingly encouraged by social media's business models. Worse, everyday uses of AI in both the managing and sabotaging of platforms are now intensifying, not easing, those vulnerabilities. That's why many experts fear that AI-driven deep fakes may sabotage a number of the national elections held in 2024.[35]

These problems are not accidents or bad fortune. They are the results of bad or reckless design. The problem that our era must uniquely face is that engineers really are now able to design the whole network of spaces where people socialise and the conditions under which they do so. Yet it has taken three decades for social space's design to enter public debate. It began to do so in May 2023 when the American Psychological Association (APA)'s Health Advisory on Social Media Use in Adolescence commented that 'designs created for adults may not be appropriate for children'.[36] That understates the problem, because children, well before they reach adolescence, are using social media platforms in many countries. By March 2024 the US Surgeon-General was calling for immediate legislation to reduce the mental health harms to young people from social media design.[37]

In 2021 ex-Instagram whistleblower Frances Haugen gave testimony to the US Congress, European and UK parliaments. One of the most shocking things she exposed was that executives knew from internal research that their platform was harming young girls through the images and competitive pressures that platform use promoted.[38] In their unguarded moments, Facebook executives, such as Andrew Bosworth (quoted at the start of the chapter – now Meta's chief technology officer), had already admitted that 'the natural state of the world is not connected', or at least not connected in the way Facebook wanted. What was not admitted was that with this unnatural connection comes an inevitable vulnerability. A vulnerability of individuals to psychic harm. A vulnerability of whole societies to more polarisation and to warped forms of socialisation.

A vulnerability that is not limited to platforms' general users. Platforms have started to spend large amounts of money on filtering out the bad stuff circulating on their platforms before you and I, or our loved ones, encounter it. They claim ever-increasing success in this, a record that the European Commission for one is closely monitoring.[39] But that has created another equally unprecedented risk: to the human screeners who have to view this horrific material first, as part of social media's hidden production line.

AI can't perform the task of automatically screening out the bad stuff without some preparation – it must, after all, be *told* what looks bad to humans, and this requires humans to do the telling. Human beings who must first look through a mountain of such material in order to provide the data that trains the so-called 'artificial' intelligence. Maybe AI will eventually take over this awful role: that's the best outcome, but it assumes AI is capable in principle of taking on that screening role. If it isn't, because the judgements needed are just too subtle, then human scanners will go on doing that corrosive work. Like a scaled-up version of the imperial taster whose job was to taste all food before it went near the emperor's mouth, those screeners protect the rest of us from psychological harm by viewing the bad stuff: not just occasionally, but all day, every working day.[40] Those screeners usually live in the Global South, where wages are lowest and people's vulnerability to exploitation highest. So, even when platforms protect us from some of the harms they have helped generate, they create a new global injustice, exporting their most toxic contents to parts of the world that, because of the long history of colonial power and global inequality, have less ability to say no.

There is a fearful symmetry between today's two unprecedented problems: digital space and the climate emergency. Not only are we coming to realise that human actions have damaged both the physical environment *and* our social environment. But we are finding that attempted solutions push most of their costs onto the disadvantaged parts of the world that had least to do with creating those harms. We can choose to ignore this. But it is surely better, quoting lawyer and environmental activist Jedediah Purdy, to take 'active responsibility for the world we make and the ways of life that world fosters or destroys'.[41]

We do indeed need to ask: what have we done?

The Great Denial

Yet many of our thought leaders, even as they acknowledge specific problems with what's circulating on social media, go on as if nothing fundamentally needs to change.

Perhaps this is not surprising. Social media companies are commercial corporations, aimed exclusively at profit: they have built their platform structures on top of the publicly subsidised invention of the internet.[42] Under public pressure they talk as if such issues can be addressed by modulating this or that design practice, tweaking this or that platform feature or moderation process. But they never ask whether the problem lies deeper: with the basic design of the new commercially driven space of the world.

In October 2021, just after Frances Haugen's devastating revelations, Meta's chief executive and lead shareholder, Mark Zuckerberg, issued a statement. He sounded pained but resolute: 'Most of us just don't recognise the false picture of the company that's being painted.' 'I just don't know,' he added, 'any tech company that sets out to build products that make people angry or depressed. The moral, business and product incentives all point in the opposite direction.'[43] Meanwhile Elon Musk, when mooting his takeover of Twitter (now arbitrarily renamed as 'X', but we'll keep to its more familiar name when referring to the platform's usage before mid-2023), called it 'the digital town square where matters vital to the future of humanity are debated'. Jack Dorsey, former Twitter CEO but more recently a critic of social media, posted on the platform that Twitter 'was the closest thing we have to a global consciousness'.[44] Yet Twitter's own research found in October 2021 that in six major democracies its algorithm gave more amplification to right-wing politicians than left-wing politicians:[45] probably not the global consciousness Dorsey intended.

It's hard to imagine everyday life any more without the internet, and many academics rightly celebrate the many positive aspects of our lives with social media – new possibilities for positive connection, exchange, collaboration.[46] And there certainly *are* things to be celebrated about social media: for example, how it enables people to have voice in unprecedented ways, or helps all sorts of group to form spontaneously. I don't deny any of that. But many other academics, as we will see in later chapters, are raising serious concerns about the dangers of social media, particularly for young people who until now have been regarded as its natural adopters. We need to ask whether there is something deeper that underlies both positive and negative features: a flaw in how our access to the internet's riches has been organised, a flaw in the design of our space of the world.

We might hope that policymakers could balance their appreciation of social media's benefits with a long-term view of the new social risks to which that flaw gives rise. But, in the heavily politicised world of public policy, Western representatives tend to claim all the good aspects of the internet and social media as achievements *for the West*, while blaming most of the bad aspects on countries outside the West, such as China.[47] The Declaration for the Future of the Internet, published with some fanfare in April 2022 by US President Biden, made exactly this mistake of proclaiming a triumph for the West without acknowledging the global complexity of what's unfolded.[48] Even if we leave political ideology aside, such appraisals make no factual sense. Take TikTok: a platform developed by ByteDance, a Chinese-owned corporation, with the aim of outcompeting Facebook, leading Meta in turn to introduce its own features that mimic TikTok such as Instagram's Reels. It emerged also that many state governments in the US rely for the functioning of their own websites on web-tracking code supplied by ByteDance.[49] So, in the sphere of global Big Tech, you can't draw a neat line between the West and what lies outside the West, as US politicians want to do.

In any case, bland celebrations of the West's vision for 'the internet' miss the key point: that the root of the problems we've identified is the idea of allowing market-based commercial corporations *anywhere* to design the space of the world. Commercial corporations were always disposed to design a certain type of space: a space managed to optimise profit from sales, rentals, traffic and, of course, advertising. Some tasks, like designing the conditions under which social life can be conducted, are just too important to be left to anyone to design, except perhaps those guided by public, indeed socially negotiated, values.[50] Put directly, this might seem obvious. Yet something has stopped us from seeing the problem.

What blocks us is the liberal market narrative which saturates our discussions of Big Tech. It is so dominant that it has become an ideology. Yes, recent events have blown its cover and revealed the real, and far from positive, social transformation that the dominant design of platforms involves, but that doesn't stop the ideology from reproducing itself. Take the political philosopher Francis Fukuyama (notorious for his 'end of history' thesis three decades ago), who recently expressed concerns about social media platforms' power, yet insisted that liberalism itself is not an ideology, and that part of the problem is those who call it out as ideological.[51] But there is ideology surely in the persistent belief in the legitimacy of social media businesses, even as the problems they generate stack up.[52] Why indeed would we give immunity to *any* corporation for its role in problems this large and this serious?

True, China (another hugely important player in building today's space of the world) does not share this liberal market ideology. Few people outside China celebrate China's use of platforms for social surveillance and of AI to build a more controlled social order. But it's interesting that, unfettered by neoliberal myths, China has been much more ready to control the damaging consequences of social media than the West. We mentioned earlier the limits imposed on gaming; strict limits also apply to young people's use of Douyin, TikTok's twin in China.[53] That's why we won't in the rest of the book focus on social media and online search in China – not because it is unimportant (far from it), but because China is already on a very different path to managing it.

In thinking about the problems raised by social media and online search outside China, we must not, however, give up on the idea that human beings *might* redesign better the technological spaces through which they currently interact. Faced with the badly designed space of the world we have, we have no choice but to hope human beings can exercise in the future this dangerous new power in a more responsible way. We cannot reverse connectivity, but we must build ways of connecting with each other on different terms, terms over which, as social actors and citizens, we have more control.

One goal of this book is to prepare us for the huge task of redesigning today's space of the world, which may mean dismantling much of its current infrastructure. Another is to show that, unless we commit to that redesign, humanity faces a social emergency that will undermine our chances of averting the wider catastrophe of climate change. From this, as from so much else, current debate about the 'existential risks' of advanced AI is a distraction.

And yet this is all so different from how those we think of as the designers of the internet and Web imagined things would turn out!

Consider Vint Cerf, a computer scientist who played a key role in designing the packet-switching process which enables information to circulate online, as well as the protocols that made this an ordered process. Today's space of the world is surely not how he imagined the open communication space he thought he was building, when he tested out ways in which computers could talk to each other.[54] He has since expressed his concerns about what followed.[55] Or take Tim Berners-Lee, the inventor of the World Wide Web. He was certain he was building a wonderful new information space, writing at the start of the century that 'the Web was not a physical "thing" that existed in a certain "place". It was a "space" in which information could exist.'[56]

Berners-Lee had no expectation – how could he? – of what would happen, a decade later, when a version of this same space, massively enlarged and reconfigured, would become a playground from which capitalist corporations could extract profit.[57] And Berners-Lee certainly did not anticipate that the World Wide Web might, within less than two decades of its invention, be comprised almost entirely of vast walled spaces controlled by profit-driven corporations where humans would not only exchange documents, but live out much of their lives, under unprecedented commercial constraints and enticements.

The internet and the Web that we now know are not the same internet and Web that Cerf and Berners-Lee imagined: Cerf worked on a small, closed network for the US defence industry, while Berners-Lee designed Web protocols for a small, closed scientific network of computers at the physics laboratory CERN. They are also very different from the now largely forgotten social computing worlds that existed before the so-called dawn of the digital age: France's state-backed Minitel system, which used phone lines for social messaging and remained popular into the mid-to-late 1990s;[58] the world of dial-up connection to home computers across the US phone system that was socially popular well into the 1990s;[59] and the communities of teachers and students in schools and colleges who connected around the time-sharing possibilities of early mainframe computers in the US back in the 1960s.[60]

A new, commercially run and massively larger infrastructure, very different from the closed world of universities and defence establishments or from those alternative community-run networks, would soon become the internet's dominant model, unleashing all the concerns with which the chapter started.

Map of the Book

The rest of the book is an attempt, in seven steps, to unravel the huge mistake we have made in designing the space of the world so badly. I will survey the damage done to the fabric of society and politics, and then offer some starting-points for building a better space of the world, in which solidarity becomes, once again, something for which we can reasonably hope.

Because the cumulative error has been so astonishing, in Chapter 1 I will tell its story in the form of a fable. I imagine there really was a coherent overall purpose behind what happened, as if the actual steps that, over time, led to a fully commercialised internet dominated by private walled platforms like Facebook and Google really did unfold according to a far-sighted plan. We'll also look at the various liberal and neoliberal myths that disguised what was actually happening. Then Chapter 2 will offer a detour via the history of political theory to show just how absurd is the idea of allowing commercial corporations to build a space for social interactions on the scale of the planet, when seen against the backdrop of two and a half millennia of thinking about the conditions and scale on which a healthy politics is possible.

Part 2 of the book lays out the evidence, from academic research and other sources, of the damage to social life, and in particular the conditions for political solidarity, wrought by today's space of the world. Chapter 3 investigates this from the perspective of the individual, who, while celebrating the vast expansion of information at her fingertips, is also increasingly exposed to risks incompatible with basic psychological health, let alone a positive engagement with civic or political life. Chapter 4 explores the flow of information online for groups and individuals, and the role digital platforms play in amplifying the risks of tainted information inevitably present when the internet's infinite space of connection was created. We will see how trust in people and institutions is a potential casualty. Chapter 5 turns to the problem of polarisation, particularly polarisation in feelings. Drawing on the latest research from political science but also a much longer tradition in social psychology, we will see how allowing commercial platforms to develop as they did contradicted everything we knew about how to limit polarisation and foster solidarity.

Part 3 turns towards the future and the prospects for rebuilding the space of the world in ways more conducive to solidarity. Chapter 6 considers the idea of solidarity itself: the cases where it appears to have been helped by digital platforms and the many cases where it hasn't. What is it about offline settings which work well for solidarity that online settings don't have? In Chapter 7, I draw the threads of the book together by asking what would it mean to rebuild the space of the world – and its platforms – as if it was society we wanted to benefit, not small elites. If sadly the term 'social media' has become almost an oxymoron, I will ask what a *socially* and *publicly* oriented approach to rebuilding social media, and perhaps online search, would look like. The solutions depend on rethinking the most basic features of how the space of the world has been designed. Instead of relying on the untrustworthy guide of commercial optimisation and the maximisation of profit at all costs, humanity will be better served by simpler and more modest principles such as resonance.

The architecture of today's space of the world has become so important in the management of daily life that it is truly difficult to imagine building, let alone inhabiting, a different architecture. But that is what we must do if lasting social harm is to be avoided and if as a species we are to confront more effectively the true existential issue of our age: the preservation of the planet. To do this, our concern for the state of the digital world must go beyond particular faults and policy fixes. We must confront the flaw in the design of our digital world as a whole: a space of the world that we allowed to be run for profit.

CHAPTER 1

Redesigning the Social World as if by Accident

'What shall I do?' presupposes 'how is communication possible?' (Karl Jaspers)[1]

Imagine a parallel human world with a global government whose policy-makers were given complete authority to redesign how information and communication flows around the planet. The year: circa 1990. The immediate aim: to ensure the freest possible flow of content from all possible sources to all possible destinations. The long-term goal: to move away from a world where communication was monopolised by large institutions such as media companies, enabling more democratic societies.

The early 1990s was the time, in the US particularly, when, after years of multiplying TV channels, there was restlessness for a different type of media: more decentralised, more open to individual production. Let 'prime time' become 'my time' announced MIT professor Nicholas Negroponte in his book *Being Digital*; let's unleash the potential of the 'Daily Me' had written Stewart Brand, creator of the Whole Earth Catalog a few years before.[2] In the early 1990s the internet was starting to become a feature of everyday life, and a period of major innovation in the internet's design followed, with the World Wide Web protocols being published in April 1993.[3] A new world of information seemed to be opening up.

What happened next was so bizarre that it makes more sense, initially, if retold in fable form. We are talking about a major step-change in the organisation of social life, or even, as one commentator put it, an evolutionary shift from one state of things to another completely different state of things[4] – or, as I put it in the introduction, the design of a new space of the world. What actually happened quickly erased earlier forms of civic and social computing, and it happened without any democratic

23

consultation. Technological elites just took on themselves the task of 're-engineer[ing] society'.[5] Let's pretend, for a moment, that everyone knew what they were doing.

How We Came to Have the Internet We Have (a Fable)

Let's suppose our imaginary policymakers met and decided on some simple steps, designed to unfold over time, that they must authorise in order to transform the world for the better. In reality, events unfolded more chaotically, but let's pretend for the moment there was a plan, that what unfolded were steps which as a sequence made sense. There were seven steps in all.

First, create a large number of computers. And give special attention to optimising for a key early feature of computers, which was to archive traces of the actions they performed: all computers track their performance and create a complete record how they are used.[6] Optimise for this feature, and you have created a world with lots of little performance archives which record, in data form, what happens on the device on which they are recorded.

Second, connect up those computers with each other, allowing them to exchange information and making it easier for computers to find information which other computers are ready to exchange. We know this step historically as the expansion of the internet, in the late 1980s and early 1990s, from a small, closed network to an infinitely expanding space of connection. This space was made massively more productive for information retrieval by Tim Berners-Lee's design of the World Wide Web protocols. The result: a much wider space of connection where all computers could exchange information and the asymmetrical extraction of information by powerful surveillant computers from countless other computers was possible.

Third, shift this vast space of connection over from public to private commercial ownership and control. This involved a number of complex technical moves, for example, encouraging the proliferation of commercial web browsers, of which the first was Mosaic, launched in 1993. The most important step was the decision to move the management of the internet's underlying infrastructure from public to private commercial hands. The closed computer network that Vint Cerf had known (called ARPANET) was in 1990 absorbed into NSFNET, an infrastructure owned by the US's National Science Foundation. Yes, there was still at that time a vision of building an 'information superhighway' whose role would be basically public and educational. But all that ended when the businesses that serviced the technical side of NSFNET insisted on offering their services direct to commercial network providers. In 1995 the publicly oriented NSFNET was retired, and all that was left was a commercialised internet infrastructure focused on delivering commercial, not public, goals.[7] Over time, other decisions were taken, at every level of the infrastructure 'stack',[8] to let market forces unfold: that's why, for example, today we have a world where commercial corporations own the 400 undersea cables that carry 99 per cent of the world's digital communications,[9] and commercial property developers own the key connection points that hold the internet together *as* an inter-net.[10] This 'privatised' model became the liberal model that underlay the internet almost everywhere in the years that followed.[11]

Once this key shift of ownership had occurred, market priorities took over completely. Rising numbers of people and daily interactions joined the emerging information space. Major voices celebrated the freedom of 'cyberspace' from political interference, including John Perry Barlow in his famous 1996 Declaration of the Independence of Cyberspace.[12] Already some marketers saw the potential for using the internet's surveillance capacity to get better informed about what their customers did, even when not in the act of buying something: devices like the cookie were invented to capture our activities online,[13] and suddenly, at a stroke, the transcripts of our computer use became open territory for commercial exploitation.[14] Yet in our fable we are still in the 1990s: the era of US internet providers like CompuServe and AOL, when many still got their internet connection via dial-up connections working across phone lines, while in the UK the internet was only slowly becoming available at home.

Then a fourth step: to embed connected computers much more deeply in everyday life. How? By massively expanding the number of computer-based *devices* that could connect us online and also capture our activities. Such devices could be of any sort; they could be a desktop or laptop, but, in time, mobile phones would be as good, provided they were connected to the internet. This began with the iPhone's launch in 2007 and the launch of Google's Android operating system in 2008. Once so many devices were connected, you had a space with vast numbers of interconnected performance archives which could record what had been done with each of those devices. Luckily for internet entrepreneurs, only a few people realised that this new connected space was potentially a vast surveillance system: at the time most of our activity online was not yet being surveilled.

By then a fifth and decisive step was also unfolding: to allow the market to generate new ways of bringing this vast new information flow into focus. For example, search engines to help people find the online information they wanted (Google had some years before developed a search engine to rival then market leader, Yahoo, while also launching Adwords in 2000 to streamline its service to advertisers). And new spaces where we could be social: what we now know as social media 'platforms'. The early social media were by no means all advertising-focused: Myspace quickly was, which was why it was bought by News Corporation, but Orkut created by Google wasn't. But those early platforms fell away when a new competitor, Facebook, grew to a huge scale in the early years of the last decade. Even Facebook, however, was not at first focused exclusively on generating advertising through every means possible. This started to change from 2008. when Sheryl Sandberg was appointed from Google to be Facebook's chief executive.[15]

Sixth step – and here the full potential and danger of the fifth step emerged: allow those who run search engines and platforms to operate them according to *whatever business model they want.* The first five steps had unfolded without developing any generally recognised way of securing payment for content or services online. But the development of platforms and interfaces cost a lot of money, costs which private corporations paid for. So, why not (the sixth step) allow search engine and platform owners to gather unlimited information about those who used their services and collaborate with marketers who aspired to do just the same and might be willing to pay for that opportunity? Why not allow data gathered for one purpose to be freely reused for any other purpose? Why not let businesses build algorithms to evaluate, predict and, in the long-term, push 'engagement' with their services?[16] Indeed, why not let businesses, in pursuit of more engagement, track any aspect of user behaviour they want? And, finally, why not allow – indeed

26

encourage – those platforms to proliferate across the world, insisting that other countries put nothing in their way, so sweeping aside rival local platforms? If you put your trust completely in self-regulating market mechanisms, there was no reason to stop any of this.

Let's pause for a moment to consider what the unfolding of the fifth and sixth steps in our fable involved, for it was here in the late 2000s and early 2010s that a crucial phase in constructing our current space of the world happened. The internet and the World Wide Web, as a presence in everyday life, had grown fast in the 1990s and the early years of this century. There were already concerns about the consequences of such expanded connection: scandals about pornography,[17] whether accessed on bulletin board sites (BBSs, a local form of connection, popular until around 1997) or just on the internet; worries about racist or extreme right-wing groups who acquired an online presence of some sort. Indeed, there was already a pushback with calls for increased media literacy, civil society campaigns and some effective moderation on networks such as America Online.[18] But the liberal model – of allowing markets and information-flows to take their course – remained dominant.

Yet something decisive, if little noticed, had changed. As step five (the expansion of platforms) and step six (unfettered business models) played out over time, a massive machine (commercial social media) emerged to transform the world of internet connection, *amplifying* all the bad things out there online and bringing them potentially much closer to everyone. Far from being neutral portals, social media platforms came to depend on us forming groups of followers who would signal their shared identity with some, and not with others. Web search shifted from Yahoo (simply a directory based on the number of links into a website) to Google's more sophisticated model, which weighted links according to whether their source was already better connected, in formulae that suited Google's wider business goals, goals that were already turned towards advertising income.[19] If you had decided on step six, there was nothing to stop search engines and platforms becoming exclusively focused on the pursuit of advertising income,[20] and the ever more precise targeting of predictable attention.[21]

Much of the story of how this unfolded is familiar from pioneering accounts by Mark Andrejevic, Julie Cohen, Christian Fuchs, Robin Mansell, Siva Vaidhyanathan, Shoshana Zuboff and many others.[22] But what has not been sufficiently appreciated was that, through these steps that I have retold in fable form, a fundamental transformation of *social space* was achieved. The space of potentially all possible social inter-actions had become the target of commercial exploitation. Our spaces online had originally been separate, if connected, streams of interaction which still felt local to particular communities, but in the late 1990s a new commercial opportunity emerged: the chance to exploit the wider space of spaces across which those online interaction streams flowed.[23] Within a decade platform business models that could take full advantage of this new possibility had emerged, and the exploitation of that space started in earnest.

This new commercially managed space of the world was more than just a portal. It was a space where all online interactions potentially could be nudged, tracked and archived: a computer-based environment, entirely under the control of networks of platform providers, where users could be enticed to live out their social lives.

Through the archiving of whatever we did on those platforms, another transformation occurred, so deep that it too passed almost unnoticed. The space of the world became a continuous space-*time,* a continuous universe of interaction that persisted in time, just as the everyday social world does, but with one key difference. The time-function or memory-capacity of the online space of the world was no longer stored in uncoordinated individual brains, as in the offline social world, but in vast corporate databases where everything any of us had ever done online was readily available for centralised comparison, measurement, analysis and intervention. In so doing, not just the space of the world, but its conti-nuity in time, became the direct target of commercial exploitation.[24]

And so to the seventh and final step in our fable, which was not really an extra step at all: because, in spite of the risks already emerging, our policymakers went on as if everything was going to plan. They decided they would do absolutely nothing, even when it became clear that dominant search engines and platforms were *ignoring* the social side-effects of their actions and designs. Our imaginary policymakers didn't react when a large industry was built to exploit all the information about the users of platforms and search engines: not just advertisers, but data brokers and countless apps and platforms that seek to profit from the vast data pools the big platforms hold, all working together in a huge ecosystem of data extraction. The reason for this inaction? Because, at least in the US, the only framework for regulating something like the internet and the new space of the world was one inherited from regulating telecommunications. That old model (at least in its neoliberal versions) was focused on keeping lines open, regardless of what passed down them.[25] A totally inadequate model for internet connections which are not just a bunch of wires, but a world of social content and social interaction in the making. This was how, without any regulatory management or even a moment's public consultation, our space of the world became a space of commercial exploitation.

These seven steps built a commercially managed online social space, radically different from the world of free information flow between peers that Tim Berners-Lee and Vint Cerf had imagined, and very different from the social computing communities of the 1970s and 1980s. That alternative online world – of peer-to-peer circulation that the early internet had presaged – was swept away.[26] As computer historian Joy Lisi Rankin puts it: 'the people computing became the people consuming',[27] people also being continuously surveilled. Worse, people adjusted their behaviour to conform to the constraints and norms of the platforms they used. The parameters of social life – of social interaction and even of socialisation – had started to change.

Those seven steps take us to the threshold of the world in mid-March 2018, just before the Cambridge Analytica scandal broke – a scandal that revealed how for years Facebook had been allowing third-party companies, good and bad, access to firehoses of data about anyone who used Facebook. The world just before the so-called TechLash of 2018 against Big Tech companies,[28] when the dark secret of our transformed space of the world emerged before everyone's eyes.

Perhaps, now we have reached the end of the fable, it is clearer why I told things that way. The point of any fable, after all, is to try and make sense of the world. Today we operate as if the design choices of the past thirty years really *did* somehow make sense, but in reality, when seen as a whole sequence, those steps never did make sense. It never made sense to allow designers and engineers inside a few commercial corporations to make choices that would result in a new space of the world managed exclusively for profit. Only a fable could convince us that this ever made sense.

Where's the Social?

There's a reason why a commercialised digital world unfolded without opposition, as if in a fable, even as the resulting damage started to accumulate. The reason is that many of those leading and promoting these changes were thinking about what they were doing only in technological and commercial terms: building the 'tech' that was needed to allow 'information' to circulate freely, and so make 'markets' function as well as possible. Any social side-effects were consistently ignored. Only the perspectives of the engineer and the platform capitalist, dominating markets and the economy in the abstract, seemed to matter.[29] The emerging story of how the internet and the space of digital platforms were built to satisfy commercial ends may prove, over the long run, one of the most significant transformations wrought by capitalism and, as Ulises Mejias and I have argued elsewhere, colonialism too.[30]

So let's rethink the steps of our fable to foreground the social consequences that were ignored.

The social world exists in space. The space of the world is made up of our interactions in space, including our interactions while circulating information. But information itself exists in a different kind of space: a space constructed from the relations between bits of information that we call information space. The World Wide Web was a revolution in information space that transformed how bits of information can be connected to each other at unprecedented scale and speed. When people in everyday life use devices that have access to information space, the properties of that information space get embedded into another space, the space of social life. This has consequences which are nothing to do with data science or engineering, but a lot to do with social interactions and social space. The technical properties of information space now directly affect the quality of social space, i.e. whether it feels good to live together or not.

The resulting power to transform the space of the world was not what data engineers signed up for when they started to write the code for the new digital platforms. At most they wanted the platforms and digital infrastructures they built to succeed in the market. In Facebook's early days, Mark Zuckerberg, it is said, would end weekly team meetings 'by raising his fist and shouting "domination"'.[31] But it is unlikely he was thinking directly about domination of the social world.

Hence this chapter's title: Redesign *as if by Accident*. We allowed data and software engineers to redesign our space of the world, not at first intentionally – there was no original conspiracy to take world power – but *recklessly*: as a side-effect of designing information systems in a competitive race to shape our everyday technology usage.

But even if there was initially no direct intention to take over the social world (hence, 'by accident'), what happened (indeed the whole fairy-tale quality of the fable I just told) was deeply shaped by the creeping marketisation of every aspect of social life since the late 1970s. Neoliberalism allowed markets to grow without limit and required individuals and institutions to adapt to whatever markets demanded. The unconstrained growth of a commercial internet and commercial digital platforms was just part of that (hence this only happened 'as if' by accident).

Seen from this broader sociological perspective, the new space of the world was far from a historical accident. It fitted perfectly into societies that for decades had relentlessly sacrificed the social to market forces. Arguably this is the deepest damage that neoliberalism has done. It encouraged us to allow commercial technological forces to take something that wasn't theirs (our space of all spaces, our space of the world), and use it as a tool to manipulate to suit *their* values. The result was what philosophers call a 'sphere transgression' of the most profound sort, converting everything that makes up *our* lives into zones of commercial and indeed colonial extraction.[32]

The result was to change our modes of communication, and so our conditions of social life. The kind of life I can lead in the world depends, as philosopher Karl Jaspers noted in the 1940s, on 'how communication is possible'. I quoted Jaspers at the start of the chapter, but let me now give the full quotation:

> The . . . question 'What shall I do?' . . . [now] has to be complemented by a foundation of every ethical act and knowledge in communication. For the truth of generally valid laws for my actions is conditioned by the kind of communication in which I act. 'What shall I do?' presupposes 'how is communication possible?'[33]

Jaspers' insight can help us see what we might otherwise miss. We know that social media and the internet have changed how we communicate with each other. What Jaspers makes clear is that there is no way such deep changes could have left the rest of our social, moral and political life unaffected. By allowing engineers and business leaders to change how communication is possible, we have changed how we act in the world; we have changed our possibilities for ethics and for politics.

Our fable of how the internet took shape, when retold from this social perspective, becomes a horror story about the risks of connecting up the world as we have done in the twenty-first century; about the social costs of allowing commercial corporations to control and dominate the surveillance space that resulted; about the highly vulnerable space of information flow and human interaction that emerges when a substantial majority of the world's population (perhaps now 65 per cent, projected to rise to 75 per cent by 2028)[34] holds in their hands a device that gives them access to a commercially shaped space of connection.

Our fable, you'll have noticed, focused almost entirely on the developments of the US tech and policy sector. That was deliberate, because it was the US that dominated narratives about the development of the internet and World Wide Web, even though many other countries (for example, China, France, South Korea and, during the internet's pre-history, Chile) developed their attempts to shape the internet.[35] But only one story normally gets told: the US version that now sets the terms for our online world across most of the planet. Meanwhile, as we noted in the introductory chapter, China has pursued similar technological goals but aimed at social order rather than market freedoms.

Look back at our fable through a social lens, and it's obvious that the particular choices our imaginary policymakers made were always likely to involve risks of social harm, and for three reasons: first, because they permitted an exclusive focus on maximising numbers (numbers of people connected, numbers of connections between them and their devices, numbers of interactions) rather than questions of quality; second, because they didn't exclude potentially toxic material from entering the vast space of connection that had been created; third, because they allowed that space to be governed by business models that were designed to maximise the circulation of content without regard to whether that material was toxic, as long as it generated engagement. Only the fog of neoliberal market ideology permitted this to make sense as social design.

It really *is* as if humanity decided three decades ago to delegate the design of the social world (the world in which communications are possible) to a small group of powerful policymakers. The mission? 'Wire up our civilisation and get billions of people to come into contact with each other.'[36] Humanity then slept soundly, as those engineers drove us downhill with only one hand on the steering wheel and no foot on the brakes. And now, as we career down the slope, we are waking up to the impending crash, and must quickly work out what evasive action would look like.

Liberal Distractions

No one, of course, as the internet step by step took on its commercial form, told exactly that fable. History always looks clearer in retrospect, but, even more important, engineers, digital businesses and vast swaths of the media and academic world were telling society an entirely different and positive story about what was going on: a fairy-tale about markets and their ability to transform society for the good through the magical force of information.

The engineers and business owners to whom three decades ago we, in effect, delegated design of the space of the world might usefully have asked themselves a question. If you create a space of social interaction where information can flow without limit on a global scale and at instantaneous speed, and focus those flows through managed portals or platforms, then won't this affect the social *boundaries* on which everyday life relies? The answer is yes: necessarily, it will, and quite possibly in ways that are toxic.

The reason is clear. Social boundaries are important.[37] They are the building blocks out of which our social world is made. Your family would not be a family in the same way if everything you know within the family were also known by everyone outside the family. You would not be an individual person in the same way if everything that you are conscious of inside your body were also known by those outside you. Boundaries are important to *building* social life, including boundaries that manage the flow of information: a point which is nothing to do with government censorship, but everything to do with making our cognitive and social lives manageable. We cannot simply ignore the impact of such boundaries on how information gets circulated and expect to sustain a stable personal life.

But the business world didn't think about that. Quite the contrary.

Liberal Information Myths and What They Obscure

The Big Tech industry stripped away all the barriers that might limit the flows of information between different social contexts. As US legal scholar Ellen Goodman put it, 'platforms have bulldozed the sources of friction that were able to disrupt the [information] loop'.[38]

It's not that the industry sought to undermine *specific* social boundaries (after all, they weren't paying attention to anything in the real social world); rather they focused on removing as many general restrictions on information flow as possible. Their hostility to social boundaries was a side-effect of a different principle: let information be free, but extract as much profit from that freedom as possible. The implications of prioritising this principle were profound. Many contextual boundaries that we take for granted to sustain the integrity of our social settings collapsed: boundaries between contexts, between stages of life development, between one group of friends and another, between family and friends, between our everyday context and the very different context of violent extremists on the other side of the world.[39] Put simply, the boundaries in space and time on which socialisation itself depends were dismantled.

It seems few ever thought about what would happen when you embedded this new, massively larger, massively more connected information domain into *social* space.[40] Not at first anyway. Then, when they realised the extraordinary power over the social this gave engineers, platform managers started to take advantage of it: recall Facebook's notorious experiment on its users a decade ago to see how design tweaks could influence their moods.[41] Bad publicity for that experiment didn't stop Facebook expanding access to users' data for its engineers, indeed for thousands of its staff.[42]

This recklessness about social consequences was driven by powerful actors in the world's most powerful economy (the USA), the economy that has been the principal beneficiary of a huge concentration of economic and soft-political power during the recent history of capitalism/colonialism. During the decades we are discussing, there was roughly a quadrupling of the global economy, so the commercial benefits of this misguided social engineering all fed into a vast increase in global wealth extraction.[43] As a result, US Big Tech's market innovations in the 1990s and early 2000s spread globally and with minimal resistance, least of all to the social harms that would come in their wake.

This social recklessness had its roots in a way of thinking about technology and markets that I'll call the *liberal imaginary*. This thinking lies at the core of neoliberalism. By the liberal imaginary, I mean the long-powerful idea that market forces are the best way of organising society. A corollary of this is the liberal myth that information needs to flow as freely as possible: 'information wants to be free', as Stewart Brand is reported to have said.

The idea of free information flow stems from what is broadly a good idea (freedom of expression). But, when no attention is paid to the social consequences of *how* information flows, this collapses into the assumption that unrestricted markets for information flow are just 'best', regardless of the consequences. But best for who? For information markets maybe, but what the liberal imaginary tends to ignore is that (unless regulated to avoid this outcome) markets generally become concentrated in monopolistic corporations, with unpredictable consequences for society. Yes, liberal frameworks rely on anti-trust interventions to correct for *market* harms caused by concentrations of economic power, but such regulatory interventions, even when they happened with the internet (which wasn't often), did not address those harms' consequences for social life. Why not? Because the liberal imaginary assumes that markets *just are* the best way of organising society, making negative social impacts completely counter-intuitive: they aren't seen to be there, because it's assumed they can't be there.[44]

This helps explain a paradox of early internet times: that leading tech commentators often *seemed* to be talking about the social, when in fact they weren't talking about social effects at all, merely projecting technology's design onto the space where the social actually happens. Think of the term 'Internet 2.0', popularised by Californian publisher Tim O'Reilly at the first Internet 2.0 conference in 2004. The phrase emphasised the expanding role of social networking and ordinary content producers, so-called 'user-generated content'. In promoting the term, no one thought about the actual consequences for human society of the space of the world being configured this way. This was engineering language with a liberal tinge, masquerading as social description.

But an important variant of the liberal information myth had a more collectivist ethos, making it seem even more attractive, indeed democratising. This version of liberalism eloquently celebrated the power of networked online communities to be creative, to innovate, to link us together in projects of solidarity. The long-term inspiration was the already mentioned heady days of the early internet with its bulletin boards and other online communities that opened new forms of public discussion.[45] A later and powerful exemplar – still to this day – is the online crowd-authored encyclopedia Wikipedia, founded in 2001. An excellent academic representative of this thinking was Yochai Benkler and his 2006 book *The Wealth of Networks*.[46] A popular version of this thinking was Charles Leadbeater, who, jokily, signed off his 2008 book *We-Think* as co-authored by him 'and 257 other people'.[47]

The liberal information myth is then not all bad, and certainly not all corporate bravado. It characterised much early thinking around individual privacy online. And it took wing in the 1990s, a time of great academic uncertainty, when even leading sociologists, such as Alberto Melucci, sensed that the intensifying globalisation of everything (from trade to travel, from communications to culture) was creating a profound new cultural, indeed theoretical, challenge. 'Never before', Melucci wrote, 'have human cultures been exposed to such a massive reciprocal confrontation.'[48] Confrontation? Maybe if people had listened to Melucci, they would have been more careful in designing a global space that brought everyone together in such a potential confrontation. But, as I have said, engineers were not thinking about social side-effects at all; they were driven by business models, crafted under the guidance of liberal informational myths, that cared only about the free flow of information, the growth of digital platforms, and of course the generation of profit. In any case, right then, almost no one seemed to sense what form those social side-effects would take.

Amid this uncertainty, a deeply optimistic and narrowly technocentric view of society steadily took hold. It sometimes acknowledged concerns about privacy and the quality of information flowing online, but it tended to converge on an optimistic view of the internet's future without questioning the basic direction of travel.[49]

To see the limits of the liberal market vision for technology most clearly, let's look at one of the smartest versions of this thinking: David Weinberger's 2011 book *Too Big to Know*. This book celebrates the internet itself, as captured in Weinberger's comment that 'the smartest person in the room is *the room itself*'.[50] This version of the liberal imaginary does not ignore space – it is much too smart for that – but it thinks about internet space *only* as a space for the infinite expansion of information flow. In fact, it goes further and argues that the benefit of the interconnected space of the internet is that it enables information to flow without gatekeepers, or with only minimal gatekeepers.

At the same time, Weinberger was aware that spatial boundaries matter in managing social interrelation; indeed his book at various points responds to concerns about online 'echo chambers' that were, by then, emerging (we'll return to 'echo chambers' in Chapter 5).[51] But Weinberger let his awareness of these concerns be overridden by an overall optimism about the direction of travel. Since, he argued, the internet allows information to flow freely across all boundaries, the issue lies with *us*, as users: 'the barriers that remain are not technology's but our own'. We as users needed to take on the challenge of 'embrac[ing] difference'. Failing which, we would miss out on an unprecedented explosion of human wisdom: 'we do not yet have any good idea of what *cannot* be done by connected humans when working at the scale of the Net'.[52] What Weinberger didn't discuss were the business models shaping this expanded information space. When he offered solutions to the problems as he saw them, they were purely technological, sidestepping the consequences of implementing those business models directly onto social space. To be fair, he was writing before social media platforms reached their current huge global size (Facebook had only 500 million active users mid-2010, when probably Weinberger was completing his book, but now has 2.9 billion active users).[53] But the limits of the liberal imaginary were already becoming clear.

Five years on from Weinberger's book, even liberals had no choice but to acknowledge the trends towards poor-quality information online and some unambiguously negative social effects, such as polarisation. US communication theorist Russell Neuman in his 2016 book *The Digital Difference* explicitly acknowledged the problem of polarisation on social media, yet talked, in liberal fashion, as if this were just an inherent feature of human life that inevitably spread to the online world.[54] Again, it is not exactly that Neuman ignored space, but he had no way of linking the polarising patterns he saw to how *space itself* was being reconfigured. So, while noticing that globalisation changed the meaning of the term 'neighbour',[55] Neuman did not ask what kind of global space was being created by digital platforms.

Meanwhile, there were intoxicating examples of boundary disruption in contemporary politics that social media platforms such as Facebook seemed to make possible. The so-called Arab Spring provided famous examples. Consider Tunisia and Mohamad Zayani's analysis of its social uprising at the beginning of the 2010s. Zayani showed that in authoritarian societies, characterised previously by restricted public networking, social media had temporary positive effects.[56] Many information boundaries really *are* bad, and the conviviality that emerges in challenging them on social media networks really *can be* positive: take for example social media's role in highly censored societies such as Saudi Arabia. But Zayani also noticed the emergence of social divisiveness on Facebook,[57] and since the time of the Arab Spring a much more cautious view of how social media contributes to political action has emerged, at least among academics.

Outside academic debates, however, the liberal mirage has continued to dominate most debates, and Big Tech's engineers went on writing code that extended the reach of the platforms through which our space of the world was transformed. Few sensed the growing tensions.

One writer who did anticipate them – and by more than a decade – was the Spanish sociologist Manuel Castells. Though sometimes criticised for his technology-driven account of the 'network society', he had a strong sense of the underlying tension between the new structure and older ways of life. Long before the emergence of social media platforms, he wrote about the other social world ignored by the headlong advance of online networks:

> infinite social distance is created between this meta-network and most individuals, activities, and locales around the world. Not that people, locales

or activities disappear. But their structural meaning does, subsumed in the unseen logic of the meta-network where value is produced, cultural codes are created, and power is decided. The new social order, the network society, increasingly appears to most people as *a meta-social disorder*.[58]

Something, in other words, deeply *anti*-social was being engineered through technological networks. Alternatively, something deeply social was being disrupted by the network society. Either way, Castells predicted disorder.

But what sort of disorder? What exactly was being disordered by the headlong growth of the internet and digital platforms? Recalling the quotation from Karl Jaspers with which the chapter started, the answer becomes clear: it was our possibilities of communicating, our social spaces of interaction, that were at risk.

Surveying the Damage

The space where you or I live includes our immediate surroundings, and the space of those with whom we live and regularly interact; there is also the broader community of resources on which I rely to live. Then there is the space where I come into contact with those I don't ordinarily meet, and become subject to wider forces and rules, including national societies and imagined communities on all scales up to the global.

What I have called 'the space of the world' is the sum of all these layers, and it comprises a space of *communications*. It might seem like a fixture of human life, or at least something that must only change very slowly. But, as I have noted, it has changed with particular rapidity in recent decades.

Through the emergence of the internet, I can, with increasing ease, reach others on the other side of the planet with information, ideas and expressions of emotion, and they can similarly touch me, even though we do not come into physical contact. Through the expansion of daily space online, I become exposed to forces that previously would not have touched me in my everyday life; countless things and ideas at a distance now come within my reach; contexts that were *not* my context suddenly intrude into mine.[59] The gradual expansion of social boundaries on which inherited models of socialisation depended collapsed at a stroke.

My everyday physical and social space became overlaid by the properties of information space, an information space built by external corporations. I said 'overlaid' because, although computer scientists used to think of data in terms of modelling the world from a distance (a model that enabled a better overview of the world's complexities), the abstract space through which platforms extract value is not just a model. It is an organisational grid imposed on the world by the rules of how platforms work,[60] and then embedded in the social world by how we use those platforms.

We are still struggling to absorb the implications of this transformation. Social theory can play an important role in unpacking those implications, as we will see in Part 2. Recent social theory already registers this damage in fragmentary form. The late Ulrich Beck wrote of the world morphing into 'indefinite numbers of "world societies"', and anthropologist Arjun Appadurai writes of a 'cellular world'.[61] What kind of world is this where, as Beck put it, 'global others are here in our midst and we are simultaneously elsewhere'?[62]

My concern in this book, however, is not the general problem of online evil which troubled Beck and Appadurai. Evil long pre-existed today's commercially saturated internet and social media: there is, after all, a certain quantity of evil in the world, and the internet, as the *searchable* space of all possible information spaces, necessarily, and from the start, increased our chances of encountering it. My concern instead is with the more specific risk factors that emerge when the internet's general potential becomes used – many would say exploited – by business: through the tracking of us by social media platforms to personalise what we see on those platforms; through the tracking of us by search engines, while amassing huge amounts of additional data, not just to personalise our search results, but to profit from that data in other ways; and through the exploitation by marketers and app developers, in countless ways, of data about us to shape how we interact with them. Those processes drive the specific risk factors that we must consider when thinking about today's space of the world.

We can picture the kaleidoscopic change of the past three decades that has resulted from those risk factors in a series of images. In its early days, the internet was just a series of *links* in a small network. Quickly it became a large *network* with some dominant nodes much more connected than others. As connections multiplied massively and in exciting ways, the world came to be experienced as full of unexpected connections: it felt like a *horizon* of expanded discovery. Increasingly, however, the space of online connection transformed into something different and more constraining: a *grid* where we have no choice but to be connected and are forced to accept multiple forms of external tracking, surveillance and influence. But that grid, from a personal perspective, increasingly feels like a *force field*, shaped by the dynamics of the information space that digital platforms have built to suit their own interests (Figure 1.1).

The problems of living in this force field were, as I have explained, not planned from the start by some malevolent god or dictator, but are a side-effect of specific and, it has proved, highly reckless business and policy decisions.[63] Call them an *emergent property*[64] of a world in which one crucial decision was taken: to allow the internet's massively expanded information space to be run by business to maximise its economic benefits, without regard to any social costs. In the fable I told, this perhaps made sense, but in our actual social world it certainly didn't. The resulting space of the world has three highly distinctive properties.

First, older social boundaries, based in the organisation of social life in physical space, get overlaid by global information space. Each person becomes exposed to excessive connection: we become, as sociologist Rogers Brubaker puts it, hyperconnected.[65] This affects us spatially: we become over-connected to distant places and contents whose production occurs far from our own life-context. It also affects our sense of time: distant content reaches us instantly in sequences that bear no relation to the rhythms of our physical and social spaces. As the philosopher Paul Virilio put it presciently a quarter of a century ago, the 'law of proximity' has been disrupted.[66]

Figure 1.1: How internet space has changed.

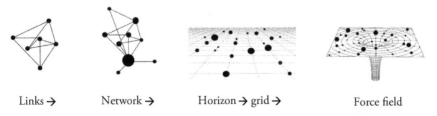

Links →   Network →   Horizon → grid →   Force field

Second, while the social logics that have always shaped human interaction don't disappear, they now play out in a space that is not just hyperconnected but integrated ever more closely with commercial logics. We spend ever more time on social platforms that are configured so as to drive ever greater personalisation of their services, through continuous data extraction. Take the domain of party politics: whether at the level of party struggles or diplomatic summits, politics is now increasingly organised less through formal meetings or phone calls and ever more through WhatsApp threads and other forms of instant messaging.[67] And consider that when we are *not* working, we spend our time on commercial platforms, including messaging services like Facebook Messenger, that afford all the personalisation opportunities that advertisers want. As the customer lead for chat agent Landbot put it in a discussion recorded with Médecins sans Frontières' head of digital, 'personalized content delivered by messaging apps and bots can be much more meaningful than a Facebook post to your entire public'.[68] But these are just a few among countless examples.

Personalisation of platform services is driven by the goal of fuelling ever more intense connection: platforms call this 'engagement'. And this self-fuelling logic links up ever more areas of everyday life into huge feedback loops, circulating messages and content ever faster to meet the imperatives of platforms, and not necessarily those of users as social beings. As a result, the basically good idea of using technology to connect humans to each other in newly effective ways has become corrupted by a very different idea: the commercial imperative of *optimising the scale and volume of all connections at all times* to generate profit, *whatever* the social costs. As tech writer and designer Ian Bogost recently put it:

> It was never a *terrible* idea, at least, to use computers to connect to one another on occasion, for justified reasons, and in moderation . . . The problem came from doing so all the time, as a lifestyle, an aspiration, an obsession . . . it's taken us two decades to realize the Faustian nature of the bargain.[69]

And now, far from reversing the problem, platforms through advanced AI are doubling down on these features. Take Meta. In the face of huge backlash against its selling of highly personalised data to third parties (including when Apple changed iPhone's terms of service to require Meta to get explicit user consent before it could extract such information), Meta is using its own AI-based tracking of users to reorganise that knowledge into ever-better advertising packages for its business clients; its profits go on growing.[70] Far from halting the advance of social media's commercialisation, AI promises only to deepen it.

Platforms have become the 'new governors' of social space, regardless of whether this is what people want, or whether it can be sustained over the long term.[71] In exercising their market freedoms, platforms have done much more: they have fundamentally re-engineered the social and political spaces from which *all* freedoms derive.[72] Meanwhile the debate about whether the resulting space of the world needs to be dismantled, or at least fundamentally redesigned, has barely started. That debate can be delayed no longer.

Some Complexities We Must Address

Social media platforms have become part of daily life in most societies across the planet. So too has access to the internet. Fixing the consequences they have for social life means therefore being realistic about the complexity of what has changed. Solutions will not come easily, because they will cut across a whole universe of habits that has emerged over two to three decades. As we diagnose the specific problems in later chapters, we need to bear in mind a few general points.

Internet use across world is growing in a linear way (from 1.8 billion users in 2010 to 5.3 billion in 2022).[73] Active social media use and mobile internet use accounts for a very high percentage of this, and fully 96 per cent of young people in the European Union use the internet every day.[74] But it remains important not to assume that even basic internet access is universal. So, for example, in Latin American market societies there can be surprisingly low levels of internet access amongst the elderly: in Argentina, 44.5 per cent of over-65s lacked the internet and 28.7 per cent lacked even a mobile phone in late 2020, while the inability to use the internet has been a key factor for non-access among the over-60s in Chile.[75] Age was also shown to be a factor in Europe, with a recent European Union survey reporting that more than 40 per cent of the over-55s in Europe do not use the internet.[76] Put the other way, according to a recent UNICEF/LSE report, fully one-third of internet users globally is aged under eighteen.[77]

In addition, what constitutes access varies greatly. So, in European countries like Germany a majority access the internet through desktop or laptop computers, but in Brazil, for example, a large majority only access the internet though their phones;[78] indeed phone-only internet access varies considerably within Europe.[79] But how you access the internet affects how you use it, as we will see shortly. Meanwhile, levels of screen and internet use from all devices increased greatly during the pandemic.[80]

This linear growth in internet access makes users highly dependent on a few very rich corporations located in a few global centres, although again the form of such dependence varies by region. So, for example, we find very high YouTube access in the UK, especially among children, where this platform is by far the primary choice for children between three and fifteen, accounting for 90 per cent of the sampled population.[81] In some countries, such as India, YouTube is also a leading news source, while Meta products are particularly important for news in Latin America.[82] TikTok, however, has also recently been rising fast and almost universally, reaching large numbers of children well under its official age limit of thirteen.[83]

Whatever the national variations, social media use has become profoundly embedded in daily life almost everywhere, because it provides young people in particular with a basic form of social connection. Ethnic differences are also important here, with social media connection especially high in the US amongst Black and Latino youths who are more likely to say they are online almost constantly.[84] While there is evidence that people do meet some people online for the first time,[85] it is unclear whether this changes completely our patterns of meeting new people.

In many countries social media have become fundamental to news access, although this too is unevenly distributed globally. In their 2021 study, the Reuters Institute for the Study of Journalism surveyed news use in forty-six countries, but only in Spain had social media not yet overtaken TV as people's main news source. A sixteen-country, five-continent study commissioned by UNESCO in 2023 found that social media was the main news source in almost all.[86] Again, TikTok's role as a news source is expanding very fast, for example in the US.[87] Yet television remains in many places a significant news source, especially among adults in Europe.[88]

How people access news (for example on laptop or desktop or on mobile) depends on how they access the internet and this, in turn, affects how they consume news. In some countries where mobile access dominates (for example, India), it is 'personalities' who focus people's attention on news: the situation is different in the USA.[89] The medium of news access even affects the context in which news is consumed: so, for example, Facebook users tend to find news incidentally, as part of some other activity,[90] rather than when choosing to consume news.

Those are just some of the complexities regarding online news consumption that are the background to the analysis in later chapters of how the space of the world may be impacting individual lives, information flows and political polarisation.

Another complexity we must bear in mind relates to the platform environment itself. The fable we told was an origin story: it explained how a huge transformation of our space of the world got under way and gained momentum, until it literally transformed the space of all spaces where we interact with each other. But the platformisation of the world, even today, is not static: it goes on developing in both scale and geography.

Since 2020, a Chinese platform has challenged the dominance of US-based global platforms: Douyin and its Western version TikTok, both owned by Bytedance (as explained in the introductory chapter. TikTok, like all Western platforms, operates under substantially less governmental control than Douyin, so we'll focus in what follows exclusively on TikTok). TikTok challenged in some ways how social media platforms operate, prioritising short-form video and shifting emphasis from users' 'social graph' (that is, the detailed analysis of their networked connections) to the new 'communities' generated by its much-vaunted algorithm corralling users around what they most like to watch.[91] But in making those changes TikTok also intensified the underlying engagement-based business model. TikTok has been extremely successful, undercutting US platforms like Instagram in advertising price and leading the world in rates of in-app purchase.[92] For all the political scandals about TikTok's hidden links with Chinese political power, the business model it represents is basically the same as those of Western platforms, only intensified.[93] So TikTok matters because it points not to a radical shift in our space of the world, but rather to an acceleration in the direction of travel taken in the West since the early 1990s.

One final complexity. The platform environment is not only formed of huge Big Tech companies; it is also where many smaller platforms thrive, driven by similar logics and often having similar social consequences. The engagement-driven platform business model is replicable on many scales, in platforms that originally seemed to offer a radical alternative to commercial platforms (like Telegram) and in others that from the start were designed in opposition to the mainstream, as enclaves for extreme opinion (Gab, Gettr, TruthOut and many others). The dangers of the new space of the world derive not just from the business models of Big Tech platforms, but also from how a similar commercial logic is replicating across social life in ever more concerning ways.

Conclusion: Getting the Whole Problem into View

The details of our lives online are inevitably complex, and so too are the details of how we came to have the platformed internet. I deliberately foreshortened them in the fable I told. A lot of researchers rightly focus on those details, sometimes celebrating them but more often these days lamenting them. But amidst the details there's a danger of missing what should concern us most of all: the fact that we have allowed into being a space of almost all possible interactions – a space of the world – whose properties undermine the *conditions* of social life, the very *possibilities* of ordering social life well. We need to keep those fundamental conditions and possibilities in view, if we are to grasp how over the past thirty years they have been transformed to suit commercial, not social or democratic, goals. As an attempt at social theory, this book focuses not so much on technology, as on changes in how societies are put together. If that sounds unfamiliar, that's because until recently it was: until the digital era, this was not something human beings could ever imagine designing or shaping. But now, as Ian Bogost put it, the Faustian bargain has been sealed.

Signs of strain are appearing. A 2023 global poll by the Open Society Foundation found that support for democracy is declining, particularly among the under-35s.[94] Even economists, long used to assuming a positive link between markets and democratic politics, are beginning to ask: what if market access to better internet connection is associated not with improved information access and political engagement, but with reduced political engagement?[95] A first crack perhaps in the liberal consensus that markets are always good.

Let's step aside from the details of how this or that platform works and ask whether today's space of the world is *overall* positive or negative for sustaining the sort of politics that human beings need, in particular the politics we need to address the climate emergency.

One thing we surely need more of in our politics is solidarity: the willingness to act and take risks together for a common purpose. Does today's space of the world help promote solidarity or not? What if it doesn't? Since positive mental health and some limits on polarisation are necessary if solidarity is to grow, does today's space of the world help sustain them? And again, what if it doesn't?

And what about the preconditions for solidarity, such as trust and a shared cognitive horizon that enables us to know that our and others' actions, however varied, are converging on the same broad goal? Are these sustained or undermined by the digital space of the world? And if undermined, what next?

The 'space of the world' is not just an academic concept; it is a practical tool. It identifies an otherwise invisible dimension of contemporary societies where digital platforms are having the most profound and dangerous consequences for social life. By isolating that dimension, it helps us think about how we can change it. It might seem strange not to focus on the more obvious question of which media provide useful information on climate change.[96] But, by focusing on the less frequently asked *ecological* issue[97] about digital platforms and the searchable internet, we can foreground four urgent social-theoretical questions about life today:

What are the <u>spatial</u> conditions under which a flourishing human society on any scale is sustainable?

What are the conditions under which a <u>cooperative</u> politics is sustainable that can address our collective global challenges, such as climate change?

Do these conditions require us to <u>reverse</u>, in some ways, the recent transformation in the space of the world and build a different space?

If yes, how can we manage that reversal and build a <u>better</u> space that really does help sustain the expanded solidarity we will need in the decades to come?

We need, in short, to imagine a new internet: 'an internet after social media', as internet historian Kevin Driscoll recently put it.[98] A social world not disfigured by the engagement-driven business models that commercial search engines and commercial social media platforms share. For some proposals on how we build that different internet, you will have to wait till the end of the book.

Before we set off on this journey, let's ask in the next chapter what guidance we can get from those who over the past two and a half millennia have thought about the conditions under which politics and solidarity are possible: political theorists. Spoiler alert: you may be disappointed.

CHAPTER 2

When Political Theory Gets Bypassed

'Facebook will not take down the Leviathan in mortal combat. But it could weaken the forces that keep modern democracy intact. Even if it can't bring its own hierarchy and network together, it could still pull the hierarchy and network of the democratic state apart.' (David Runciman)[1]

No one asked citizens: would you like us to redesign your space of the world? Platforms, search engine owners and other businesses just did it anyway, and all citizens are now living the consequences. But Big Tech engineers and managers bypassed politics in another, more subtle way too: they designed a space of the world with features that contradicted all the advice over two and a half thousand years from those who have thought hard about what makes politics possible. Not just any politics, but a politics which is more than a 'war of every man against every man', as seventeenth-century English philosopher Thomas Hobbes famously put it.[2]

Big Tech did this by bolting onto the world of everyday interactions a separate shadow world, made possible by computer software and hardware, which had very different features from the world of everyday life before the internet and digital platforms came along. We'll unpack the detailed consequences in Part 2, but Chapter 1's fable has already sketched the five key features of that shadow world.

First, everyone in principle is continuously connected to the full universe of information *and* to everyone else. Second, anyone can perform key actions (accessing information, commenting, uploading more information or media, forwarding information and media that's already online) with great ease. Third, all of this can happen instantaneously and without regard to physical or social distance. Fourth, none of those operations happens autonomously; they only happen under the constraints and subject to the incentives that Big Tech sets. Fifth, the constraints and incentives that Big Tech sets are driven by the desire to make profit, not by any desire to make society or politics function better, let alone democracy. In fact, as we will see, the new space of the world was designed in direct *contradiction* to what might have been learned from political theory. Profit tends to be defined in this context by reference to maximising what platforms call 'engagement',[3] the attentive engagement that attracts advertisers: clearly this is not the same as political or social good (how could it be?).

We can also add a sixth feature: that none of the first five features was negotiable by citizens or even, excepting some powerful authoritarian states like China and Russia, by governments. All these things unfolded as *fait accompli*.

Big Tech has bypassed politics, democratic or otherwise, by transforming our space of the world without consultation, designing a world that, by the standards of most theories of politics, makes little sense. This chapter will concentrate on this latter point: the bizarreness of treating network societies as models for healthy politics. This will require a short detour via political theory.

Why Political Theory Matters

Philosophers, political scientists and historians (and here, for brevity, I'll confine the discussion to 'Western' political theory) have reflected for two and a half millennia on the conditions under which politics is feasible, and on what scale. Those conditions, in turn, underlie any possibility we have for political and social solidarity. Political theory assumes that we need to take care of those conditions, if we care about the health of our politics. There are basically two theories about those conditions.

The *positive* theory (most famously represented by Aristotle) argues that politics has a natural basis in underlying human needs and feelings: as such, politics may be subject to necessary limits on geographical scale, since there are practical limits to the scale on which the satisfaction of human needs can be organised effectively. The *negative* theory (most famously represented by Thomas Hobbes) argues that politics is anything but natural: what is natural instead is the competitive war to the death of individuals and groups against each other, which makes collective decision-making impossible, and even economic productivity. To correct for this, the negative theory proposes as its solution respect for the common authority implied in all our mutual transactions with each other, an authority that Hobbes called 'Leviathan'.

We'll need shortly to look at these rival theories of politics in a little more detail, not for their own sake, but to show that, for different reasons, both theories risk being consigned to irrelevance by today's space of the world. That's why, as I suggested at the end of Chapter 1, you may be disappointed by what we discover.

Briefly, the positive theory of politics is breaking down because people are being drawn into informational relations – and therefore social relations too – on scales incompatible with a sustainable politics. It is also breaking down because, at all scales, people are exposed to other people's content under conditions that make polarisation and other undesirable social feelings more likely. Meanwhile, what I called the negative theory of politics is breaking down, perhaps more slowly and subtly, because our lateral connections online are becoming ever more salient in everyday life *at the expense of* vertical connections to the institutions which until recently have symbolised the central social and political authority that should underpin everyday interactions. Worse, those new lateral connections are not based on the reciprocal play of rights and obligations between citizens, as Hobbes and others assumed, but on those citizens' individual dependence on an external, private *and entirely non-political* authority, that of the platform.

If our two rival theories of politics – which in turn underpin liberal, republican and even radical democratic models of practical politics – become irrelevant, we may have little left in our toolkit to explain how politics is possible, except an authoritarian politics, for which, disturbingly, the new space of the world offers major opportunities. That would be an alarming outcome: a technologically connected world that *appears* social, free and positive for political mobilisation (that is, for getting political activity started), but which in reality is strongly negative for politics, and particularly for the building of solidarity around constructive programmes of social change.

The problem has been a long time building. As I already hinted in the last chapter, neoliberal trends in policy and societal organisation – above all, the relentless individualisation of everything that was once based on socialised provision, and, with this, a declining belief in social institutions – have been undermining democratic politics for a long time.

51

Indeed, digital platforms, where as isolated individuals we fight to be heard, do our shopping, promote business ideas, and raise finance, are a perfect example of a neoliberal social world.[4] The inadequate regulatory response to digital platforms' rise that we noted in Chapter 1 embodies the neoliberal principle that 'markets always know best'. But there is something deeper about the *space* of digital platforms that is particularly problematic for democratic politics, and that's what we will try to get clear in this chapter, as part of our theory of what has changed about societies in the digital age.

Getting clear about this problem is of more than intellectual interest. We need this clarity if we are ever to have a chance of answering the test eloquently formulated by Jedediah Purdy: 'whether citizens can form the kind of democracy, that can address the Anthropocene question, the question of what kind of world to make'.[5] Quite simply, if our space of the world undermines the very possibility of flourishing democratic politics, then we have built the wrong kind of world.

Politics as Natural Community?

By no means everyone likes politics, but what I call the 'positive' theory of politics insists nonetheless that politics is a natural activity for human beings. As Aristotle put it, 'man is by nature a political animal'.[6] Aristotle was not talking about a particular form of party-based or other politics, but politics in general. He meant that it is impossible to imagine human beings living without something like politics. But what is politics for Aristotle? It is what human beings do to protect their 'self-sufficiency', which for Aristotle meant that politics has a natural scale: the scale of a self-sufficient city.

The term in Aristotle's text we tend to translate as 'state' is *polis*, the Greek word for city. In the classical world, the city was the natural unit for politics for a number of reasons. First, it was the scale on which families, and the groups of families that made up villages, needed to come together to ensure self-sufficiency in food.[7] Second, it was the scale on which it was still possible for citizens to come together to reflect on and decide – that is, to deliberate[8] – about what to do to protect that self-sufficiency. (Aristotle's definition of who could be a member of a city was scandalously exclusive: no women, no slaves and probably no workmen or tradespeople, but we're only looking here at the general features of his model, so we will put that to one side.) Third, the city was a scale on which some social order could be maintained: one reason was that in a city (at least in ancient Greece) it was still possible to know who was around and spot people who were not members of the city, that is, its permanent inhabitants.[9] To sum up, Aristotle says that 'an excessively large number [of citizens] cannot take on any degree of order; that would require the operation of a divine power'.[10] Without divine intervention and to avoid lapsing into total disorder, life needs to be managed on the scale of the city.

Aristotle's idea of a natural scale of politics was revived in the modern world by Jean-Jacques Rousseau, even though his formulation via a 'social contract' drew also on the negative theory of politics to which we'll come in a moment. Rousseau's view of the natural scale of politics was not very different from Aristotle's. If the essence of the social contract was the expression of a 'general will', this was, Rousseau believed, naturally present in a small territory and expressed through appropriate forms of collaborative decision-making. Rousseau insisted that democratic politics could only take place on a scale small enough for a state's members to vote on all its decisions, rather like in ancient Greece.[11]

This view of politics influenced those who thought about the direction of the French revolution, but its problems were quickly recognised. Problems not just of physical scale, but also of time. There were simply too many decisions to be made for citizens to vote on everything, so some form of *representative* authority was essential: but how long was the delegation that chose representatives to act on voters' behalf good for? When did that authority need reviewing? What happened to the legitimacy of government pending that review?

Looking back on the French revolution, political historian and theorist Pierre Rosanvallon notes that today the issue of the general will has become a puzzle not just in relation to geographical scale, but also space-*time*.[12] In today's media-saturated world, the 'general will' can and must be continually renewed in an interface with what he calls 'the manifold negativities of the social'.[13] It's good that modern broadcasting enables the 'general will' to move from a purely fictional unity achieved every few years at election time to become something more fluid and open to renewal: 'a territory of shared trials, similar situations and parallel histories'.[14] Talk shows and social media commentary are potentially part of that.

Other theorists, responding to the world of global information flows, have gone further and argued that the subject of *demo*cratic politics and community – the *demos*, or people in Greek – can be sustained across and not just within national borders. Political theorist James Bohman in his book *Democracy Across Borders* recognises the challenges of maintaining democratic decision-making on a large scale, but argues that the globalisation of contemporary life requires politics to expand in scale too.[15] But how is this possible? Bohman imagines 'new relations between institutions and publics'[16] that he believes will emerge by building human beings' 'common life' in new and larger spaces, perhaps through our ways of interacting via 'computer-mediated communication'.[17]

Bohman's book was written in 2007, and we cannot imagine such tentativeness now. Of course, computers are involved in our forms of politics: we hold them in our hands as we speak, message and scroll! Communications researchers, even if not all political theorists, have caught up with this, celebrating the rise of 'networked publics' on all scales up to the global.[18] Yet the question remains as to whether Aristotle's intuitive idea of the physical political community can be stretched so far from its starting-point.

What seems to allow this stretch is another idea, developed in the modern era (it was only implicit in Aristotle), that individuals become *socialised* into political engagement through their interactions. From the eighteenth century onwards, the idea developed that politics was associated with a common culture or a common spirit of freedom, that was assumed to be distinctive of not just cities, but even of nations.[19] Edmund Burke expressed this by arguing that politics grows out of the bonds of family and close friendship within a nation's religious and institutional culture.[20] Alexis de Tocqueville found politics in the 'patriotic zeal' of a US state, province or district.[21] These political thinkers, of course, realised that face-to-face discussion had its natural physical limits but believed that structures could be built between natural political communities to create a larger and more effective representative state or federation.[22]

The intuition of some common *social* core from which politics springs was most clearly expressed by Hannah Arendt. She saw a shared 'space of appearances' (not necessarily in the form of a city square) as the place 'where the reality of the world is guaranteed by appearing to all'.[23] But Arendt warned that this space is 'only potentially [there], not necessarily or forever'; it is always, in other words, vulnerable to being undermined by external forces.[24]

Indeed in a globalised world, the idea of a natural basis of politics hits against some basic constraints. The first is language. How *can* the world appear to all, as Arendt puts it, unless those people share a common language in which they can express this? Will Kymlicka challenges recent cosmopolitan ambitions of democratic solidarity across national borders (such as James Bohman's) by pointing to the basic fact that political interactions (deliberating on what is to be done) require not only a common language but an immediate life-context in which to ground trust: without that context, no one will be prepared to talk about sorting out their differences on matters of common concern.[25] From this point of view, expanding the spaces across which information and messages circulate beyond natural language communities, as today's space of the world does, raises potential problems.

This links to the question of civility which Philip Pettit argues is one of politics' basic preconditions.[26] Civility is the basis not just of politics, but of the law too, a civility that makes possible what Pettit calls 'a politics of common concern'.[27] People need a sense of their 'non-vulnerability to the will of others' if they are going to entertain even the *possibility* of political discussion.[28] Where can such a sense come from? There are no obvious recipes for building civility according to Pettit: 'we know little or nothing about how to generate widespread civility where it has more or less ceased to exist'.[29] So if, as we will find in Part 2, civility is being undermined online, it will not be easy to regenerate it.

But even if we could resolve the conundrum of what is the 'right' scale for politics, today's space of the world has already *imposed* a scale on life today that no political thinker ever thought practicable for politics: a global scale without limits. Today people routinely encounter people on the other side of the world: for cultural exchange or political insight, games or sex. What if they are being socialised too, in part, on the scale of the whole internet? That would have implications for our model of politics.

No political theorist has ever thought that politics could be sustained in a space whose extent was fully global (James Bohman, at most, talked of democracy *across* borders). And that's because no one has ever believed you could socialise people – for politics or anything else – within a completely borderless space. The very idea of *social*isation implies some specific and, in some ways, locally limited social context of knowledge, what Robin Berjon in a powerful recent essay calls 'the local anchoring of knowledge':[30] recall our discussion of social boundaries in Chapter 1. But today's space of the world embeds an unlimited, potentially global space of information exchange into everyone's daily life. Little wonder then that social theory, as we saw in the last chapter, is starting to worry about living in a socially disconnected 'cellular world'. Little wonder that political scientists, like David Runciman quoted at the start of the chapter, are worrying that Facebook may 'pull the hierarchy and network of the democratic state apart'.

This is a problem to which classical political theory so far appears to have no answer. The reason is simple: no one ever imagined the possibility of such an extreme redesign of the space of the world. Even the most globalist of all Enlightenment political philosophers, the Marquis de Condorcet, who believed the goal of politics was to guarantee human rights and ensure their equal distribution 'over the largest area', insisted that, in order to assure those globally applicable rights, you needed universal rules decided upon by the majority in each society.[31]

Even worse, as we will see clearly in later chapters, platforms build into our online exchanges special features that are really not conducive to solidarity and community, or perhaps even to basic peace. Here Pettit's worry about civility is very much to the point. There are many examples of polarised political conflict played out on social media, but what if their rise can be traced *directly* to particular features of platform design and the business models that drive them? There is nothing in the idea of 'networked publics' to resolve those problems: networks are just bundles of connections that become more powerful, the larger they get. Larger networks don't bring new solutions with them as they expand, just larger problems.

The idea that politics is a natural activity with a limited natural scale is therefore now under great strain. Our algorithmically managed platform-driven space of the world bears little relation to the physical space of the agora that Aristotle once had in mind, or even to the small societies that inspired eighteenth- and nineteenth-century political thinkers. For sure, it can be argued that modern democracy has long been in tension with Aristotle's idea of scale, but that tension has now stretched to breaking point. Figure 2.1 summarises the impact of the internet's spatial transformation on political socialisation.

Maybe we should turn to what I've called the 'negative' model of politics, which doesn't assume that politics is natural to human beings. Does this fare any better in today's space of the world?

Politics as a Contract of Mutual Protection?

The negative theory of politics sees it not as something intrinsically positive, but purely as an arrangement of mutual protection against something much worse. In his book *Leviathan* Thomas Hobbes explained that the 'Commonwealth' – his term that replaces 'city' or polis – was based on a contract of mutual self-restraint. Writing in the mid-seventeenth century during the English Civil War, Hobbes argued that the social contract protected its members from a violent state of nature.

Politics on this view was therefore precisely *not* natural: it was an artificial contract ('the mutuall transferring of Right') which human beings entered into to avoid an unsustainable conflict and have the chance by their 'industry' to attain 'such things as are necessary to commodious living'.[32] The means? Individuals ceding their will to an artificial authority, a fictional person or Leviathan. Provided it was based on this universal contract, the Leviathan could, according to Hobbes, be validly and authoritatively represented in any human form, for example a 'Sovereign'.

Figure 2.1: How political socialisation has changed.

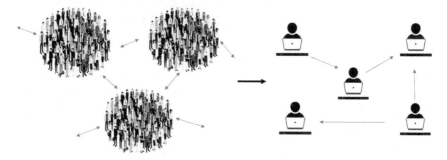

This model of politics, because it assumes nothing natural about political involvement that needs protecting, makes the scale of politics less problematic. When John Locke, writing in more peaceful times at the end of the seventeenth century, extended the idea of the social contract, he saw its role as protection against risks to property and sustaining a growing colonial economy. He could imagine its scale as much larger than just the city, at the very least on the scale of a nation.[33] Within the social contract model, such larger structures didn't require citizens to deliberate together, because power was delegated to a central authority, for certain limited purposes, to achieve the cooperation at scale that a peaceable economy and society required.

This negative model of politics, based on the necessity of individuals accepting mutually binding rights and obligations, because it potentially applies to all scales, has had enormous influence. It is very much alive in twenty-first-century neoliberal models of market societies.[34] Its influence can even be traced in versions of radical democratic theory.[35] It underpins all versions of liberal theory, which assume that freedom of exchange generates healthy order in economy, politics and society, through the mutuality of the rights and obligations that regulate such free exchange.

And yet there is something paradoxical about this model. Because it doesn't believe mutual relations are held together by anything positive, it relies entirely on the practical effectiveness of its central binding authority. Some later philosophers such as Hegel tried to temper this idea with an emphasis on the positive value of recognition between human beings: individuals cementing their loyalty to society by recognising each other's worth.[36] But, as we'll see in Part 2, the idea of recognition may be very far from the society of algorithmic platforms in which we live. Unsurprisingly perhaps, there has been a trend to see in algorithmic power precisely the sort of *impersonal* authority for managing the social that Hobbes had in mind: an 'algorithmic leviathan'.[37] We'll return to that point.

Whether that's plausible or not, today's world poses an interesting question for the negative theory of politics. Does today's space of the world, given the obvious limits of the positive model of politics, make Hobbes' negative and deeply sceptical understanding of politics ever more necessary? Or does today's space of the world expose precisely the tension that was always there at the heart of Hobbes' idea of the social contract: the tension between the celebration of mutuality (contractual obligations to each other) and reliance on an absolute authority that rules over human relations. I will argue it is the latter, and that the Hobbesian model of politics is now breaking apart. Since the negative theory of politics does not assume any natural basis for politics, there really is nothing to stop its collapse, if the conditions are right. What if, by creating commercial social media platforms, we have engineered exactly those conditions?

Think of the most famous image associated with Hobbes' work: the front cover of the first edition of *Leviathan*, reproduced countless times (see Figure 2.2). It shows the giant figure of Leviathan – with the head of a king – as it engulfs a mass of mainly male citizens, all looking obediently towards it. This, it seemed, was the political reality that regulated the city and land spread out below.[38]

What have the growth of the internet and the rise of social media problems done to this model of all-encompassing social authority?

Figure 2.2: Hobbes' Leviathan model of political/social authority.

For sure, the boundaries around the informational flows which reach each member of the masses under Leviathan's authority have changed: everyone now has access to informational worlds far beyond that encompassed by their Leviathan (unless we improbably assume that the Leviathan is itself now global).

No one today, unlike the bodies represented in the picture, has their eyes only directed at Leviathan, represented in the image by a king. Quite the contrary: more and more of our attention in everyday life is today directed, not at what central institutions of government, the law or society are saying, but much more towards what those in our online groups are saying: those in our own groups, and those in all the other groups online, news of whose exchanges also reaches us via social media.

The vision of a population organised around one central point of authority – and one central source of authoritative information – may once have been persuasive, perhaps until the end of the twentieth century, given the success of national broadcasting institutions. But it is much less plausible today. To take a recent example: in March 2023, a financial crisis in a particular part of the US banking sector emerged. The problem was the withdrawal of deposits from Silicon Valley Bank, itself linked to its excessive exposure to failing cryptocurrency businesses. But for some weeks there was fear of a wider global banking crisis, and there was talk of a 'Twitter-fuelled bank run',[39] even though national banking authorities had been very active in combating the issues. If he were alive today, this is no doubt what social contract theorist Locke would have wanted to prevent: surely, he might have said, we need a social contract to prevent an authority breakdown that endangers assets? But it is exactly such a contract to govern social media rumours that we lack, because of our space of the world.

Today's space of the world requires us to redraw the famous image of the Leviathan (Figure 2.3). The people are the same, they still stand close to those they were close to in the original drawing; and their eyes still *seem* directed to the central authority. But they are organised in smaller online groups, which focus much of their attention. They are continually reminded (as represented by the arrows) of their group's relation to *other* online groups. Instead of information flows coming mainly from centralised media or representatives of the state, more important is the information they get from fellow group members or from other groups,

Figure 2.3: Leviathan in fragments.

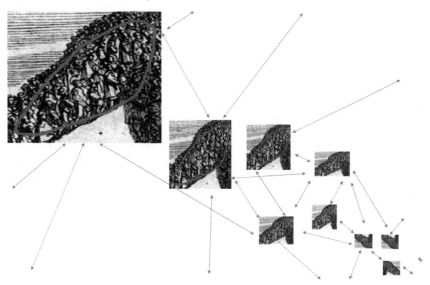

material recirculated via social media platforms. All of this against the background of the global, not just local, information-horizon that each person now has.

The Leviathan is now in fragments. Its authority – the absolute authority that stemmed from the fact that everyone was looking towards it in the same way – is potentially in fragments too. Over three decades, we have transformed the ordered space of the Leviathan into a situation that *might* easily revert to war – a war not of 'every man against every man', as Hobbes once said, but of every group against every other group.

A diagram, of course, proves nothing. But if it successfully captures the radical change that our space of the world has undergone in the past thirty years, something so deep and seemingly abstract that it is hard to capture except in image form, then we really do need to revisit our inherited models of politics and ask whether they still work.

It is not that proponents of the social contract theory of politics were naive about the existence of external influences that might complicate, even destabilise, the Leviathan. They noted the problem, even if in terms that today seem a little quaint. So, for example, Hobbes noted that young men's reading of the heroic stories of ancient Greece and Rome could distort their view of how citizens should act: stories that, of course, they knew only through media (at that time, books).[40] Nearly a century later, Montesquieu noted the destabilising role that cultural experience might play for democracy: the sheer variety of the moral models people came across, as they travelled widely in ways that were becoming normal in the modern era, undermined, he thought, their sense of the authority of any one moral model in a way he believed didn't happen in Aristotle's world or that of ancient Rome.[41] Montesquieu also noted the destabilising impact of flows of goods and money which operate outside the confines of any one nation-state and according to their own dynamics.[42]

But Hobbes and Montesquieu could never have imagined the changes we have recently lived through: the introduction of a computer-based space that can, simultaneously, connect each of us to any of us *and* to the entire sum of knowledge. They could not have imagined the sorts of influence that arise when external information flows are expanded almost infinitely and this expansion is, in turn, managed so as to organise us into ever more distinctive groups whose attention can be distinctively targeted by advertisers. The last chapter's fable would have seemed absurd to them: absurd because the means to achieve it just didn't exist, and couldn't have been imagined. But now they can be imagined, and those means do exist.

In an essay on Facebook, legal scholar Tomer Shadmy proposes a further twist in the fate of the negative model of politics.[43] Key players such as Facebook appear to be something like the Leviathan. The platform exercises an impersonal authority over us, and we have little choice but to obey it, a sort of 'internal, political-like, hierarchical order'.[44] Facebook enforces this order not by giving us instructions, but through what its software permits or doesn't permit: if Facebook doesn't give you the option to 'dislike' another's post, you just don't have that power.[45]

But this new social contract is highly distorted, retaining only the authority side of Hobbes' model. There is no mutuality between you and Facebook, or between you and other Facebook users. The rights of expression each of us has on the platform stem only from our individual contractual relationship *with Facebook*, as the owner of the platform. The fact that I am on the platform does not imply I have obligations towards other users. Facebook's community, seen from the perspective of social relations, is an imposed community, a top-down authority structure hidden beneath our relations with others on the platform. This arrangement risks erasing people's sense of their obligations to others while on the platform: all they feel is the right to express themselves, which depends not on their balancing responsibilities to others, but on whether they fulfil their limited obligations to Facebook, who may, of course, try to limit their speech in certain ways.[46]

The result, Shadmy suggests, may be to undermine the sense inherited from other social contexts that we must be tolerant or civil: on the contrary, I may just feel this is *my* chance, as Manuel Castells put it, to 'mass self-communicate',[47] and no one should interfere. But if that is what is happening with social media platforms, then this must also undermine further the positive model of politics, which requires some degree of civility as a basic precondition of political involvement.

Although, once again, this is just a diagram of what's happening out there in the social world, not social proof,[48] we will find plenty of evidence in Part 2 for believing it is alarmingly accurate. It is no longer hyperbolic to say, as did the US-based NGO the Center for Countering Digital Hate:

> Digital spaces have been colonized and their unique dynamics exploited by malignant actors that instrumentalize hate and misinformation . . . over time these malignant actors . . . have formed a digital Counter-Enlightenment. The disinformation they spread to bolster their cases has socialized the offline world for the worse.[49]

If that's even halfway right, then urgent action needs to be taken.

Conclusion: *The Triumph of Neoliberal Markets, or a Chance for Democratic Experiment?*

From some perspectives, none of this is surprising. Modern democracy has always been in tension with inherited models of politics. In addition, over nearly half a century, we have come to realise that markets – the neoliberal practice of making markets the privileged reference-point for social and political organisation – have eviscerated our politics.[50] As Wendy Brown puts it, 'casting every actor and activity in market terms [neoliberalism] vanquishes the political meaning of citizenship and erases the crucial distinction between economic and political orders essential to the most modest version of popular sovereignty'.[51] Markets are a general force that are eroding our sense of what democracy means: market-based social media platforms are, in the end perhaps, just a symptom of that.

Even this, however, is part of a larger picture. Many forces, not just neoliberalism, have weakened the ability of nation-states to manage their territories, without abolishing the nation-state itself: nation-states have become ever more enmeshed in global market powers that their governments increasingly struggle to regulate.[52] Maybe, over the longer run, we are losing touch with the idea that politics on *any* scale is about building forms of inclusion, as earlier political thinkers supposed: maybe it is today more about forces of exclusion, or as political economist Saskia Sassen says, 'expulsion'.[53] But if so, that's a much bleaker story about our relations to politics and community than Big Tech and digital platforms like to tell.

It is not just in politics or markets where the problems lie. Brazilian computer scientists worry about the long-term consequences of what they call 'algorithmic institutionalism': the installation of algorithmic power at the heart of social and political organisation.[54] Legal theorists worry about the implications of AI and platform power on the institutions of the law.[55] And, if platforms and their advertising-driven business models really are contributing to polarisation, then a basic dimension of human capabilities – our capability to have affiliation with, and to recognise, others – may be being undermined, as philosopher Martha Nussbaum suggests.[56]

We have here a meta-problem: the basic ways life can be organised in space have been disrupted. The space of the world, this book's main term, is itself a meta-concept: it refers to the space of *almost all possible* spaces that the internet and digital platforms have introduced. Get the design of that wrong, and you have a deep problem with how life is organised everywhere and along every dimension.

The space of the world is fundamentally out of kilter with our inherited models for how politics (and society) can be organised. In the absence of any alternative theory of how politics might work, we must ask seriously whether we need, instead, to reorganise our space of the world.

Since the current space of the world came, basically, from the commercialisation of the internet, adjusting it will mean challenging markets' role in how we organise technology; and putting politics and society first, over economics. As some US legal scholars recently argued, 'the substance of economic life must support democratic self-rule',[57] not hinder it. We can't just let market forces undermine the solidarity amid genuine diversity that is needed to address the immense life changes required by the climate emergency.

After fifty years of neoliberalism this change of direction will for sure be difficult. We will need to reject what Brazilian legal and social theorist Roberto Unger calls the 'false necessity' of our current space of the world to unleash a new 'democratic experimentalism'.[58] We will need to reconsider how we organise the spaces and platforms where politics goes on.

Given the scale of this challenge, let's end Part 1 of the book on an optimistic note. Consider one final political theorist, Jens Bartelson from Sweden. In a book written a decade and a half ago, *Visions of World Community*, he admits that the difficulties of forming coherent political communities cannot be simply resolved at any scale, but he then turns the tables. What if we already have within our grasp, through our experiences of diversity in the modern world, an *intuition* of 'a more comprehensive human community than commonly exemplified by the nation'?[59] What if this is the basis on which a new politics could be built? An idea present, but suppressed, in political thinking for two centuries or more: the idea of a natural cosmopolitanism, based in a sense of our shared humanity.

Ambitious yes, but Bartelson calls on us to reformulate 'our conceptions of community in the light of our cosmological beliefs about the human habitat'.[60] Our beliefs about our habitat surely, for many, *have* changed radically in the past decade. It must be worth then putting on the table the redesign of our platform-built space of the world, if the prize is to protect possibilities for solidarity everywhere.

In Part 2 of the book, we will examine the full evidence for the damage that has been done. It is stark. We could, of course, run away from the problem. But the only people likely to benefit from that failure would be authoritarian politicians: they don't need genuine solidarity, only uniformity of adulation. So, let's open the box and see what range of detailed problems must now be confronted.

PART 2

CHAPTER 3

The World at My Fingertips?

'I grew up in Australia but truthfully I grew up on the Internet. I grew up without television or movies as cultural touchstones. I learned about the world, its inhabitants and ideas online.' (Ton-That, founder of Clearview AI)[1]

We find ourselves in a world saturated with social media, but Part 1 identified the fundamental error this involved: allowing software engineers and code writers, overwhelmingly male, white and based in elite cities of the world's richest country, to build a shadow social world that, once bolted onto our actual social world, disrupted the conditions under which democracy, or even just a tolerably peaceful social life, is possible.

In Part 2, I will lay out the evidence for believing that social media platforms have done the exact opposite of what we needed from them. They have accentuated and hard-wired the problems that were already inherent in the connected space of the internet, rather than doing everything they could to mitigate them. The result is a space of the world that makes individuals ever less likely to draw on values of togetherness, to build political bonds, or perhaps even to trust in external facts or authority. If so, this will fatally undermine our two inherited models for how a positive politics is possible.

This is controversial territory, given the disruptions to everyday life that questioning social media's role in our lives may cause. We will need to draw on academic research that debates the overall 'effects' of new technologies. So, a health warning is in order. More than two generations of media and technology researchers have warned against assuming such effects: for surely it is not technologies in themselves, but what humans do with technologies in their particular social and cultural contexts that really matters?[2] That's without doubt correct, but not the end of the story.

Our interactions with digital technologies are not simply free choices. They are shaped by the options and contexts that those platforms offer to us: the menus of interaction they allow, the possibilities of circulation they permit or indeed incentivise. So too with the wider space of the internet itself which, though it seems unbounded and unconstrained, in fact has features that limit what we can do, even if they don't determine what we do moment to moment.[3] This makes it unsettling that some key insights for understanding what's wrong with today's space of the world may already have been known to tech elites a quarter-century ago *before* social media platforms were invented: insights that were ignored or quickly forgotten.

A Path Not Taken

Consider an article published by two MIT management theorists in June 2005,[4] a few months before Facebook (launched the previous year) expanded to US high schools and non-US universities.[5]

Some research underlying this article had already been done in the 1990s, with one paper published in that decade.[6] In the 2005 piece, published when memories of the early internet communities of bulletin boards and listservs were still relatively fresh,[7] Marshall Van Alstyne and Erik Brynjolfsson challenged the widespread assumption that online space would necessarily become more socially integrated. They modelled what happened when individuals, able to use basic search and filtering functions, took advantage of the internet's space of infinite connectability, but with one proviso: that they preferred to have more contact with 'like-minded individuals' than would be normal face-to-face.

Hardly a shocking assumption, you might think, given that everyone has specific interests and limited time to pursue them and given the infinite connections the internet now provide us with. But the result, their model showed, was an online world that, over time, became increasingly segregated into mutually exclusive groups. As the authors put it: 'local heterogeneity can give rise to virtual homogeneity'.[8] What drove this seemingly strange result was the infinite space and connectivity of the internet, and the lack of constraints, online, on people moving around in space until they found a place that exactly suited them.

Yet Van Alstyne and Brynjolfsson were not pessimistic. They hoped that the counter-force of the internet – the way it makes vast informational variety available to everyone at their fingertips – would win out against this darker, segregating force. However, the conclusion to their paper was pointed: 'we can and should explicitly consider *what we value* as we shape the nature of our networks and infrastructures – with no illusions that a greater sense of community will inexorably result'.[9] The moral was that we all needed to work harder than had been anticipated to prevent the internet's dark force – a tendency towards segregation – from winning out. And, to do that, we needed to be clear, as we expanded the architecture of the internet, that our social values were the values that really mattered as we designed online space.

The authors were here echoing 1970s work by Nobel-prize-winning economist Thomas Schelling on how housing neighbourhoods become segregated, and subsequent work by legal scholar Cass Sunstein that had concluded that polarisation was a likely outcome of an online world – again, all predating social media.[10] While the question of online polarisation is more complicated than initially appears, the basic insight – that spaces such as the internet, where people are free to make ever more network connections without limit, are *potentially* polarising – endures. A few popular commentators picked up on this,[11] but the MIT theorists' insight was ignored by those developing and expanding social media platforms such as Facebook, and in public debate from the early 2010s, when social media's tendencies towards polarisation became more generally visible.

The challenge of overcoming the risks inherent in the internet's openness was sidestepped by the very people (social media's engineers) who needed to address it. Profit prevailed, and a business model that insisted on driving engagement with the platform at all costs. Designers prioritised *shallow* community (meeting more people like us, but measured only according to a few variables).[12] The typical TikTok 'community', organised around a hashtag, itself constructed to ensure that exactly *this* video goes viral (in order to ensure higher visibility for its producer's next video), is the most developed version of this drive towards shallow community.

The wider consequences of this research amnesia have been momentous. In this chapter we'll explore this from the perspective of the individual who may still hope that the abundance of information online can leave them better informed to participate in politics or civic discussion. After all, we can't simply abandon that optimism, given the essential role that information plays in understanding and combatting climate change. We'll return to the question of polarisation in Chapter 5.

Yes, the World Is at Our Fingertips . . .

Through the internet, the world's information seems to be just there, available at the touch of our fingertips, whether we are individuals or institutions.

No doubt, for reasons of literacy, skills and network access, individuals have varying relations to this cornucopia (this is the tough reality of 'digital inequality').[13] But informational abundance may be a general experience. Even those in Global South countries who can only access the internet via Facebook's Free Basics will have access to information shared via Facebook which may *seem like* abundance. Or consider this US system designer who uses Twitter (the pre-Musk version at least) as 'a notification system, always up', commenting that 'Twitter is becoming, for me, a coral reef [of information]'.[14]

Recent surveys of the world's children reflect their happiness at this transformation, particularly in the Global South, where in the pre-digital era information was considerably scarcer than in the Global North. This is not just about information access, but also access to people: 59 per cent of global children surveyed by UNICEF think that meeting new people online is important to them (27 per cent said it is 'very important').[15] And listen to the thirteen-year-old Serbian boy quoted in a UNICEF/LSE report from 2019: 'the internet is like a book without a cover: we can search for information, we can have fun when we have a bad day'.[16]

The sense that daily life has been transformed for the better through the basic features of the internet and social media is widespread. A 2015 Pew Research Center study on US teens reported that 76 per cent use social media and, of those, 83 per cent felt it made them more connected with what's happening in their friends' lives and even (67 per cent) their friends' feelings.[17] A 2022 Pew study confirmed a similar result: 80 per cent of US teens felt social media made them feel 'more connected with their friends' lives'.[18] The ease of sharing information online with those you know is also felt to be positive, according to a 2017 survey by UK regulator Ofcom, because it gives access to more content.[19] Meanwhile, the many types of interactions that social media platforms have facilitated

– locating old school friends, keeping in touch with people as you move region or country, creating casual groups around any activity or interest whatsoever – must add *something* positive to social life and our possibilities for becoming civic and political actors, surely?

But it's easy to exaggerate the benefits social media brought, dazzled by the dramatic nature of the change in our space of the world over recent decades. Take music recommendations: the opportunities to share them have expanded massively with social media, but so far there isn't evidence that people are sharing music recommendations amongst a wider range of people than before. Sharing among friends and family still seems the usual way to share knowledge of music,[20] and in some cultures (for example China) in-group sharing remains stronger than out-of-group sharing.[21]

More importantly, it's not just transformations for the better we need to think about. Even in positive accounts of the internet and social media, a sense of risk is present. Already back in 2016, 80 per cent of kids surveyed globally by UNICEF acknowledged the risks that they face online of being 'sexually abused or taken advantage of online'.[22] The sense of risk was higher in some countries than others: according to the already quoted UNICEF/LSE report, children's sense of being unable to verify information online can be as high as 77 per cent (Philippines) or as low as 36 per cent (Montenegro), and the percentage of children exposed to sexual content online varies from 16 per cent (Albania) to 51 per cent (South Africa).[23] Indeed there are risks for people of all ages in relying on what one participant in a 2012 *New York Times* debate called the 'meta-layer of information' circulated by our friends and acquaintances.[24]

The key question for children in particular, as UNICEF/LSE note, is how we address such risks without losing all the opportunities from the internet's open information flow. Improving individual and group literacy with media must surely be part of the solution.[25] Nonetheless people's general sense of the risks of online space has grown significantly in recent years, so let's look more closely at what form these risks take.

. . . But There Is a Growing Sense of the Riskiness of Online Space

From very early on in the internet's development, some researchers have suspected that there could be a negative correlation between our time spent online and our psychological wellbeing: in other words, more time spent online means less wellbeing.[26] They worried about what economists call the opportunity costs of our media usage: could more time spent searching the internet mean less time spent socialising with others? Similar concerns were once expressed about television.[27]

Two decades on, there is consistent evidence from multiple academic studies of an association between *problematic* social media use and wider mental health problems.[28] You might ask: what does 'problematic' mean here? A whole line of academic research has measured problematic social media use, with indices for Facebook addiction and more recently a 'social media disorder scale' developed by Dutch researchers.[29] So-called 'internet addiction' has consistently been found in global research, especially among men.[30] Economists have even tried to prove the existence of social media addiction from the statistical variations in how social media are used and by whom,[31] but that remains speculative. Meanwhile, findings from the UK Millennium Cohort Study suggest that almost half (48 per cent) of 16–18-year-olds in the UK *feel* addicted to social media.[32]

It is hard indeed to separate out what's problematic about social media use from the psychological problems which may already afflict particular social media users. We would expect the influence to run both ways: those with chronic social or mental health problems retreating to social media as face-to-face interactions become more difficult for them, but also (potentially) social media use negatively affecting, for example, people's sense of self-esteem. And this two-way relationship is exactly what one key study found, without being able to show definitively which was more important: loneliness driving higher social media use or higher social media use driving loneliness?[33]

The perennial difficulty of working out the direction of causality is compounded because most research in this field is only set up to establish correlations, not causation. Showing that one (preceding) factor 'causes' a subsequent one requires a series of statistical measures to establish a stable pattern of influence *over time* from one factor to another. In a rare US study that did this,[34] higher Facebook use over time was shown to have caused a reduction of wellbeing, while more offline interactions were shown (though less strongly) to cause an increase in wellbeing. One variable tracked was the objective measure of body-mass index, but when they tracked 'wellbeing', the authors meant self-reported wellbeing, so preconceived ideas of such effects may have played some role. The pattern revealed was nonetheless striking.

Studies of the correlations that exist or *don't exist* between multiple contextual factors may give us important clues about the larger ecological patterns at play here. So, in a review of the worldwide increase in adolescent loneliness in thirty-seven countries between 2000 and 2018, based on the world's only global educational survey (PISA), Jean Twenge and colleagues found some interesting patterns.[35] First, adolescent loneliness increased, often by 100 per cent or more, in thirty-six out of thirty-seven countries in that period. Second, almost all of that increase happened between 2012 and 2018, exactly the period when in those countries smartphone usage and heavy internet usage among adolescents became normalised. The only country that did not see such an overall increase (South Korea) was, the authors note, one of the countries whose adolescent smartphone use had already reached saturation by 2012.[36] Third, those contextual factors (smartphone usage, internet use) were more than just a loose association: they increased and decreased *in step with* rises in adolescent loneliness in all the thirty-six countries, whereas some other likely contextual factors (for example, parental unemployment or family size) didn't.

Such correlations, in themselves, can of course only be suggestive, and their meaning remains open to debate. After all, if we define loneliness as a 'discrepancy between one's achieved and desired social relations', it is likely that social media also change perceptions of what volume of social relations is normal and desirable.[37] Nor is anyone denying that, during times of enforced isolation, such as the COVID-19 pandemic, social media helped stave off loneliness for many people.[38] Larger claims that a whole generation has been damaged by the smartphone have rightly proved controversial: so many factors feed into generational differences, including changing levels of economic inequality and social mobility.[39] But the idea that there is *no* connection between the largest media trend of the past decade (the universalisation of social media use) and other major social trends is surely just as implausible.

These general studies of internet pathology may hint at broad factors (for example, the loss of face-to-face social interactions due to time spent on smartphones, or the 'fear of missing out' (FOMO) that may drive internet addiction).[40] But they do not get us much closer to under-standing what *exactly* about social media or internet use drives these problems. There are pathological forms of almost every activity from collecting to eating to playing games, but precisely because they are exceptional, pathologies don't automatically imply problems with the underlying activity. We need to look closer.

When the Online World Closes In

One starting-point for understanding problematic forms of internet and social media use is to consider how we interact in online spaces, as distinct to offline spaces (and yes, the distinction is today sometimes hard to draw, but when we look back historically, the differences become clearer). For example, online, much of the context present in face-to-face interactions may be missing, including real names.[41] This may lead to more risky behaviour, which in turn may have negative consequences that further shape individuals' behaviour.

Another starting-point is that many social media platforms incen-tivise us to add more and more platform 'friends' or connections.[42] People can easily have 300 or more friends on Facebook and of course thousands of followers on Twitter, Instagram or TikTok.[43] But, whatever that actual number is, it is likely to be much larger than the actual number of social connections human beings can meaningfully sustain. A key study on the topic, while confirming other research that people's offline networks are generally between 100 and 200, found their closer contacts are likely to be far less – between ten and twenty, with less than ten of these really close. Tracing online traffic suggested that numbers of closer relationships on social media are not much different.[44] As a result, our *average* interactions with those defined as our online 'friends' risk being lower than with our friends in the offline world: shallow commu-nities indeed.[45]

Some General Factors

Important research has established for the post-school population that negative experiences on social media are associated with social isolation. One study looked at subjective social isolation among US university students – their own *sense* of being isolated – and examined how it was correlated with social media use across multiple platforms.[46] It found that high time spent on social media was associated with *double* the likelihood of 'perceived social isolation' (PSI) and frequency of social media use was associated with *triple* the likelihood, each time comparing the highest and lowest quartiles (25 per cent blocks) of the population. Inevitably, there is some evidence to the contrary (for example, a Korean study linking higher social media study and better attitudes towards suicide).[47] More research therefore needs to be done, but this is a striking starting-point.

We are far from having a complete understanding of these potential connections. But there are some important clues. One study found a correlation between less social support in everyday life and higher social media use.[48] This might, of course, suggest that social media use has a compensatory role, but things could be more complicated.

Certainly, we would expect these causal patterns to be multi-directional, but one study throws some light on a potential vicious circle in operation here. Although derived from a small sample, it found that having more online contacts is *not* associated with reduced loneliness; meanwhile, pre-existing loneliness itself *can* incite internet addiction.[49] Someone therefore who is already lonely will have a reason to spend more time online, but even if they make more online contacts, spending more time online will not necessarily decrease their loneliness. Indeed, because of the opportunity costs, that time online will likely mean spending less time with face-to-face contacts, so potentially increasing loneliness and the incentive to spend even more time online. A possible vicious circle.

A second strand of psychological research concerns issues of self-esteem rather than social isolation. A factor that may drive certain uses of social media is the need for what psychologists call 'social comparison'.[50] People who have a need to keep comparing themselves to others (so-called 'social comparison orientation') will be drawn to platforms that encourage that activity. But there is a risk also that spending time on platforms engaging in social comparison will fuel exactly the anxiety that drives the need for social comparison in the first place. Another potential vicious circle.

Earlier researchers had explored the association between higher Facebook use and a sense that others have happier lives (that is, a *negative* social comparison).[51] Their explanation was convincing: as the sheer number of friends and interactions online increases, it becomes increasingly impossible to monitor all of them closely, in the way one monitors face-to-face interactions. As a result, social media users adopt a shorthand: they judge others exclusively more and more on their social media performance. Because of the particular incentives of social media platforms, people come to act on platforms in ways that exaggerate the positives of their life over the negatives. But this tendency towards shorthand judgement will, over time and as the volume of interactions builds, generate a negative sense of self-worth in the viewer, especially the person with 'social comparison orientation' that other research identifies as at risk.[52]

We start to see here – in the psychological cycles to which an over-large space of online social interaction may give rise – some reasons why today's space of the world *as a whole* might be toxic for individual interaction, at least for those in the population who use social media more than most.[53] It is, after all, always *as individuals* that we interact on social media: it is my phone into which I type, it is my phone or laptop through which I look at the world, when I am online. The features of our collective space of the world must therefore be experienced individually. That does not remove the need to address individual usage's wider social context. Of course not. But we can expect individual vulnerabilities to play a major role, even in a social media space that might otherwise seem suited to coordinating action and solidarity. Let's look now at what platforms' own business models add to the mix.

Specific Platform Dynamics

For a decade, journalists have been suggesting that social media use was associated with particular psychological consequences. Already in 2012 an article in *The Atlantic* asked 'Is Facebook Making Us Lonely?'[54] Drawing on existing research, the author was careful not to simply blame Facebook itself for our loneliness, since, as noted at the start of the chapter, it is not technology itself but our relations to each other that cause our loneliness. But the author did not yet consider that something about how the space of social media had been designed might be amplifying loneliness, at least for some people.

Move on a decade, and the discussion was not about the general phenomenon of loneliness, but direct psychological harm, with the blame firmly targeted at specific social media platforms. Much discussion was prompted in 2022 by the UK coroner's verdict that social media practice contributed to the tragic suicide of fourteen-year-old Molly Russell. The report was striking in its detail: social media platforms, it argued, contained content unsuitable for a fourteen-year-old, delivered that material often algorithmically without any need for a prior search, and 'normalised' depression and its links to self-harm and suicide.[55]

Recently we have come to know more precisely how the features of platforms such as Instagram can engender specific psychological harms. For a long while those detailed workings remained hidden from us, 'under the hood' of platforms' commercial secrets. But the revelations of Instagram whistleblower Frances Haugen in September 2021 changed all that. Based on internal documents and particularly discussions of Instagram's own internal research that she witnessed, Haugen's testimony was devastating.

Haugen, whose documentary evidence was extensively reviewed by the *Wall Street Journal* and others, showed that Facebook (as it was still then called) was perfectly well aware of the pressure that its platforms put on users to be visible, and to perform for each other (after all, that's part of the design and purpose of Instagram). Whether or not they read the psychological literature we have reviewed, Facebook managers' own commissioned research told them things like: 'Thirty-two percent of teen girls said that when they felt bad about their bodies, Instagram made them feel worse.'[56] They knew that a significant minority of their users traced their suicidal thoughts to the platform, and that the platform's negative effects could be long-term. They also knew that those effects were heightened by the isolation of the pandemic, when as one seventeen-year-old from Wisconsin put it, 'if you wanted to show your friends what you were doing, you had to go on Instagram'. Meanwhile, the sense of compulsory presence encouraged by the platform made it hard to log off, *even when you felt it was harming you.*[57]

Far from reading this as a signal to reverse or abandon its business models, Instagram's owner, Facebook, chose to double down. Driven by emerging fierce competition with external platforms such as TikTok, Facebook dreamed of reaching ever younger segments of the young population, including preteens (so-called 'tweens'), with seemingly little thought as to the wider ethics of *any* business targeting children in this way. Why not see tweens, they mused, as a 'valuable but untapped resource' and why not 'leverage [their] playdates'?[58] The goal after all was to achieve 'message primacy' amongst US tweens, and so achieve greater dominance among future teenagers.

Instagram acknowledged that its own users might see things differently. In fact, they feared what they called the 'myth' spread by teenagers to their younger friends or siblings (that is, tweens) that there is a psychological risk of overexposing oneself on the platform.[59] But rather than taking teenagers' own opinions as confirmation of what their own research was telling them – that the space of Instagram itself was the problem – managers instead sought to undermine those opinions, just the sort of schizophrenic strategy seen decades earlier when tobacco corporations undermined scientific evidence of the very same cancerous effects of their products they *already knew about*. The Facebook corporation did, however, change its name to Meta on 28 October 2021, as if that made things better!

In response to these revelations, campaigners immediately called for more insight into how Instagram's algorithms achieved this malevolent impact.[60] But can tweaking the algorithm be enough to halt the damage being done by the very idea of allowing *any* business to exploit young people's lives as raw input to its profit machine? Isn't the real problem that business was allowed to design spaces that made this even possible?

Needless to say, Instagram's CEO Adam Mosseri had a different perspective. He was quoted as dismissing the social costs of Instagram as like the percentage risks associated with any other socially beneficial technology: 'we know more people die than would otherwise because of car accidents, but, by and large, cars create way more value in the world than they destroy. I think media is similar.'[61] To which the obvious response is: from whose perspective? Who calculates the value/harm that Instagram creates? Who counts the deaths, or indeed the other serious harms, to which today's space of the world gives rise? For sure, platforms' profit motive disqualifies them as objective commentators on the matter. Note also what Mosseri inadvertently admitted: that Instagram *was* a designed social space, one with inherent dangers.

We confront here a fundamental flaw in Instagram's (indeed Meta's and perhaps many other platforms') understanding of what they do in the world. They talk about young people as if they are merely audiences to be marketed at. But that is not how their own platforms work. Platforms do something much more consequential in shaping the conditions *under which young people relate to each other*. They do this by creating a space of the world where young people, in their daily actions, can reproduce the conditions of their own lives, including long-term risks of psychological harm. This is radically different from the harm caused for decades by images of impossibly glamorous celebrities in mass-produced magazines. The way today's social media images get presented to young people – images circulated between friends via their phones rather than via the pages of a glossy magazine – makes all the difference. Even Instagram's own research admitted as much, noting that the video-performance style of TikTok and the jokey emphasis of Snapchat, helped reduce the impact that Instagram's static full-body images had.[62]

When we put these alarming insights into the internal thinking of one Big Tech corporation in the context of what we know from independent psychological research, it's clear that it's not just Instagram that is at fault. We see here the consequences of a *type* of business model that treats platforms as spaces where engagement can be incentivised without limit, a model that characterises many platforms, both large and small, mainstream and alternative.

Consider how those with psychological issues are distributed across social media platforms. Whereas we might expect those people to be less visible in face-to-face space (through their own withdrawal and also stigmatisation), the situation with online space may be different. The inventors of the respected 'social media disorder scale' suggest that 'disordered users differed from non-disordered users particularly in the [large] number of posts that they place on Facebook, Instagram and WhatsApp'.[63] Given that, to pursue their business models, those same platforms *incentivise* those who post more, we can expect that, on average, social media spaces will be disproportionately populated by disordered users and their posts.

Evidence is indeed emerging of links between attachment disorders and excessive social media use.[64] Anxieties that drive attention-seeking behaviour could well be a reason why Facebook seemed an initially attractive space for those with attachment disorders, and yet in the long run proved deeply unsatisfying for them.[65] Whatever the wider practical uses of social media platforms, this suggests that, from the point of view of the individual user, there is a potential problem, and *particularly for heavy social media users*. Social media platforms, with their particular drive towards pushing engagement and risky self-performance, are spaces of increased psychological vulnerability.

We are only now starting to get the larger picture of what this means for personal development on a societal scale. Two leading UK surveys (Understanding Society and the Millennium Cohort Study) provide clear evidence that, for particular age-ranges (during part of adolescence and early adulthood), higher social media use is associated with lower life satisfaction.[66] Because the developmental trajectory in adolescence of girls and boys is different, the age-brackets where this negative association plays out also differ between girls and boys. The periods of greatest risk appear to be 11–13 for girls and 14–15 for boys, with another period of worrying negative correlations occurring for both sexes at the start of their university years. The 2022 study that argued this provides some of our clearest evidence so far that social media platforms are negatively affecting the psychic growth of young people. But it is only part of a huge wave of research that has investigated how social media use might be associated with young people's mental health.[67]

A controversy has erupted about whether a larger causal relation can be proven between social media use and mental illness generally. One author of the study just quoted, Amy Orben of Cambridge University, is sceptical.[68] But, as a sign of how fast this debate has moved, in 2019 she and another of her co-authors published a highly influential paper which suggested that the statistical links between 'digital technology use' and 'adolescent wellbeing' were negligible. This apparently positive finding unsurprisingly was seized upon by many in Big Tech.[69] But 'digital technology use' and 'adolescent wellbeing' are two very large objects to investigate: what type of digital technology are we talking about? Could different patterns be found with social media in particular? And whose wellbeing in particular? Does it make a difference if we look at boys or girls, as indeed Orben's later study suggests?

Along those lines, Jean Twenge and Jonathan Haidt in the US have controversially argued that the associations between mental illness for girls and more intensive social media use *are* sizeable and found across the majority of studies using all methodologies, including when they themselves reworked the same data that Orben used in her 2019 study.[70] Other research has found connections between depression specifically and high social media use, particularly among girls.[71] Meanwhile, academics even dispute how to interpret the many meta-reviews of multiple past studies.[72] Such debates have inevitably spilled out into mainstream media, and we would certainly expect sceptical positions to be echoed in industry research.[73]

I can't resolve those detailed disputes here. Given the extreme multi-layeredness of social life and the fuzziness of much social behaviour, would we *really* expect to have found yet definitive statistical proof of major correlations between social media practices and society-wide mental illness, let alone proof that social media had caused such mental illness? Similarly, would we *already* expect definitive evidence that broad measures of social media use are associated with such general phenomena as self-reports of life satisfaction and positive or negative experiences, as measured through large-scale surveys?[74]

Surely, we wouldn't. Not only are mental illness or life-satisfaction very complex, but when we discuss mental health and people's sense of life satisfaction or experience, we are talking about people's perceptions of how they stand *in relation* to others. At the level of a whole societal cohort, many such differences, being relational and driven by personal competition and rivalry, may well cancel themselves out, especially for a cohort that lives much of its life in social media spaces.[75] But, even if definitive proof of social media's negative consequences may for now be elusive, there are a number of red lights flashing on the dashboard of social life.

Concerns about social esteem and social media use noted earlier are particularly worrying. Either social media platforms are taking advantage of children who already feel badly about their lives or they are directly causing them to feel badly about their lives – or both! The US is not the only country where evidence about low bodily self-esteem exists. For example, in Barcelona, 55 per cent of adolescent boys and 63 per cent of adolescent girls feel a lack of satisfaction with their body (in Spanish, *insatisfacción corporal*).[76] The evidence suggests that it is young girls in particular who are worst affected by these trends. Definitive evidence proving the statistical links between this and social media may be a while coming, but is that reason to ignore the issue, given what we already know about how social media spaces work?

Even the basic affordances of contemporary platforms – for example, their easy searchability and search optimisation through hashtags – can be problematic when matched with content that is intrinsically harmful: for example, sexually exploitative posts by men about women's bodies, such as up-skirting. According to two academics who have studied the phenomenon, the hashtag searchability feature in itself creates an 'architecture of voyeurism and objectification'.[77] Or as one blogger, Lily, put it of grooming videos found on the platform Discord: 'these videos can only exist because it is so easy to find them online'.[78] Lily's point is presumably not that such videos are literally created by the process of searching for them, but that the easy-to-search nature of these platform spaces creates ever greater incentives to produce them. The issue is not just with how general search engines like Google work, but it concerns the search functions within platforms, which, like everything else on the platform, are designed to drive engagement.

The issue is not: are all, or even a majority, of social media users negatively affected by these trends? Because the social world is always relational and competitive, cohort effects may, as we have said, remain unclear on the largest scale. But there appear to be sizeable minorities, for whom all this is by no means a good deal – a point downplayed in narratives that celebrate a majority who are broadly happy about a world dominated by social media. The Pew 2022 study which headlined that 'majorities of teens credit social media with strengthening their friend-ships and providing support' also noted that 23 per cent of US teens say social media 'make them feel worse about their own life', including 28 per cent of girls (as opposed to 18 per cent of boys).

Can we really be relaxed about a space of the world that has such a negative effect, and impacts girls twice as negatively as it does boys? What if today's social media platforms have created a 'perfect storm' for many individuals?[79] A world not of empowering social networks, but perhaps, as communications scholar Jack Bratich puts it, of 'lonely social networks', echoing David Riesman's sociological classic *The Lonely Crowd*.[80]

Risks to/from the Isolated User

We have already seen plenty of evidence of the risks that social media platforms pose for those who are already isolated or have a disposition to become isolated. The Japanese trend of *hikokimori* (remaining isolated at home for at least six months) may be exceptional,[81] but there are plenty of isolated people everywhere.

There are of course counter-factors to be considered too. The internet may allow those who are socially isolated to go online and find people with whom they have things in common. For example, parents of an autistic child can join communities with other such parents; single mothers living in communities dominated by traditional family structures can find solidarity with other single mothers online. Queer people, and increasingly those who are gender non-conforming, may well benefit from accessing the community that online discussion groups can bring.

A decade ago anthropologist Mary Gray's beautifully researched study *Out in the Country* told this important story for gay and lesbian young people in US rural districts.[82] The study was researched in the pre-social media era, where it was civil society-backed websites and email discussion forums, or blogs under the exclusive control of authors, that provided the online 'meeting places'.[83] As one said, 'online you're able to meet a lot more people than you are offline . . . Online I can talk to maybe twenty LGBT people in an hour.'[84] Similar possibilities obviously now exist on social media, even if the public dimensions of some platforms (especially Facebook) create complex risks, alongside possibilities of support.[85]

Sexuality may indeed be an area where platforms *not* structured around direct social interaction like TikTok have an advantage: according to a recent study, TikTok was the only major social media platform where more than half of LGBTQ people of colour in the US felt safe.[86] That said, the relative freedom of self-expression currently on TikTok has, because of the connectedness of the internet, been used to fuel prejudice on other platforms: the polemicist X account Libs of TikTok is known to have broadcast material there to scandalise US conservatives.[87]

In the field of politics, digital platforms can have an equally crucial role for individuals or groups who are isolated or oppressed. A small Turkish social media platform, You Won't Walk Alone, which allowed anonymous contributions, enabled women to post messages to protest the enforcement of strict Islamic dress on women.[88] A similar process played out with women's protests against the strict imposition of the hijab in Iran.[89]

But against the background of these important and positive stories, there are also specific concerns with how other users of social media platforms overcome their isolation. What of those who 'grow up online', in isolation from face-to-face social encounters? I raised this issue for political socialisation in Chapter 2, but it applies to socialisation more generally.

It is exactly the impossibility of being not just diverted and entertained, but *socialised* online that the founder of Clearview AI raised in the opening quote of the chapter. The potential instability of identity was noted by psychologists working at the very start of the online era.[90] Rather than our identity morphing randomly, it is more likely that those already isolated from face-to-face contact risk getting drawn in directions that reinforce social stereotypes and hostilities, for example gendered hostility by men towards women. Think of the so-called 'incel community' of involuntarily celibate men and the acts of violence with which they are increasingly associated, as cultural studies scholar Sarah Banet-Weiser notes.[91]

We reach here the problem of 'identity fundamentalism'.[92] In a space of infinite connectability and searchability (the internet), a person who has become unmoored from the restraints of offline family, friends or acquaintances risks going ever deeper down rabbit holes. After all, the internet is home to a high percentage of all the *other* isolated people on the planet, including those with various extreme opinions. And what if the internet's infinite space of connection itself challenges fragile identities by making more easily visible the others with whom one does *not* feel something in common? If so, then people may feel increasingly tempted to invest in 'fixed identities' that are produced, as anthropologist Arjun Appadurai suggests, 'to *allay* the uncertainty about identity that global flows invariably produce'?[93] If that's the case, we have a double-bind in the making.

It is hard to see such risks being eliminated without closing down the internet as a whole. No one wants that, and anyway it's not feasible. Our energies instead should be focused on whether the way online search engines work – general ones like Google or the search engines embedded into platforms like Twitter, YouTube or TikTok – *accentuates* rather than diminishes such underlying risks. How do we weigh up the benefits to each of us (the example is Cory Doctorow's) of easily finding highly specialised carpentry videos when we need to build a cabinet at home – or indeed the music we really like on a streaming site – against the societal risks of putting individuals on a path that leads to ever more extreme social content being consumed without any offline context?[94] Are we happy that platforms, especially TikTok, tend to drive individuals down rabbit holes, both cultural and political, based on the closest tracking of how they have consumed what those platforms' algorithms push at them?[95] Maybe we need new principles that rethink how recommendation algorithms should work if they are to avoid anti-social risks. Mozilla, drawing on detailed fieldwork with YouTube users, is currently developing draft Principles on Content Recommendation.[96]

There's a basic idea that lies deep in all platform design thinking: 'homophily', the idea that 'birds of a feather stick together' or, more precisely, that 'similarity breeds connection'.[97] If the point of most online spaces is to encourage more connection, then the homophily principle requires content to be distributed so as to produce ever more groups receiving material that is ever more personalised to them. Maybe that is what consumers want, considered as consumers, but it can also seem like a trap: as one interviewed TikTok user put it, 'I don't know how to get away from what I'm typically seeing.'[98] The homophily principle is pretty much what management theorists Van Alstyne and Brynjolfsson assumed as their baseline when predicting ever-growing segregation in the 2005 paper discussed at the start of the chapter.

In the space of politics, the homophily principle could easily have perverse effects. What if, for reasons perhaps nothing to do with social media or the internet, it turned out that a preference for cognitive environments characterised by greater stability, clarity and familiarity is associated with those who are both more conservative and more politically extreme? Then we would have installed in the *basic operating system* of digital platforms a bias towards environments that suit right-wing extremists. And that is exactly what political psychologists have found, summing up all the fears that have surfaced in this chapter:

networks that embed their members in denser webs of like-minded associa-tions, which could then insulate individuals from the demotivating effects of dissenting views, and may enable [extreme] political behaviors to spread faster than they would through sparser networks . . . [producing] a structural advantage to the mobilization of right-wing or politically extreme social movements relative to left-wing or moderate ones.[99]

Indeed there is evidence from Canada that during the COVID-19 pandemic such right-wing extremist messaging expanded.[100] If these patterns regarding politics sounds eerily familiar, it is because they express exactly the trajectory that we have heard so many times in the life stories of mass shooters.

Social media platforms of all sorts, because of their openness, inevi-tably expose people to the risk of evil predators. But the issue is also more specific: the risk that already isolated people get exposed to ever more extreme material, including material previously posted by mass murderers. There are many examples of mass murderers finding in their social media audience imaginary validation for their acts as they film them live. Think of the Christchurch mosque murderer who in March 2018 livestreamed his atrocities via a GoPro camera direct to Facebook.[101] That killer, in turn, was a direct inspiration to the mass killer in Buffalo, New York State in May 2022, who also livestreamed his murder.[102] Many other mass killers have used social media to post material anticipating their murders (for example the murderers of Uvalde, Texas, in May 2022 and Highland Park, Chicago, in July 2022).

These forms of 'reality murder', as one expert on mass shootings calls them,[103] use social media to amplify their impact. The ideologies that motivate them, of course, have many sources, including television (in the US, former Fox TV star Tucker Carlson's championing of the so-called 'great replacement theory'). But at their core lies a deep pattern of isolation and perverted connection summed up in the answer that the Buffalo murderer, in his manifesto, gave to his own question, 'where did you get your current beliefs?': 'Mostly from the internet. There was little influence on my personal beliefs by people I met in person.'[104] So, although the process of online isolation is necessarily individualised, the wider costs to society and the social fabric may be traumatic. Those costs stem directly from the way our space of the world has been configured.

Conclusion: Empowerment and Vulnerability

The infinitely connected space of the searchable internet inevitably poses risks for society, alongside the obvious benefits. The reasons for fearing that differences between people might be accentuated online had been identified before social media platforms were built, and certainly well before platforms were transformed into today's algorithmic engagement machines.[105] But, by the time Facebook, Instagram and Twitter switched from simple chronological timelines, those platforms' commitment to business models that amplified underlying social harms was already well under way.

Whatever the risks it poses, we can't uninvent the connected space of the internet and worldwide web. Nor is anyone suggesting that search engines should be uninvented. Given the almost infinite volume of content that the internet archives, it is unusable without search engines. But we need to be clear-sighted about the risks that an infinitely searchable space of connection unavoidably poses for individuals, especially those who are already vulnerable: risks of easy connection to shallow community, risks of rabbit holes detached from any social context. If the internet is 'a volume knob, an amplifier, and accelerant',[106] we really do need the institutions that have taken on responsibility for configuring the space of the world (above all, digital platforms) to *mitigate,* rather than amplify, those risks. But it appears that commercial social media have done the exact opposite.

If the response to much of the evidence collected in this chapter is that it only concerns young people (the familiar 'they'll grow out of it' argument), we can respond: aren't childhood and adolescence exactly the periods of life when society should be preparing people for their full participation in society, indeed, preparing them for citizenship? Heightening psychological risks is not a good way of going about this. Here the perspectives from social psychology on which I have relied in this chapter connect with sociological theory on generational difference and the risks to socialisation from social and technological acceleration.[107]

It is easy to dismiss some of the themes of this chapter as the plight of a sad minority. But rising loneliness is, as the philosopher Hannah Arendt once noted, always a political and not just an individual issue. Why? Because the experience of 'not belonging to the world at all', expressed so vividly by Ton-That in the chapter's opening quote, is a resource on which authoritarian rulers have historically built.[108]

So too with falling institutional authority and trust. Trust in information is exactly what is in short supply in today's space of the world, as we'll see in the next chapter.

CHAPTER 4

When Trust Starts to Fail

'We need a web that spreads truth more than rubbish.' (Tim Berners-Lee)[1]

Social media are not the only cause of contemporary societies' growing mental health problems. Of course not. There is also the profound impact of the growing climate emergency. Sixty per cent of the UK population say the climate crisis is having a negative effect on their mental health, rising to 73 per cent amongst 16–24-year-olds.[2] Global reports by the World Health Organisation and for Lancet Planet Health have raised similar concerns.[3] However we reform social media environments, this growing mental health issue will still be with us. The same goes for the mental health impacts of inequality that is growing sharply both on a global scale and within nations.

But that doesn't end the debate about social media. Our possibilities for action always depend on a background flow of information. What if social media platforms, as news sources and places to hang out, make our problems worse by encouraging misinformation and outright disinformation on climate change, the one subject where above all we need reliable facts? Then we would be compounding the problem of climate change, making consensus on collective action ever more unattainable. Sadly, as Tim Berners-Lee, the Web's founder, appears to fear, this may be exactly how things stand: more rubbish than truth spreading online.

There are actually two, interlocking problems with social media platforms' relationship to information. One is the way social media platforms' engagement-focused business models drive polarisation, shaping how otherwise reasonable people *interpret* the information that circulates there – we'll leave that issue to Chapter 5.

The more basic problem that we'll tackle in this chapter is how the global connected space of social media, *merely by the fact that it exists*, creates a space of the world that optimises for rumour and so creates opportunities for malevolent or careless information actors, whose effect, maybe intent, is to undermine trust. Digital societies face increased risks of what political scientist Henry Farrell and security expert Bruce Schneier call 'common knowledge attacks':[4] that is, attacks on 'the consensus beliefs that hold political systems such as democracies together'. Autocracies may be different since they depend on common ignorance about how politics operates, although they may benefit indirectly from the problems democracies face, as the case of Russia makes very clear. But let's for now keep our focus on democracies, because acting together in democracies *depends* on the quality of our common knowledge.

Assuming we care about common knowledge problems, we need to start protecting the internet as an information environment.[5] We need to protect something very basic that the philosopher Bernard Williams called the possibility of using language under 'conditions which enable it to be . . . co-operative'.[6] Disinformation is the key enemy. Disinformation has been defined by a European Commission High Level Expert group as 'all forms of false, inaccurate, or misleading information designed, presented and promoted to intentionally cause public harm or for profit'[7] – basically: intentional misstatements, the worst form of misinformation. There is a lot of disinformation and misinformation online and on social media, much of it enabled and encouraged by how platforms operate.

The Commercialisation of Gossip

Gossip – by everyone, weak or powerful – is part of life, but in excess it degrades our information ecosystem. Equally problematic are the ill-thought-out ideas we all have from time to time, if they spread beyond our thoughts and immediate surroundings. The problem is not just what we say, but what we believe. Belief grows in a non-linear way, feeding on multiple sources including gossip and half-baked ideas, and then growing on itself in a self-justifying cycle.[8]

Consider COVID-19, a very serious shared health risk from which thankfully the world has largely, if not completely, recovered. This two-to-three-year crisis saw major problems with the quality of health-related information online, particularly on social media platforms. One false and fast-spreading claim was that COVID-19 itself was unreal; the claim's propagators relied on pictures and videos of empty hospitals under the tag #FilmYourHospital, all started by just one original tweet.[9] After being amplified by right-wing politicians and activists, this false claim generated nearly 100,000 posts in ten days in early 2020, spreading beyond the US, where it started, to many other countries. Yes, COVID-19's features at the start were poorly understood. And yes, in spite of this false claim, in Europe at least, trust in health professionals and health authorities as information sources on the pandemic remained overall high.[10] But that there was a problem with COVID-19 misinformation is undeniable.

The problem was not just the circulation of misinformation, but its escalation. While COVID-19 misinformation was a phenomenon in many countries, often shaped by local political factors,[11] the US can serve as an exemplary case. US Facebook groups that started, quite reasonably, by protesting against the educational and family impacts of school closures morphed into anti-vax groups. A woman who had initially been mocked by other parents on social media for complaining about school closures' impact gravitated towards those online who shared her concerns: 'I found my people,' as she put it.[12] Social media activity spilled over to Instagram and Telegram, and groups shifted from being pro-school to anti-mask and then to anti-vaccine. Members came to see themselves as single-issue voters, a version of the online radicalisation process we saw already in Chapter 3.

The issue didn't affect only large platforms. Smaller pregnancy apps proved an important site for the spread of misinformation about vaccinations and their consequences. I say misinformation, rather than disinformation, since the issue of intentionality was unclear. Really small apps, such as the US pregnancy app Glow, lacked the vast moderation resources of Facebook or YouTube, so were poorly placed to act on bad information circulating. Medium-sized apps such as What to Expect's 'Pregnancy and Baby Tracker' with 2 million users a week found they had to invest suddenly to counter the rise of misinformation on their platform. The problem went far beyond those particular apps in the Global North: there is a wider problem of pregnancy misinformation on social media, for example in African countries.[13]

One academic commented: 'You have some sympathy for the people that run these platforms wanting to just provide a forum for people to discuss these issues . . . and then suddenly they're thrust into this unenviable role of deciding the boundaries of public conversation.'[14] But look a little closer at what those pregnancy apps were doing, and something different emerges. Judging by the accounts of a number of users whom the *Washington Post* interviewed, those platforms were *pushing* posts and email threads towards users, just as do the largest platforms, presumably through an algorithm: posts and threads that included conspiracy theories about vaccinations.[15] They were doing this because this is how platforms normally run: driving engagement by circulating what is likely to cause engagement. Things only improved when What to Expect invested in a 24/7 moderation service, built a keyword detector and invested in additional third-party support, measures that, as an app owned by media conglomerate Ziff Davis, it could afford.

The issues go far beyond specific platforms. First, if platforms' only goal was to *enable* public discussion to happen, why did they need to push it in any particular direction? Second, why does society need today's type of platform as the spaces to discuss such issues? What sort of community exactly is being encouraged here? Platform advocates talked of the 'word of mom',[16] an important feature for sure, but what if such communities had no offline contact with each other that might act as a check on radicalisation? Could that itself be problematic?

There is something distinctive about how information circulates in online space. As the authors of a paper on health misinformation during earlier pandemics note:

> historically, naturally limiting factors such as geography and communication barriers inhibited opportunities for strengthening networks with outlying views. Risky behaviors . . . such as opting out of recommended childhood vaccination schedules . . . reverberated in existing small networks *without necessarily scaling to dangerous magnitudes.*[17]

But, they go on, an 'online social network allows greater connectivity among networks through the increased visibility of group behaviors [with the result that] previously non-normative behaviors can thus become normative'. More bluntly, in online spaces there is 'a *hidden-to-visible* switch' which changes the balance of risk in everyday discussion.[18] Behaviours that before were socially hidden become visible and available for comment and emulation, just because a platform exists. When this happens, expert opinion that contradicts such information may be insufficient to dampen its circulation.

The pandemic was too complex and fast-moving to yield any definitive evidence linking social media use and individual decisions on vaccination, but evidence from Germany suggests that vaccine hesitancy was associated with those who heard about vaccines via messenger services or online video platforms: that is, in the context of social media commentary.[19] Certain Twitter hashtags had major impact in the US, for example (#cdcwhistleblower and #vaxxed). Medical researchers suspect that social media was where the promotion of vaccine hesitancy had special success.[20] The videos that these papers studied, circulated by non-experts, tended to contain no scientific evidence. Levels of scepticism in vaccine safety, in the UK at least, were anything but trivial during the pandemic, and remained so even after the epidemic peak was long gone, with 26 per cent in February 2023 still thinking that 'vaccines have harmful effects which are not being disclosed'.[21]

The issue is not that people were completely cut off from mainstream facts and views opposing theirs (we'll see in Chapter 5 that the popular 'echo chamber' hypothesis is rarely accurate). An older study of vaccine hesitancy found vaccine-hesitant groups drawing on mainstream information as the basis for their own counter-claims.[22] What mattered more was how people interpreted and commented upon that information. A key factor was the space where people encountered information. An interesting study by UK political scientists looked at how people talked about the pandemic. It was often social pressure that prevented challenges to false information circulating: people were embarrassed to create conflict by challenging claims they knew to be false, especially in public-facing online social groups, where the price of challenge was higher.[23]

Researchers once hoped that the 'spiral of silence' so dangerous in offline talk would disappear online. But on the contrary, the evidence now is of an intensified spiral of silence in a world where people fear being attacked on social media.[24] This matters most when it is disinformation that's being freely circulated. As Farrell and Schneier point out, any disinformation that attacks a society's common knowledge harms that society *as a whole* and provides an opportunity for its enemies. It appears that some undemocratic foreign powers, like Russia, saw the encouragement of vaccine disbelief in the US exactly in these terms.[25]

A number of themes have emerged from the COVID-19 example. First, there are inherent risks to quality of information that derive from the nature of online space. Second, there are risks from the type of space that existing social media platforms have designed for us, which, in turn, risk disincentivising debate based on facts. Third, there is a particular risk from bad actors, some of them in external non-democratic societies, who take advantage of these problems. The second point leads us quickly into the question of polarisation, which we will defer until the next chapter. For now, let's just focus on the first and third points.

A Space Connected for Disinformation

Why haven't we talked yet about 'fake news'? The reason is that this term is deeply unhelpful: first, because what's called 'fake news' is, by definition, already in a practical sense news for many people, so 'fake news' is at best a matter of perspective. Second, the tag 'fake news' has been adopted by politicians such as Donald Trump to attack the claims about them (claims many reputable sources regard as true), and so has become 'irredeemably polarized'.[26] 'Fake news' is a term of abuse, rather than a clarifying term.

The flood of claims of fake news has also generated excited academic claims that we live in a '"post-truth" era'.[27] We need to be careful here too. Obviously their authors did not intend to give up on truth themselves, but why suppose there is something general and cultural about the spread of 'fake news'? That can generate a dangerous fatalism. An actual 'post-truth' domain would be a world in which human beings could not function at all, because they would have no reliable basis on which to interact. Anything less is a metaphorical form of 'post-truth'.[28]

A better term, as we have seen, is disinformation. Disinformation, like gossip, has been a feature of human life from the start. People's lurking desire to take advantage of others by spreading poor-quality information is not new. The question is: how do forces of disinformation play out in today's space of connected platforms where information can spread asymmetrically across the world within a matter of minutes?

Most posts don't go very far: only a very small minority become viral. A key factor limiting circulation is the limited attention-space of every user.[29] We can take some comfort from that. But, when posts do spread, which ones are likely to go viral? Here the news is less encouraging.

Rather than the truth always winning out, it's the opposite: it is 'falsehood [that] diffuse[s] significantly farther, faster, deeper, and more broadly than the truth' across all categories of information.[30] This key finding comes from an important 2018 paper by MIT researchers on 'rumor cascades' which modelled all the claims circulated on Twitter since its launch in 2007 that had been fact-checked. They used a robust definition of truth and falsity, as confirmed by a very high percentage of reputable fact-checkers. Their findings did not rely on any specific features of Twitter as a platform or the details of its business model, and so they have broad relevance. The conclusion was alarming: 'whereas the truth rarely diffused to more than 1,000 people, the top 1 per cent of false news cascades routinely diffused to between 1,000 and 100,000 people'.[31]

When those researchers reflected on why falsehoods spread more effectively, the answers were also striking. Not, as one might expect, because those propagating falsehoods had more followers or were more active on the platform: the opposite was the case. Instead the reason was that falsehood is more likely to be *novel* and more likely to excite *strong emotion* such as surprise: the sort of emotion that, under platform conditions (easy spreadability, easy searchability of what's spread) induces people to circulate content further, possibly with an endorsement. Interestingly, they found this effect was more pronounced with false *political* news than other types of news (disasters, terrorism, science).

Perhaps the long-polarised political context of US made a difference here, but even so this finding remains of huge importance, including for the many polarised countries outside the US. It might explain for example why 'anti-vaccine' tweets have been found to be much more likely (by more than fourfold) to be retweeted than neutral tweets, and three times more likely than pro-vaccine tweets.[32] It also has relevance beyond Twitter, because Twitter is just one example of a platform designed to maximise information circulation. Under platform conditions, the natural human propensity to pass on information which is emotionally stimulating has amplified effects. The MIT authors conclude that, in the spread of disinformation, humans are generally more important than 'automated robots'.[33] But this provides little consolation, for, as we shall see, robots are perfectly able to exploit this human weakness for their own programmed goals.

A second recent research finding is that the people who are sources of online disinformation are few in number and highly untypical of the general population using online platforms.[34] According to one paper (which still used the term 'fake news'), 'only 1% of individuals accounted for 80% of fake news source exposures' – that is, acted as the initial source – and just '0.1% accounted for nearly 80% of fake news shared' – that is, acted as the onward spreader of that fake news source. This high concentration in the sources of disinformation has been confirmed by studies of content circulation on Facebook: according to a 2021 study just ten key influencer accounts played a disproportionate role in spreading misinformation on the climate emergency.[35] In the US at least, the audience for tainted information seems likely to be older, more conservative and more highly engaged in political news: that is, devoted news 'fans', whose higher exposure to political news means higher exposure to disinformation![36] In a different study, users over sixty-five, regardless of their political leanings, were found to be seven times more likely to share fake news than the youngest age group, and the sources were again usually conservative-leaning users.[37] More evidence is needed to confirm these findings, but what matters is that platform dynamics allow such small sources to have disproportionate effects in our space of the world.

A third recent finding concerns how platforms users react over the longer-term to the circulation of such claims. An experiment conducted at Yale during the 2016 US Presidential election found that it was enough for a claim to have been presented to people just once to increase the chances of its being believed a second time around.[38] Naturally when a dubious claim *is* circulated more than once, its valence increases further. How the statement was labelled and the political ideology of the audience made no difference. Even warnings in the experiment about credibility seemed to have little impact.

There is something, in other words, that we might call *circulation bias*: information gets believed (and so circulates more) just because it is already seen to be circulating. This is how virality gets going. The risks of virality are accentuated in a world of digital platforms set up to maximise circulation to generate profit.[39] And, although virality is still the exception rather than the norm, when it happens, it has major impacts, not just locally but right across social space.

Meanwhile the record of individual platforms in addressing such risks is poor. The Australian Competition and Consumer Commission in March 2022 sued Meta for allowing a false advertising campaigning to encourage Australians to use cryptocurrencies: the campaign depended on linking images of Australian celebrities to false media articles.[40] Facebook's failure to manage such information problems has been noted by regulators in many countries. A particularly important insight on this emerged from whistleblower Sophie Zhang, who was fired by Facebook in early 2021.[41]

Zhang's published account accused Facebook's multiple process failings in relation to false information generated by undemocratic governments or campaigners right across the world. Facebook cared, it seems, rather less when the problems emerged in the Global South, rather than the Global North. As one manager cited by Zhang put it, 'I don't think Honduras is high on people's minds here.'[42] Part of the problem was that Facebook didn't have enough moderators in relevant local languages.[43] But the main point was more basic: that, even if moderation processes were better resourced and more efficient, we should not be relying on individual people in *any* organisation to fix issues that affect the political culture of whole countries. As Zhang said, 'it was just very overwhelming and frustrating because, frankly, I should never have had this much responsibility and power'. But nor should anyone else! Only our contemporary space of the world makes it so.

The issue goes far beyond Facebook. Many other platforms have become unwitting gatekeepers of the quality of our informational 'air', but without the necessary expertise. Take Spotify, the music- and audio-streaming platform. When its top podcaster, Joe Rogan, became associated with vaccine misinformation, it struggled to deal with the protests by another celebrity Spotify user, Neil Young.[44]

At bottom, this is an issue about our space of the world and how it is configured. Our information space is constructed to incentivise repetition as an end in itself, removing barriers to circulation. This encourages social validation: what circulates more among us tends for that reason to acquire higher social validity, a very different standard from scientific validation. This creates pressures towards what political scientists Russell Muirhead and Nancy Rosenblum call an 'indiscriminate denial of standing of knowledge-producing institutions'.[45] Against this backdrop, existing knowledge institutions may struggle to be heard, because it is precisely their older ways of supporting and disseminating their expertise that play badly on social media.[46]

We shouldn't exaggerate. After all, television, not social media, was named in a 2021 European survey by most people as one of their three main sources of information about climate change (61 per cent of people as against 48 per cent for 'internet or social media').[47] But higher numbers named 'internet or social media' in some countries, and 76 per cent of the 15–24 age group named Facebook as one of their main news sources.[48] Indeed, given the recent explosion in TikTok use among young people,[49] such a survey, if repeated today, would likely show TikTok as a prominent source. The impact of social media as an informational ecology, including for climate debates, can never therefore be ignored. The signs are worrying.[50]

Pleading the Case for Social Media Platforms

What is the case for the defence of social media?

The simplest argument is that social media platforms should be free from interference because they, and those who use them, have an overriding right of free speech. If it were only individuals who suffered from these consequences, this would be a strong argument. But the problems that social media platforms cause operate on the scale of whole societies: common knowledge problems affect *society's* cognitive functioning and indeed the context in which individual rights (such as freedom of speech) make sense at all.[51]

Then there is the argument that disinformation only represents a very small proportion of the information which an average person accesses during a news cycle. In a much-cited article on the 2016 US Presidential election, economists Hunt Allcott and Matthew Gentzkow (again, still using the term 'fake news') estimated that during the election period 'the average adult saw and remembered . . . 1.14 fake news articles' (from a specially constructed 'fake news database') and that their news memory was more dominated by stories that were not demonstrably fake.[52] Perhaps then the whole problem of waning trust in information on social media platforms has been exaggerated? This study, however, depended on an artificial way of measuring effects: how much more likely, the researchers asked, was someone to remember a fake news item than another item not in the fake news database (a so-called 'placebo')? Other researchers have suggested a much higher salience for misinformation.[53] Misinformation, in any case, may have consequences beyond direct recall: it may shape unconsciously how I frame an issue, how I interpret a particular story that is true, and do so even if I can't remember the actual 'fake' source.[54] Crucially also, the Allcott and Gentzkow study excluded stories accessed via mobile devices, even though that is where so much of people's news is accessed.[55]

A broader argument that excuses social media platforms from much of the blame for misinformation and disinformation has been made by Harvard researchers Yochai Benkler, Rob Faris and Hal Roberts.[56] These authors foreground the distinctive nexus of broadcast and press news producers that has existed for a decade on the US far right. This alternative news ecology, they argue, exists with limited overlap with the US's mainstream news. As an explanation of the *distinctively* unstable and polarised US political environment, this is in large part convincing.

Less convincing is those authors' attempt to downplay the role of technological design in political change. They argue that political culture matters much more than social media: 'it is only when the underlying institutional and political-cultural fabric is frayed that technology can exacerbate existing problems and dynamics to the point of crisis'.[57] But our argument has not been that social media are the first mover in information distortion in societies as vast and complex as the USA. That would go too far.

A better question to ask is whether platforms' business model *contributes* to making toxic information flow worse than it would otherwise have been. And here it is hard to avoid the evidence.[58] As Benkler and colleagues themselves acknowledge, 'misinformation [on social media] may play a larger role in fields that are not populated by intentional, well-organised and well-resourced actors' such as politicians, for example in the health field and, perhaps, climate change.[59] Consider also the dynamic uncovered by Alice Marwick and Rebecca

Lewis for the New York think tank Data & Society: the way platforms give initial visibility to extreme political voices and then, through their powers of 'strategic amplification and framing', help those messages move 'up the chain' of media to the mainstream, or at least the alternative mainstream.[60] The symbiotic relationship between (extreme) social media and (more or less extreme) broadcasting/press media ends up amplifying content that would otherwise have been invisible except to very specialised audiences: exactly the hidden-to-visible shift we noted in the vaccine misinformation context. The result is a pressure towards political radicalisation, which in turn amounts, potentially, to a societal 'radicalisation'.[61]

The issue, then, is not whether social media platforms aim to promote right-wing propaganda, though Elon Musk's X raises some doubts. The issue is the ecological consequences for societies' whole information landscape that flow from the underlying features of today's commercial platforms. Misinformation and disinformation are inherent to human communication, but the sheer size and intense interconnectivity of today's platform ecology (which has no precedent) creates forces large enough to be powerful pollutants of our space of the world. Recall, for example, that Google once claimed it would root out climate misinformation but was found afterwards to still generate much of YouTube's income from videos associated with such misinformation.[62] Such things matter for how we know the world in which we act.

Bad Knowledge Actors

All this creates a huge opportunity for bad knowledge actors: those who are hell-bent on causing collective knowledge problems.

It has for some time been recognised that bots (automated software agents) and fake accounts of various sorts are the source of a major disinformation problem on digital platforms.[63] Part of the problem is platform scale: as one commentator put it, 'fake users have become more difficult to identity as [Facebook] has grown', while Pieter Zatko, a Twitter whistleblower, claimed, after Musk announced his takeover, that Twitter had even more fake accounts than Musk had admitted.[64] There is a problem of automated nuisance messaging in all forms of internet-based communication:[65] the internet, as a vast collection of interconnected machines, is open to manipulation at a scale and speed different from humans. Bad actors are increasingly imitating human voice and appearance through AI agents, a risk that ChatGPT will only intensify, according to Sam Altman of OpenAI.[66] Fears are growing, more generally, that generative AI will 'supercharge online disinformation'.[67]

However we design digital platforms, there will be a need to root out this sort of deception, and it will require considerable technological resource. But bots are not the only problem. There are state actors powerful enough and well enough resourced to fund human armies of communicators to simulate robots that, in turn, are simulating human beings. Russia's Internet Research Agency boasted it had a key role in propelling Donald Trump to victory in 2016, and armies of Russian operatives are generating false information to influence news in Africa.[68] The Agency is keen to undermine 'Western agendas' such as feminism, for example by targeting feminist activists, like Linda Sansour, one of the leaders of the 2017 Women's March on Washington.[69] In July 2021, internal documents from the Russian government emerged which, if authentic (and of course that is denied), indicate that Russia's leadership decided, already in January 2016, to take advantage of what they saw as the USA's key weakness: its 'media-information space'.[70] Social media platforms were seen as the best entry-point for intervention. When hostile governments see the new space of the world as a strategic *weakness* of the most powerful nation on the planet, we know we are dealing with a major ecological transformation.[71]

Meanwhile China's '50 cent army' generates vast amounts of social media posts, while from its base in Israel the shadowy Team Jorge pursues disinformation projects worldwide. India's rulers rely on right-wing groups acting under cover of 'open source intelligence' (OSINT) to target those who dare oppose the government.[72] Disinformation has notably played a major role in two conflicts that are current as I write: the Russian invasion of Ukraine, particularly from the Russian side, and, in the opinion of many commentators, the Israel–Palestine conflict. The list could go on.

The implications of these developments for how we think about the relations between technology and democracy are profound. The old assumption that online space is necessarily good for democracy has been proved false: on the contrary, as Farrell and Schneier argue, the wider flow of information about common knowledge only increases the 'attack space' at which hostile actors can aim.[73]

Think of a platform like Facebook with around 3 billion users and reaching 72 per cent of the US adult population.[74] Facebook's size creates more than a problem that expands proportionately as its user numbers do. Facebook's huge dominance, especially in US society, creates an entirely *new type* of societal problem by being a massive target attractive to forces that want, for geopolitical reasons, to sway whole societies. Suppose you do want to influence two large (indeed overlapping) groups in US society: Christians and Blacks. Then social media platforms give you the perfect entry-point, or, in the military jargon, 'attack surface'. In an important investigative piece, then MIT Tech Review journalist Karen Hao discovered that, as at October 2019, all fifteen of the top Facebook pages targeting Christian Americans and ten of the top fifteen pages targeting Black Americans were run not by human beings but by troll farms.[75] Such influential fakes are, probably, still influencing opinion in those groups. Worse, they can circulate materials on a vast scale to seed discussion among real Facebook users.[76] Meanwhile, clickbait farms present a wider problem for Facebook (for example, its advertising-driven Instant Articles feature) and for Google (its AdSense programme), since both rely for their impact on content generated by clickbait farms.[77]

Why expect other platforms to be exempt from this? TikTok with well over 1.5 billion users also presents a huge attack surface to overseas powers, even if configured differently from Facebook. The cycle of potential manipulation across and between platforms is potentially endless. But let's not, finally, discount the possibility that the ultimate human factor in disinformation is sometimes a single powerful individual. Cornell University reported early in the pandemic that the single biggest spreader of 'coronavirus misinformation' was not bot armies, but then US President Donald Trump. But again what mattered most was that the whole social media ecology was there to amplify him.[78]

How to avoid the conclusion that, as Renee DiResta of Stanford's Internet Observatory put it, 'our information ecosystem is trending toward unreality'?[79]

The Redistribution of Social Attention

Platforms do not act in isolation. Though themselves ecological in scale, they are part of an even wider information environment shaped by political and social factors. For one thing, legacy media (television, radio, the press) play a major role in amplifying what is circulating on social media. Mainstream media's solemn repetition of whatever former President Trump had tweeted is the paradigmatic example.[80] There are also many reasons why both attention and authority in the political domain are increasingly in short supply in contemporary societies.[81]

The liberal myth that the internet frees up information to circulate might tell us otherwise, but many aspects of our information environment are a zero-sum game. While information sources are effectively infinite, human attention is not. There is no reason to believe that human attention has increased in volume during the internet age: deeper factors regarding mental and physical capacity, the accelerating pace of life, and so on, may be more decisive.

That finite fund of attention can always be redistributed, and in today's information ecology it has been, with our attention being redistributed away from some traditional news sources, such as local newspapers.[82] It is a matter of redistributing not just attention, but also the advertising income targeted at that attention.[83] Social media are driving this particular zero-sum game, and so far they are the winners.

Not only politicians and governments, but also marketers want to influence information production. Take climate change. Over time, marketers have played a decisive role in reframing that debate towards what Melissa Aronczyk, a leading expert on strategic communication, has called 'the wrong kind of problem: a problem of information, politics, and publicity instead of a problem of our continued existence'.[84] The result is an even wider disconnect between most politics and humanity's actual needs for climate action. Here, political advertisers' uses of both traditional media and social media played a crucial role.[85]

What can we do about this? Some argue that the solution must lie in intensified vigilance of the professional standards of media institutions: after all, the 'marketplace of ideas' (of which platforms are just an extension) is not best designed to adjudicate between truth and falsity.[86] But, given the zero-sum game in which social media and traditional media are engaged (we'll return to its impacts in Chapter 7), we can't be confident that traditional media institutions will correct for the intense flow of disinformation and misinformation on social media. Traditional media are themselves increasingly reliant on the audiences that social media platforms divert to them.[87] As a result, our overall information ecology is becoming skewed in favour of exactly the party (social media) that most needs reform.

The result is an ecological problem for which, as with all ecological problems, we need public policy solutions.[88] Technical solutions will never be enough: as Farrell and Schneier say, 'technologists don't usually think systematically about broader knowledge system and expectations', even when they have helped cause them.[89]

It makes little sense to blame society here, although commentators are often tempted by labels such as 'misinformation society' or 'disinformation order'.[90] Big Tech never asked any society if it wanted the current space of the world! Whatever the social consequences that are unfolding, we need to place the focus firmly back on the design choices that built the space of the world that we inhabit.

The Undermining of Trust

We can't, however, stop our diagnosis at information. The connections between information form a key connective tissue for many other activities in society, especially political deliberation. So, if their quality suffers, we can expect consequences across the whole of politics. This is where trust comes in. Suspicion of government and scientific claims are certainly not new, and some suspicion is healthy for politics, and indeed for media too. Which is not to say that it makes sense, as some fear many are doing,[91] to bypass traditional media outputs altogether, when other means to correct misinformation are in short supply.

We are currently in a paradoxical position. On the one hand, according to one recent international survey (Edelman's 2022 annual survey of trust),[92] technology is the globally most trusted sector of society at 74 per cent. In Europe a slightly older survey reported similarly high trust in search results.[93] Yet trust in one key product of technology companies – social media content – is falling rapidly everywhere, and 76 per cent of those asked by the Edelman survey were concerned about 'fake news': disinformation in which social media are widely perceived to play a major role.[94] Unsurprisingly social media platforms were the news source in which *trust fell* most sharply during the pandemic.[95] But this general problem with trustworthy information predated the pandemic, as another European survey noted: 71 per cent of Europeans said in 2019 they came across false information online at least 'several times a month'.[96]

At the same time, there is what leading marketers Edelman call a 'vicious cycle of distrust' fuelled by government and media.[97] The false perception of diversity we get on social media doesn't help, since it may block us from seeing the underlying problem.[98] According to some researchers, 'the less one trusts in news media and politics, the more one believes in online disinformation'.[99] It is not as if people can automatically turn to a source *outside* social media to validate claims made on social media that don't sound immediately plausible. Increasingly questions of believability – and indeed doubt – are themselves being decided *within* social media platforms, so compounding the ecological problem.[100]

As long as we don't challenge today's social-media-driven space of the world, we will get nowhere. External institutional authority (including journalistic or scientific expertise) has taken years to build and depends not on what someone just said on Facebook or TikTok but on institutional spaces such as the newsroom, the courtroom and the university lecture hall. Such institutionally based authority has ever less weight in today's space of the world. Challenge people's beliefs in what they learn from social media, and the most likely response is for people to double down, relying on the *apparent* social authority of what 'a lot of people are saying' on digital platforms.[101] People in any case do tend to double down on their beliefs, rather than adapt them in the face of contrary evidence, especially if the contrary evidence is about something bad, rather than something good.[102]

How is this affecting engagement in science? We may be only in the early stages of the problem. After a social crisis (the COVID-19 pandemic) in which, for most people, scientific fact was central, three-quarters of US adults said they were interested in science news, although the same number were frustrated by political disagreement about science.[103] Only a third of social media users said they sought out scientific sources via social media,[104] suggesting that legacy media or educational resources are still important. Older research had found a positive, if general, association between using social media for news and trust in science, but this was maybe explained by underlying demographic factors.[105] Since then, it has become generally acknowledged that a considerable amount of scientific misinformation spreads on mainstream social media. But will blocking it just drive it to less mainstream sites, which all lie within the wider social media ecology?[106]

However hard misinformation about science is to combat, a worrying further trend has emerged in the highly polarised US. While belief in the *fact* of climate change remained high (94 per cent), when people were asked whether they believed that 'scientists adjust their findings to get the results they want' (that is, tamper with the truth!), a significant minority (41 per cent) said yes.[107] This minority belief turned out to be heavily influenced not just by low educational level (unsurprising), but also by political leanings (if they were Republican or Republican-leaning). This scepticism extended to specific findings on climate change.

Returning to the COVID-19 pandemic, European adults who lack confidence in vaccines are much less likely to trust in professional health sources. Yes, only 5 per cent of people named social media as one of their main sources of trustworthy information on the pandemic, but it is unclear, once trust in mainstream sources has been tainted, what alternative sources are left to compensate.[108]

Meanwhile levels of trust in government are variable, with some countries experiencing major rises in trust in government in the pandemic, and others a major fall.[109] Such trust is also polarised, for example in the US, where as few as 9 per cent of Republicans and 29 per cent of Democrats trust government 'always or most of the time'.[110]

All of this suits bad knowledge actors whose goal is not to convince us of their truth, only to distract us from what might otherwise be our truth. In a space of the world configured *for* disinformation, distraction is all that is needed to shift opinion substantially.[111] Distraction is the purpose for which social media platforms might as well have been designed.

What are the consequences of this for the trust on which most forms of political power depend? If all political parties and positions were affected equally by falling trust in information and knowledge authority, there might be common ground from which to build a cross-partisan basis for social media reform. But recent US research suggests a more worrying possibility: that, while misinformation in the long run reduces everyone's trust in mainstream media, trust in government is more unevenly affected, with right-wing users of social media having their belief in a right-wing government *supported* by exactly the misinformation that undermines their trust in mainstream media.[112] That risk is reinforced when the right-wing government in question exploits such misinformation, as Trump's 2016–20 administration did. A problem specific to the US perhaps, but, given the rise of so-called populist parties in many countries that often trade in debunking myths and circulating 'fake news', not a problem that can be ignored anywhere.

Philosophy has worried for centuries about what happens when in societies or communities trust fails. This is one way of understanding the famous Prisoners' Dilemma, which models the impossibility of individuals reaching good decisions about what to do when they don't trust each other sufficiently. The problem is as much about perceptions of likelihood to cooperate as about actual willingness to cooperate. As a leading sociologist of trust, Diego Gambetta, put it:

> The problem is essentially one of communication: even if people have perfectly adequate motives for cooperation they still need to know about each other's motives and to trust each other, or at least [to trust] the effectiveness of their motives. It is necessary not only to trust others before acting cooperatively, but also to believe that one is trusted by others.[113]

Could climate change action be one area particularly vulnerable to such a collapse of trust?[114] If so, we need a space of the world that works to repair both trust and the quality of information. Right now, it is very unclear that is what we have.

Conclusion

Is this too pessimistic? Might not social media become an alternative source of informational authority (social validation via social media circulation), especially for younger people who, as one report put it, feel that social media is 'their own medium'?[115] The rise of influencers on social media offers potential new sources of authority. Social media companies and consumer culture brands have built up 'ordinary' influ-encers as a bridge between major celebrities and individual users, with TikTok now being the fastest-expanding space. 'Liveshopping' – buying as you follow an influencer online who tells you the value of a product – has become normal. [116]

Critiques of the influencer phenomenon's impact abound, for example on the wage economy or children's extended exposure to adverts,[117] even while others defend the new economic opportunities that are emerging for and around influencers.[118] Whatever the potential benefits, influencers operate very much within the limits set by social media's business goals, as well as the wider logic of celebrity.[119] The influencer movement has already generated its own refuseniks or de-influencers.[120] If engagement is what matters for platforms, it is no surprise that influencers willing to challenge boundaries in the pursuit of virality have flourished: a whole subculture of toxic male charisma (think of Andrew Tate and Russell Brand) has emerged, entirely dependent on the unprecedented monetisation opportunities offered by digital platforms.[121]

The influencer movement would be a credible part of the solution to informational mistrust, if there were evidence it genuinely encouraged people to turn to alternative sources of fact and ideas. But one of the few pieces of research on what makes influencing work in practice suggests otherwise. Although limited to only one country (Finland), its finding was intriguing: that what mattered was the homogeneity of the networks targeted. The more homogeneous the network, the more likely influencers were to have influence there.[122] But isn't that exactly what we should fear: a new form of online authority that feeds off the segregation, even polarisation, of communities, the very weakness of online spaces that we explored in Chapter 3? Meanwhile, if we look specifically at the fastest-growing global platform, TikTok, current research indicates that far-right propaganda, anti-Semitism and anti-feminism are alive and kicking there.[123]

Outright censorship is clearly not the answer, but ideas for countering misinformation online abound, some of them sensible.[124] But they fall short of the actual problem, which is not a localised fall in trust on this or that issue, but a deeper change in the conditions under which trust in quality information is possible at all.

No one would claim, of course, that challenges to authority are in themselves bad: who now laments the profound social changes wrought by the spread of books through society in early modernity? But each major historical transformation must be judged on its own merits. A space of the world constituted by a hyperconnected internet and engagement-driven commercial platforms appears to be undermining the social bases for reliable knowledge in fundamental ways, with uncertain implications for democratic politics.

What if social media also dispose us to be more polarised in how we interpret whatever circulates online? That is the topic of the next chapter.

CHAPTER 5

Uncivil Societies

'Madness is no madness when shared.' (Zygmunt Bauman)[1]

In the last two chapters, we have considered the space of the world from the perspective of individuals and how information circulates there. But, as this space has been transformed by the dynamics of social media platforms and the searchable internet, what has become of society, in particular political and civil society?

It's not that Facebook, Google, WeChat or TikTok *want* to destabilise social life: they want to make money. But platforms that choose to make money by reconfiguring our space of the world generate risks, and accrue responsibilities, to which platforms have generally not lived up. At various points in the past half-decade public anger has erupted against platforms' lack of responsibility. This anger has focused particularly on Facebook and been centred in the US: the Cambridge Analytica revelations of March/April 2018; Facebook's failure to dampen down those plotting the January 2021 attack on the US Capitol;[2] the whistleblower testimony in autumn 2021 of Frances Haugen which lifted the cover on Facebook internal discussions about its social harms. A legal action started in October 2023 by thirty-three US states against Meta and Instagram for damaging young people's mental health has brought all these issues into focus.

But the issue goes far wider than the US. Think of the scandal in Kenya, where Facebook's failure to effectively manage hate speech has led to government legal action.[3] Think of whistleblower Sophie Zhang's revelations in 2020 about Facebook's inability to manage hate speech by extremist groups in Myanmar against its Muslim Rohingya minority. Zhang summarised the problem as inadequate investment in moderation based on priorities focused on the US and Europe: 'it's an open secret . . . that Facebook's short-term decisions are largely motivated by PR and the potential for negative attention'.[4] Finally, a UNESCO-commissioned survey reported in September 2023 that, across the sixteen countries due to hold an election in 2024, 87 per cent of people believed that online disinformation had harmed their country's politics, with 68 per cent principally blaming social media.[5] These and many other examples from around the world evidence how business and technical choices by platforms are having serious impacts on civil society, and potentially politics too.

Standard explanations of what has gone wrong with politics are insufficient. To blame 'populism', Russia expert Peter Pomerantsev points out, is to focus on the symptom and miss the disease: '"populism" is not a sign of "the people" coming together in a great groundswell of unity, but is actually a consequence of the people being more fractured than ever, of their barely existing as one nation'.[6] The idea of 'populism', after all, still assumes there *is* a 'people' there, waiting to be spoken for. But maybe the real problem is how a certain *formation* of 'the people' has been constructed online and left to play out, with insufficient monitoring of the consequences (a situation that our Leviathan in fragments image in Chapter 2 tried to capture). Many cultural, economic and social forces contribute to this construction, but social media platforms are the key player. They are spaces that make money by ensuring that a particular type of 'we' comes together online.[7]

Neither advertisers nor social media companies are interested in us sitting quietly, reading a book, meeting up in a café, listening to music with friends and occasionally looking at what people post on social media without commenting. What they need is our 'engagement': our posts, our comments, our efforts to recirculate what others post. Attempts to generate engagement, regardless of quality, are taking increasingly bizarre forms, for example, on the world's new rising platform, TikTok.[8] The more 'engaged' the better, and perhaps the more *polarised and uncivil* the better. In this chapter we will look at how this process of escalation starts, how it derives from design choices in our space of the world, why it is hard to stop, and what its wider consequences might be for civil society and politics everywhere.

False Leads

Researchers in political communication and social psychology have spent a decade or more thinking about the difference that social media platforms make to politics and our collective life more generally. Although there remain some optimists,[9] the overwhelming prognosis has been negative. A recent review of 500 academic articles found that, while there were some positive consequences of digital media for democracy, there was also consistent concern at negative consequences, especially in more established democracies.[10] As we saw, while causal effects are generally hard to *prove* without large longitudinal studies of a sort that is rarely feasible, the overall pattern of research about social media's political consequences is clear. Among the warning lights flashing are declining political trust (discussed in the last chapter) and growing polarisation (this chapter's focus).[11]

Yet for a while academic research was distracted by two over-simple ideas of how digital media changes our relations to information: the 'filter bubble' and the 'echo chamber'. Let's review these quickly before we move onto more plausible explanations of what has changed.

Bursting of the Filter Bubble

One early intuition about how a platformed space of the world might limit, rather than enhance, wider information space was the 'filter bubble'. The idea depended on the features of search engines, not of social media platforms. Responding to Google's increasing personalisation of its search results to fit the search history of individual users, Eli Pariser, an important critical voice in the US tech industry and once chief executive of Moveon.org – a US-based public policy advocacy group – argued in a popular 2011 book that the search filters generated by Google's search algorithm *itself* caused an individualised information bubble.[12] If so, letting information flow freely in a Google-dominated internet would not serve liberalism in the long run, quite the opposite. This was certainly a provocative challenge to the liberal vision of information markets.

However, despite the provocation, this account of how search engines have impact has not been upheld: it turns out that Google search overall tends to broaden our news sources over time, not narrow them,[13] although later we'll discuss one case where filter bubbles might be growing. The underlying reason for why we don't, most of the time, live in filter bubbles is relatively simple.[14] Historically, individuals' range of news sources was limited (a favourite news bulletin, a favourite newspaper, perhaps one or two news aggregator sites), but a search engine like Google, by searching the whole web, almost inevitably generates a wider news-source selection.[15] The current internet-driven news and information environment also gives a major role to self-selection: people put together their own regular mix of sources, but also supplement this from time to time by listening to others.[16]

So, even if Google worked in an exclusively personalised way, the broader information space each of us *actually* accesses would still be more diversified than it had been before Google. In case this seems counter-intuitive, consider that surveys provide plenty of evidence that most people now get news inputs from a range of sources and media, which, even if still relatively small, is significantly wider than the old diet of one or two broadcast bulletins a day and a single newspaper.[17]

A key error of the filter bubble approach was to imagine the individual as if she were an isolated window on the world, completely reliant on the design of that window. Yes, there *are* issues to be considered about the changing position of individuals in information space (already noted in Chapter 3), but they are more subtle than the recursive biases of a single general search engine.

Few *Live* in an Echo Chamber

Another false lead, although it seemed initially promising, was that of the sealed-off echo chamber. The basic idea can be quickly summarised: a 'setting' inside which 'people . . . will only encounter things they already agree with', which creates the worry that 'without free movement of ideas and information inside the echo chamber [people] will believe that this is all there is'.[18]

The problem is not that there are absolutely no information spaces that operate like echo chambers. So, for example, the huge mainstream surprise at the attempted coup in Washington, DC on 6 January 2021 demonstrated a sort of large-scale echo chamber in operation, while those who planned and developed the coup had operated mainly in their own echo chambers, such as the talk platform Parler.[19] Indeed there is evidence that online spaces focused around one prevalent viewpoint where openness to the opposed viewpoint is tightly limited (a space with echo-chamber-like effects) *do* exist and *may* influence how particular views on, for example, climate change emerge.[20] Those in echo chambers are most likely to be those with less diverse offline networks.[21]

But this may not be a widespread phenomenon. A further study across seven countries found that left- or right-wing echo chambers did exist online, but only 5 per cent of internet news users were in them, and only in the USA were those echo chambers configured around particular news outlets.[22] The number of those not consuming any online news at all may be larger than those in echo chambers.[23] Which is not to say those small online echo chambers have no wider consequences for democratic culture.

The deeper problem with the echo chamber idea was its assumption that there might exist in real life lots of *individuals* who are locked into perfect echo chambers that let in nothing that clashes with their dominant perspective on the world. People always have agency, and the chance to make myriad selections about what they follow online. As people make those choices and get on with life, they come across many things: some they agree with, some they viscerally disagree with. Given that people's online networks are much larger often than their face-to-face networks (see Chapter 3), people's exposure to information sources tends to be expanded by joining social media.[24] This means that the people imagined by the echo chamber thesis – individuals who exist in a complete echo chamber – are likely to be relatively rare.

What drove the echo chamber debate, however, was a concern about growing polarisation. That, as we shall see, is a very valid concern, but the mistake was to assume that polarisation is caused by exclusivity of news sources. Not only does exclusivity not straightforwardly exist in the real world, but a large-scale US experiment with adult Facebook users found that exposing them to more sources that were neutral at least (if not necessarily opposed) did not affect their underlying polarisation.[25] In any case, those whose views of the world are *most* polarised may be quite happy to sample a wide range of news sources, because they are completely confident what they find won't challenge their views. This phenomenon is not new.

Take the controversial social media commentator Megan Phelps-Roper, who recalls growing up in an extremely narrow Baptist Church community in the US South and enjoying a wide range of information sources, long before the age of social media: 'we had wide latitude in our consumption of books, television, film, and music, and for much the same reason we attended public schools: our parents weren't particularly worried about negative influences slipping into our minds undetected'.[26] As a reviewer of her memoir comments, 'Westboro members understood that they could despise the rest of the world without withdrawing from it.' It's not surprising, therefore, that, according to one survey, a majority of people have 'rarely or never' discovered information that changed their opinion.[27]

In short, the echo chamber and filter bubble hypotheses distracted us from the real issue, which is what people do with the information sources to which they are exposed. This takes us to the wider forces of polarisation at work online.[28]

How Social Media Platforms Fuel Polarisation

We need *some* differences in opinion, belief and worldview to have political debate at all. If there were no discernible sides in collective discussion – if there was nothing to argue about – why would we have politics?[29] Often, such differences will give rise to situations that appear polarised, and with justification. But that doesn't mean that all differences in belief are good: why should there be a two sided-debate about the basic facts of climate change? Nor does it mean that, in the long run, forces that fuel polarisation more widely are good.

Over the past decade, many have come to believe that politics in many parts of the world is becoming more polarised, and that social media are a key factor causing this. Even researchers who are sceptical about whether polarised behaviour is increasing absolutely still insist that hostile behaviour is becoming more *visible* through social media. Perhaps those who are disposed to 'status-driven risk taking' (another way of describing polarising behaviour) see opportunities in the higher visibility that social media gives to their actions?[30] Could this be changing how people feel about social media? A 2019 survey across eleven Global South countries found that overall 46 per cent of people felt they would be 'uncomfortable . . . discussing political issues or news on social media', although the figure varied between countries (27 per cent in India but 67 per cent in Colombia).[31] As we saw when discussing trust in the last chapter, our mutual perceptions of each other's readiness for politics matter just as much as the reality.

Clearly it was not the intention of social media's creators to make them hostile places for political discussion. Indeed their initial design seemed aimed at encouraging positive, not negative, emotions: you cannot 'dislike' a post on Facebook, WhatsApp, Instagram or Twitter. More recently Alphabet's YouTube platform which *did* have a dislike button and, because of its commentary function and the algorithm it uses to drive engagement, certainly qualifies here as social media, has hidden numbers of dislikes on its platform, although the button remains.[32] In addition, platforms based around indications of connection ('friending') open up the possibility of people unfriending others, often in highly polarised situations.[33]

Media have in recent years become full of claims that social media are polarising politics. Those claims reached fever pitch in the US in 2021, a year after a tense – and indeed by some still disputed – Presidential election.[34] The Sophie Zhang and Frances Haugen revelations added fuel to the fire. In 2022, Jonathan Haidt, a psychologist and columnist for *The Atlantic*, argued in two controversial articles that 'social media really is undermining democracy'; in the second article, under pressure from Facebook, he conceded that 'social media may not be the primary cause of polarization', though it remains 'an important cause, and one we can do something about'.[35] This sort of claim would have been unthinkable a decade earlier. It only began to become mainstream in the past five years, anticipated by pioneering academic research undermining the earlier consensus that social media platforms support political engagement.[36]

Before this particular 'TechLash', things were very different. A research paper that suggested Facebook use helped reduce ideological polarisation became very highly cited,[37] even though its authors were themselves from Facebook and were only confirming what later became established, that true echo chambers are relatively rare. Also seized upon was research by economist Matthew Gentzkow and colleagues that apparently showed greater use of the internet and social media are not associated with increased political polarisation.[38] The basis for this claim was, however, rather speculative: an assumption about which demographic groups are 'least likely to use the internet and social media'. The research modelled correlations between *those (proxy) demographic groups* and broad statistics about political polarisation. The possibility that other factors than social media use might be at play in generating polarisation (for example, age or class) was not studied.

But the debate moved on, and, in a later paper, Gentzkow led an experiment that suggested a very different outcome: when people were asked to deactivate Facebook for the four weeks of the US 2018 midterm elections, this improved their wellbeing, even though it reduced their intake of factual news input, perhaps because it also reduced their sense of political polarisation.[39] 'The downsides of Facebook use', the economists now concluded, 'are real.'[40]

Other work by economists on a country (Germany) with high anti-migrant sentiment has studied the correlation between posts to the Facebook page of the right-wing party AfD (Alternative für Deustchland) and racist attacks against migrants. Startlingly, it found that when local internet outages blocked Facebook access in an area, racist attacks disappeared. As the researchers put it: 'without outages, there is a strong correlation of refugee posts and attacks. During outages, the correlation is essentially zero.'[41]

There is good reason then for concern that social media platforms may be polarising, not just in the hyper-polarised context of the US. But why exactly?

The Deeper Roots of Polarisation

The diversionary debate about filter bubbles and echo chambers was fixed on the wrong target: people's information sources. Yes, there is something that political scientists call 'ideological polarisation' (splits in opinion over facts), but just as important is another type of polarisation, *affective polarisation*: polarisation based in opposed, perhaps mutually hostile, feelings.[42]

Our understanding of affective polarisation and what drives it has been advanced by political scientists, particularly Stanford's Shanto Iyengar. Incontrovertible evidence for a decade has shown that, in the US at least, affective polarisation is steeply on the rise, posing 'considerable challenges to the democratic process'.[43] Iyengar has been particularly concerned with the form of affective polarisation taken by political partisanship in the US, as shaped by the binary US party system. Such polarisation may have consequences for the other sort of polarisation, which is focused more on facts and fact-based opinion. As one psychologist argues, 'when societal risks [i.e. facts] become suffused with antagonistic social meanings [i.e. emotions]', ordinary members of the public start to attend to information in a potentially polarised way,[44] which presumably, in turn, reinforces polarised feelings about others' opinions, a vicious circle.

The US, although highly distinctive, is only one country among many where there have in the past decade been signs of growing polarisation: other clear examples are Argentina, Brazil, India, Kenya, the Netherlands, Poland and the UK. The result is a world where everyone is 'collectively worse off', because democratic consensus, for example about climate change, becomes ever less likely.[45] In a later paper, Iyengar, drawing now on social media evidence too, went further and concluded that 'the sense of partisan identification is all encompassing and affects behavior in both political and non-political contexts'.[46] Polarisation, in other words, has become a way of life.

Let's defer for now the question of what the space of social media might have to do with this and look back to some insights from some earlier research in social psychology, on which Iyengar's research has consistently drawn. 'Social Identity Theory' in the 1980s was a dominant strand in social psychology. This theory tried to explain how differentiated groups emerge in society. It is hard to object to its starting-point: that, to explain people's sense of identity, we shouldn't assume either a completely autonomous individual (the monad) or a pre-existing group identity, but think instead of the constant interactions between individual and group that help a sense of identity to form. Individuals acquire their sense of who they, individually, are by reference to their changing perceptions of the groups to which they might belong. This approach had much in common with important sociological thinking, also from the 1980s,[47] and offers a refreshing change from the highly individualist thinking that for decades before and since has dominated economics and neoliberal thought.

By developing a series of experiments in which they closely observed people's sense of group membership, the proponents of Social Identity Theory found that group allegiance is very basic in humans, even more basic perhaps than acting out of self-interest.[48] The gravitational force of group identity is powerful, they found, whatever the criteria used to form those groups, which can be as minimal as random selection.

After Social Identity Theory established that the human sense of group identity is basic, two psychologists went further and developed an interesting theory of why groups under certain circumstances become polarised from other groups.[49] Imagine some people in a room, and imagine that a subset is told they form a 'group' for whatever reason, perhaps even for no good reason. Those latter people, they argued, will tend to conform to social norms associated with whatever categories over time come to distinguish their in-group. They will regard as valid whatever is stereotypically associated with those categories. The more a particular individual seems to represent the group's consensus and its core behaviour patterns (say, a particular action or opinion), the more influence she will gain in the group.[50]

But in the process the average or mean behaviour of the in-group may shift from what was originally the mean behaviour of people in the room. If so, the in-group will go on orientating to *its* internal reference-point, while in reality shifting ever more to one extreme, relative to the room as a whole. The in-group's differences from the behaviour of everyone else in the room will become accentuated: the room's in-group and out-group will have become polarised.[51]

The question of what might drive that shift in the in-group's internal reference-points is left open by Social Identity Theory, as well it might have been, since its proponents, writing in the 1970s, 1980s and early 1990s, could never have imagined the polarising pressures of today's space of the world. What this early theory did, however, was highlight the deep underlying pressures towards group conformity and group polarisation that arise from just two simple conditions: one, that perceptions of who and what is prototypical of a group are *made explicit*, and two, that people feel group membership to be *salient* to them. Salience can be imposed in an artificial experimental situation, or it can arise from an inherited sense of identity, or it can emerge from what Iyengar and colleagues (also not writing initially with social media in mind) call the 'characteristics of the information environment, such as the number of times the individual is reminded of her affiliation to some group'.[52]

Social Identity Theory seems to speak from a distant world where psychologists could experiment on people's sense of identity against the background of a social and cultural world more stable than today's.[53] But its account of group loyalty and potential polarisation has huge relevance to today's seemingly fluid online identities.[54] It gives us the tools to think about a world where we *are* incentivised moment to moment to make explicit (to signal) our identification with others (liking what they post, sending that post on to others in our group with our endorsement or tagging a photo with the names of other members of our group); and where, as we do so, our group and its behaviour *do* become ever more salient to us (we get told, for example, who has liked our post, who has tagged us and so on).

Social Identity Theory gives us the lens to see our space of the world for what it is: a world, where the 'expressive incentives' to signal one's group membership on social media platforms have become unimaginably intense, compared with three or four decades ago.[55] So let's look again at how social media platforms work, but with these lessons from social psychology in mind.

Social Media as Polarisation Machines

Social media platforms are spaces where we are incentivised to signal our identity and therefore how we are distinct from others: when we 'like' something someone posts, what is this but a signal attached to that person (and therefore presumably not attached to *another* person with whom we don't have a like-relationship)? By building those signals into everyday interaction, indeed incentivising people to send such signals, social media created a space that, as Turkish-US scholar Zeynep Tufekci puts it, is affectively simplified, overriding the actual ambiguities of everyday life before social media:

> when we encounter opposing views in the age and context of social media, it's not like reading them in a newspaper while sitting alone. It's like hearing them from the opposing team while sitting with our fellow fans in a football stadium. Online we're connected with our communities, and we seek approval from our like-minded peers.[56]

On social media platforms, we sit in the middle of an ongoing social identity/group polarisation experiment:[57] not by accident, but because social media platforms have progressively focused on maximising the engagement, and potential economic value, that comes from increased identity-signalling.[58]

Twitter introduced a 'favourite' button in 2006 and a 'retweet' button in 2009. When much later people realised the impact, Twitter started to have second thoughts. While still Twitter CEO, Jack Dorsey expressed regret for introducing the 'favourite' button on the ground that 'it doesn't actually push what we believe *now* to be the most important thing, which is *healthy* contribution back to the network'.[59] Meanwhile one of Twitter's developers called the retweet function (still existing) a 'loaded weapon'.[60]

Facebook, after growing its knowledge of people's social networks, introduced the 'like' button in 2009 and in 2011 a 'send' button (allowing the forwarding of posted material to friends). It did not originally have the AI power to personalise the news it presented to users in newsfeeds (the first developers of such personalised recommendation algorithms were Amazon and Netflix, not social media).[61] But Facebook's delayed introduction of buttons was part of a crucial switch, which soon affected almost all social networks: the move from an initial *subscription* model under which users only saw posts of people they had chosen to follow, to a *network* model (which allowed the forwarding of material from people they originally didn't know), to today's *algorithmic* model, where it is mainly algorithms that drive what we see most prominently.[62]

TikTok represents the ultimate version of the algorithmic model, bypassing the first two stages. Abandoning reliance on tracking detailed social interactions, TikTok uses its algorithm to recommend videos to users and then closely tracks how they respond. Not only does its design involve more signals that users can send ('like', dislike', 'upvote', 'downvote'), but it puts special emphasis on how long people linger over videos and how often they return to them.[63] Most importantly, by foregrounding its 'For You' recommendations as the main interaction-point, TikTok, in effect, locks users into a continuous experimental zone that guarantees maximum data inputs to its algorithm. The result is the most sophisticated personalisation machine yet built, based on what has been vividly called a 'virality-centric logic'.[64] In spite of TikTok's protests to the contrary, research has shown that the TikTok algorithm works relentlessly to further promote virality-producing content, for example misogynistic material among lonely young men.[65]

Whatever the differences in their detailed features, the goal of all social media algorithms is, basically, to drive engagement, as the short-term proxy for making money. As leading algorithm expert Arvind Narayanan puts it, in something of an understatement, 'the details that matter from a[n] . . . engineering perspective are subtly different from those that matter to users and society'. [66] 'Besides', as Narayanan continues, 'companies have shared precious little about the *effects* of algorithms'. What we do know is that, while engagement is overall what platforms optimise for, how you measure engagement is much more complex, based on detailed evaluations of content and what we do in relation to content. But there is little to stop these profit-focused calculations from feeding back into the dynamics of how emotive material circulates (discussed in Chapter 4), or into the pressures towards polarisation just discussed.

Yes, platforms *can* reduce virality via their algorithms, if they want. Indeed when Twitter recently, and exceptionally, published its algorithm for calculating engagement, it revealed ways it can do this, for example through a mathematical formula that dampens the circulation of material likely to lead someone to block the person who posted it.[67] But 'can' probably won't mean 'will', since maximising circulation (including through virality) remains a basic goal of platforms that make money from engagement.

We inhabit this social media space, constantly aware of the potential state of mind of others. What psychologists call 'pluralistic ignorance' (I don't know right now what most people in the streets around me are thinking), which was once in the offline world a key factor *slowing down* social processes, becomes ever harder to sustain, when social media constantly tells us what others are thinking.[68] The issue is not yet whether these features of social media are undermining cohesion at the level of whole societies.[69] Social media have only been fully at work for a decade and a half. The issue is whether we are on that path, with some countries more drastically committed to it than others.

By multiplying 'the occasions for social comparison' and for continuously ranking oneself against others,[70] social media platforms drive an *identification logic* that fuels inherent human tendencies towards polarisation. Social media supply the final missing ingredient when, through their engagement-focused business models, they incentivise people to do whatever will attract people's attention and engage them just a little more, becoming more emotive, more extreme, relative to the previous norm.

The dial of information production, and not just emotions and behaviour, has shifted. When such group dynamics occur, people are tempted to join an emerging consensus, even if it is associated with false information.[71] In fact, the sheer profusion of other people signalling *their* opinion, *their* status, encourages another phenomenon that's not new, but is now an ever more ordinary feature of our lives, the 'availability cascade': defined as 'a self-reinforcing process of collective belief formation' whereby expressing a perception triggers a chain reaction, with the perception becoming ever more plausible as it passes down the chain and becomes more available in public discourse'.[72] We might think we can ignore the pressures of particular people's opinions in a work meeting or a classroom, but it is much difficult to ignore whole *cascades* of other people's opinions online, especially in a space (like social media) where people are primed to signal their opinions.[73]

Social media have not created the possibility of availability cascades, any more than they created the possibility of polarisation. But they have, through their spatial design and particular business models, created a mechanism (an *enzyme*, as it were) for hugely speeding up how polarisation processes operate in the social world.

Seven Rules of Hyper-polarisation

The result is that we live in an era of emerging *hyper*-polarisation. Here are its rules:

First, social media spaces are perfect spaces for amplifying messages along polarised lines (some have called this 'participatory propaganda').[74] Donald Trump, for example, retained considerable media reach, even after being banned on mainstream platforms in 2021, because individuals there circulated his content onto those sites.[75] The mainstream is therefore never fully quarantined from extremist spaces.

Second, polarising effects will be particularly prominent in groups characterised by homophily (that is, 'birds of a feather', grouped together because they share some feature, for example interest in a particular type of content: see also Chapter 4).[76] Social media platforms encourage such groupings. So too do the algorithmic recommendation systems of other platforms such as YouTube, Netflix and TikTok. Polarisation in such groups may matter less if those in the group can't or don't tend to communicate with each other, but what if they *do* communicate, as for example on YouTube via the comments function? We need to look at what happens with those polarised groups more closely.

In a remarkable study, two German researchers, Jonas Kaiser and Adrian Rauchfleisch, conducted fieldwork in 2018 which showed that YouTube, through its automated system for recommending channels, helped create homophilous groups that view ever more closely overlapping content. This is the precondition for a filter bubble, but it emerged through YouTube's general recommendations, not specifically personalised recommendations! Worse, in relation to politics, the algorithm seemed to push people particularly towards the right, including the extreme right, and asymmetrically: from centre out to the right and beyond, but never the other way (from the right back to the centre). Indeed the problem was hardwired into the workings of YouTube: *if* you watched YouTube content via its many channels, no channel would ever be recommended to you unless it had already embedded Google's recommendation system (that's just the way channels are set up on YouTube!).[77] A more recent study noted that YouTube made changes to its recommender system in 2019, following which only 3 per cent of YouTube users appeared to start viewing alt-right channels, if not already subscribed to them. But as that recent paper's authors also noted, 'even low levels of algorithmic amplification can have damaging consequences when extrapolated over YouTube's vast user base and across time'.[78]

YouTube in any case is just one of many examples of how radicalisation arises from the *ordinary* operation of recommendation algorithms. Nobel Prize winner Maria Ressa gives a similar account of how Facebook thread recommendations contributed to the rise in the Philippines of right-wing populist President Duterte.[79]

Then there is a third rule: when we consider what content is actively circulated by members of such groups, we already know from Chapter 4 (the celebrated MIT study) that virally spreading content is more likely to be false than true, especially if it is political. It is also, according to earlier research, more likely to have a moral-emotional content, for example a moral judgement. Such content is also more likely to be spread within already polarised groups than between them. The result is to reinforce the bonds within those groups in a sort of 'moral contagion'.[80]

Fourth, these polarised spaces which, as we just pointed out, can be caused by something as seemingly innocent as a platform's general recommendation algorithm, are perfect places for people to experiment with stretching the boundaries of group norms: saying yet more outrageous things about those outside the group, hoping others will follow them, and so shifting the dial of group behaviour still further from previous norms. Those whose views are less partisan are less likely to gain attention in online networks than those who are partisan, simply because of how platforms drive engagement.[81] The result is that behaviour that might once have been hidden now becomes fully visible and so able to influence others: exactly the hidden-to-visible shift that we found in Chapter 3.[82]

Fifth, media coverage of political polarisation may itself amplify perceptions of affective polarisation, reinforcing polarised attitudes still further. It may do this by the simplest move of all: reporting that 'a lot of people are saying this', or even that one very powerful person (followed by a lot people) is saying this.[83]

Sixth, search engines can also play an amplifying role, even though, on the face of it, a search engine like Google is not social media. While there is no reason to expect that Googling a term in mainstream political debate would throw up extremist sites, the less mainstream the language, the more likely extremist sites are to feature prominently in search results, according to research on migration debates in Germany and Sweden. Even searches for mainstream terms are likely to include links to social media sites like Facebook which we can expect, from examples already discussed, to include less mainstream opinions.[84]

Seventh, bots (or human armies set up to simulate them) can easily be directed to intensify all or any of these effects.[85] Social-media-driven polarisation is now a weapon in geopolitics, as we saw in Chapter 4.

This is all so astonishing that it is worth pausing a moment to consider what it means. Just two decades ago, political communications researchers could still reflect on the need to encourage local communities, with their own independent media systems and social networks, to engage more in politics.[86] Maybe – hopefully – they still can, but today it is the fractured, polarising, emotionally charged, commercially managed space of social media from which all discussions of our political future have to start.

Social media's enzyme for accelerating polarisation has created a *polarisation machine* on the scale of the planet, an experiment in which there is nothing to stop ever more extreme behaviour being incentivised every day. As two US philosophers concerned about the trends in political life comment, 'the social environment' can 'trigger extremity shifts'.[87]

Right now, all the signs are that, without fundamental redesign of our space of the world, things will go on getting worse. TikTok, the latest version of large-scale social media, with approximately 1.6 billion global users,[88] has less interest in our actual social networks than in using formidable algorithms to create its own artificial groupings, curated by its algorithm. Arguably TikTok is closer to a pure filter bubble than anything we have seen before.

Welcome to the world of hyper-polarisation!

Why Hyper-polarisation Matters for All of Us

Some polarisation, or at least clear differences of opinion, is, as we said, good: the issue is degree, and whether its dynamics remain under any sort of social control. But, through the actions of social media platforms, polarisation seems to have escaped from our social control.

This matters, first, because affective polarisation soon bleeds into perceptions of facts and the shaping of specific opinions. It has been known for some time that people choose their media to fit their political opinions – so-called *selective exposure* – and there is every reason to think this continues with social media: indeed the case of right-wing filter bubbles on YouTube, just discussed, is a frightening example.[89] Algorithms are an excellent way to drive the increasingly polarised circulation of content, which, in turn, is likely to intensify already polarised emotions.[90]

We are talking not just about one's own selective exposure to content, but also, perhaps even more strongly, about selective sharing of content to others.[91] The loaded weapon of the retweet can indeed be 'a function of partisanship' and so a direct instrument of polarisation within the perspective of Social Identity Theory.[92] This impacts on platforms' and civil society organisations' attempts to 'fact-check' messages, which can easily be undermined when retweeted with a dismissive message that polarises feelings still more.[93]

Second, when polarised groups do form, they really matter. When you have a group with homogeneous moral views and emotional responses, you have the starting-point for what we generally call radicalisation.[94] As Social Identity Theory predicted, the key dynamic is identity formation: what a leading expert on political and religious radicalisation, Kevin McDonald, calls 'radicalization constructed in relation to "I", to "you" and to "us"'.[95] Such groups can form exclusively online, unconnected to offline solidarity networks and without the constraint of face-to-face contexts. They are groups formed in a sort of 'networked intimacy'.[96]

The implications of affective polarisation on information flows are particularly important in relation to climate change, where, after all, we need the most truth-coherent information possible. Sadly the evidence is that political polarisation is likely to shape this all-important landscape of beliefs. People are naturally resistant to doing anything to drive a wedge between themselves and their peers, so when views have become polarised around a major topic like this, they may, all too rationally, prefer to follow the group view rather than take the risk of individually advocating a counter-position online.[97]

In any case people's perception of the facts may themselves be closely shaped by their political views and general ideological framework. This was the conclusion of research that synthesised studies on climate change opinions across fifty-six countries.[98] Experimental work in Australia also suggests that people's factual beliefs and policy positions are shaped by politics, while trust in scientists, at least in the US, is evolving similarly.[99]

The US, which has the strongest counter-movement against accepting the reality of climate change, may be the most extreme case here.[100] The partisan gap between Democrats and Republicans on climate change has been widening since early in the century.[101] More recently some have found hope that US climate change sceptics are becoming more willing to shift their position, perhaps under pressure from the experience of climate change itself.[102] But the widespread pressure to take up polarised positions, and indeed the polarised information flows on social media themselves, have been growing for at least a decade,[103] and this has a very credible connection with the increasingly polarised political debate in the US. This matters hugely because, according to a leading review of the topic, it is willingness or not to reflect on the need for change *in the wider capitalist system* that predicts most strongly for views on climate change, rather than people's underlying economic status.[104] Social media play a key role as sites where people learn and perform their willingness (or otherwise) to reflect on the need for change. It is hard to see how our current platforms make such reflexivity any easier.

For sure, social media are only one contributing factor to polarised conflict. There are many other factors which inevitably have deep historical roots.[105] But if social media 'naturally' (i.e. by virtue solely of how they were designed as spaces) work to accentuate polarisation, then social media are potentially a trigger towards a radically more unstable social and political world than we had before.

This increasingly unstable political world is incompatible with solidarity. Indeed it exhibits a very new political culture. Just as all individuals can today show 'agency' in selecting from an infinite range of material online, so bad individuals can profit from the special opportunities that social media space offers to them. For example, the opportunity to become the sort of person that consistently 'trolls' others;[106] the opportunity to create the sort of content (for example, a visual meme that mocks a political opponent) that is designed to spread fast and effectively within and between social media groups.[107] We discussed these features from the perspective of trust and charismatic authority in Chapter 4.

Platform algorithms are often involved here, but they need not be. The platform 4Chan, which, independently of the aims of its founders, has come to host groups for right-wing extremism, does not use algorithms to drive content: it is a just a platform where many types of groups can gather and has a search function to help you find them.[108] But, whatever the mechanics, the outcome has been devastating for US political debate. Joan Donovan, a leading researcher on the US alt right, summed this up powerfully in her recent book with Emily Dreyfuss and Brian Friedberg: if, as the late doyen of the US alt right, Andrew Breitbart, is supposed to have said, politics is downstream from culture, now we must face a grimmer truth, that 'culture is downstream from infrastructure'.[109]

Put plainly, our digital infrastructure – our digital space of the world – has a built-in propensity towards polarisation (see figure 5.1). If so, it

Figure 5.1: Today's polarisation machine.

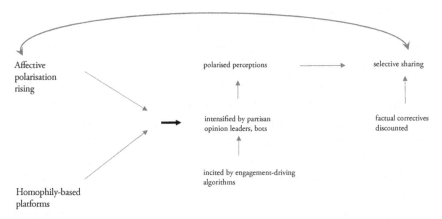

may well be, to quote Donovan again, that 'the only way to win is not to play'.[110] Having fashioned the enzyme of polarisation, Big Tech has no idea how to slow down the psychological reactions it has set in motion.

From Incivility to Disengagement?

But someone might say: polarised conflicts, terrible though they are, remain exceptional and are always driven by complex local conditions, not least in the USA, which overshadows too much of the global discussion. Can the polarisation problem *really* be so bad that it forces us to redesign social media, maybe even the internet, on a global scale? To address that sceptic, let's turn finally to a phenomenon, associated with polarised conflict, that in itself seems more low-key: incivility.[111]

Some are sceptical about whether in the twenty-first century we have seen an objective increase on political incivility.[112] Certainly a brief glance into English politics in the nineteenth century or US politics in the pre-Civil War era would correct the idea that politics then was anything like civil.[113]

Others ask: what is wrong with incivility? Surely enthusiasm is how one gets involved on one side of a political debate, and there's evidence to suggest that some incivility can help to stimulate enthusiastic engagement in politics much more than bland agreement.[114] Maybe, if, as some researchers suggest, incivility tends to stay *within* political groups rather than worsening polarisation between them, we should be less worried about it.[115]

That said, incivility today has many new technical resources at its disposal: no longer just a mocking comment to someone's face or a slur in a press article, radio monologue or TV chat show. Today we are rightly worried about police officers routinely swapping abusive pictures and messages on WhatsApp, or the sudden rise of anti-Semitic posts on Twitter in the months after Musk slashed its moderation staff, or people regularly taking mocking videos of passers-by or dancers on dance-floors and circulating them for amusement on TikTok or Instagram.[116]

No one knows when habits of incivility shared online start to stabilise into something much more worrying: cultures of hate. There are certainly cultures of hate online, and particularly on the Dark Web, many of them focused on ethnic minorities or on women.[117] Beyond these fundamental fault-lines of contemporary society, incivility is a feature of many banal or temporary public spaces: for example, comment streams on the *New York Times* website; or social media commentary in the early days of the COVID-19 pandemic.[118] And it is found in China and many other countries, not just in the US, on which so much of the academic debate has been focused.[119]

It is important not to exaggerate the prevalence of incivility: we can hope that it's not a majority, just a significant minority, who have experienced incivility direct online. The cumulative impact on society, however, goes on growing. After all, as one Irish schoolgirl interviewed by researchers put it, 'it's easy to be bitchy on Facebook because you don't have to see the person – you just have to write it'.[120] Indeed, those who comment *most* on Facebook are also those most likely to use toxic language there, as if they have internalised exactly that lesson.[121]

Social media have therefore expanded the domain of incivility, making it seamless to propagate. What sorts of consequence might this have for society? Take, for example, the hostile online culture against women, whose excesses often extend well beyond mere incivility. Amnesty International reported that 76 per cent of women who had been abused or harassed online said their behaviour had changed, with them refraining, for example, from posting content.[122]

Another impact could be on trust, touched on in Chapter 4: in an experiment where Facebook users were exposed to civil and uncivil comments and asked if this increased their level of trust, it turned out that encountering *civility* led to a strong positive increase in trusting behaviour, even in anonymous interactions, while encountering incivility did not affect trust levels at all, presumably because for participants incivility was now just the norm, so nothing out of the ordinary.[123]

Another impact could be on political discussion itself. A 2016 Pew study conducted before the latest huge rise in political controversy found that a majority of US citizens already found discussing politics online was 'stressful and frustrating', and likely to generate less rather than more political common ground.[124] The impression politics gave to US citizens, already in 2016, was negative, whether this referred to policy-focus, respectfulness, civility or other factors.[125]

There may be other impacts too, for example, on how people interpret what they find online: exposure to uncivil comments around an issue of social risk was found in one study to polarise people's perceptions of that risk, especially if they didn't know much about the issue beforehand.[126] This is clearly one driver of the wider polarisation of public opinion on climate change.

Turning to everyday politics, incivility against politicians online is common,[127] and the dominance of politicians' social media interactions by dispute and abuse was found in Greece to undermine the chance for something more constructive: for example, discussion of actual policies.[128]

Most concerning of all, but so far not backed up by systematic research, is the fear that the recent increase in abuse online against women politicians is discouraging women from entering or remaining in politics. Consider New Zealand's Prime Minister Jacinda Ardern, who resigned suddenly in January 2023, later citing as a reason the toxic nature of online politics.[129] Being targeted for abuse via social media affects women activists at all levels and in many countries, as a study by the campaign #ShePersisted across Africa, Asia, Europe and Latin America found.[130] The same reason seems to have influenced the resignation of Sanna Marin, former Prime Minister of Finland, Nicola Sturgeon, former First Minister of Scotland, and most recently the Deputy Prime Minister of the Netherlands, Sigrid Kaag.[131] And even if that isn't the case, there are good reasons to believe that perceptions of an abusive political culture make everyday talk about politics 'beyond our most intimate circles', as

US researchers Jeffrey Berry and Sarah Sobieraj put it, 'extraordinarily difficult', at least in the US.[132]

Conclusion

In a recent survey of Global South countries, most adults thought access to the digital world has made people 'more divided in their political opinions',[133] while talking to people in person was seen as a better way of 'keeping up with political news' than social media. Often this conclusion was reached not by a narrow, but by a very large, majority.[134]

The question is clear: can humanity afford to go on allowing social platforms to set the terms and conditions for social life from which all politics emerges? We can consign the question to the 'too hard to answer' basket. But that would mean accepting as unavoidable, even normal, what the philosopher Roberto Esposito has called the 'perversion of community into its opposite'.[135] It might mean accepting the perversion of solidarity into a war of all against all. This is madness if we want a democratic route to confronting the climate emergency. But to challenge this madness we must wake up from our delusion – so well captured by the sociologist Zygmunt Bauman in the quotation at the chapter's start – that 'madness is no madness when shared'. It is precisely how we *share* opinions, feelings and information in digital culture that needs to change.

Community of some sort – not necessarily a close local community, but some form of common feeling – is one of the few routes to sustaining politics at all. Avoiding difficult questions about our digital space of the world is no longer an option – if we want to find political solutions to the challenges humanity faces.

In Part 3 we address directly how, in the light of Part 2's findings, we might rethink our digital space of the world.

PART 3

PART 3

CHAPTER 6

Can Solidarity Survive?

'Increasingly people are turning their backs on the values of trust and solidarity in one another – the very values we need to rebuild our world and secure a better, more sustainable future for our people and our planet.' (António Guterres, UN Secretary-General, 2021)[1]

Part 2 has given us reasons to be pessimistic about our current space of the world, and the chances of building solidarity on *any* issue. And yet, we need solidarity more than ever to coordinate our response to the most complex, globally integrated and challenging issue of all: climate change. We need solidarity that is able to forge new connections across otherwise unbridgeable differences of interest.[2] This means we must address practically the problems which today's space of the world poses for building solidarity. That is the goal of Part 3.

In her eloquent play *All of Us* Francesca Martinez offers a way to think about this.[3] Martinez has cerebral palsy, and the play is, at one level, about disability. It doesn't comment directly about the online world. But it shows a human compassion even to those characters (scheming politicians, angry citizens) who are doing most harm to disabled people. In one scene, a heated public meeting, people shout over each other: disabled people attacking the insensitivity of politicians, others attacking the disabled for taking advantage of the welfare state. The result is chaos, and nothing gets understood. But in another scene, the lead character, played by Martinez herself, is interviewed by a woman bureaucrat who unwittingly uses language and gestures that draw on abled people's misjudging of disabled people over millennia. Instead of shouting in angry condemnation, Martinez sits quietly, allowing the woman bureaucrat to gradually realise what is wrong with how she spoke.

The roots of solidarity lie, the play shows us, in the possibility of reflecting honestly on what we get wrong and, through that, learning how it is often *we*, not others, who must change. Building solidarity does not come from abuse or mutual attacks or overheated spaces of confrontation. The play asks how, without compassion, can any of us come together, but also shows us that solidarity is possible, even when not expected.

In this chapter, we will look at the prospects for solidarity in our current space of the world, without assuming any changes to the social media infrastructure. Then, in the book's final chapter, we'll turn directly to how we can redesign our social media infrastructure to preserve key conditions for building solidarity.

But solidarity is nothing more than inflated self-interest unless it is built across difference: differences of all sorts, not just in economic and social interests, but in identity, life experience, and world view. And it is precisely such solidarity we need in the face of climate change that endangers everyone's world.

General Difficulties

There are many forces beyond social media that make building real solidarity hard.

In many countries recent political conflict and divided histories affect people's basic trust in each other. This is often reinforced by the huge global increase in inequality.[4] In the US, where inequality has grown hugely in the past five decades, trust in government has fallen strongly in the same period and is now well below the OECD average, while general interpersonal trust has also fallen.[5] Many countries in Latin America also have levels of interpersonal trust considerably below the global average, along with high inequality.[6] Interpersonal trust is also considerably lower in many rich countries amongst younger age groups.[7]

Meanwhile, climate change itself is intensifying existing inequalities between richer and poorer countries and causing huge population displacements, which are putting great pressure on societies' existing resources of solidarity. On the largest scale, it is impossible to make sense of the climate crisis without recognising that its costs will be suffered most by the victims of earlier colonial dispossession: confronting this will not lead to any quick consensus.

So, wherever we look, there are obstacles to building solidarity.[8] Indeed some, such as the UN Secretary-General, building on the worries about reliability of information discussed in Chapter 4, fear that the values of trust and solidarity are under threat. But, although everything seems to stand in the way of building solidarity, we cannot afford to lose hope.

Let's also not fetishise solidarity as something to be achieved at all costs: when inequality is rising, when recognition of fundamental rights and identities (based on race, sexuality, disability, history) is refused, this will rightly be resisted, and the result may not be an increase in solidarity between those on either side of such issues. Polarisation often exists for good reasons, as political communication researchers Daniel Kreiss and Shannon McGregor forcefully argue. Research that worries about rises in polarisation but ignores the conflicts driving them is unhelpful.[9]

But avoiding that error should not lead us to ignore the continuing need for new solidarities in the face of climate change. Yes, it is poorer countries where the highest costs of climate catastrophe are suffered, although rich countries caused the overwhelming bulk of historic climate damage; and, within countries, the costs of adjusting lifestyles often fall more heavily on the poorest. But a world with less solidarity, less commensurability of viewpoints, is unlikely in the long run to address the climate emergency, when the political 'we' needed for major change in our lifestyles has not yet been constructed anywhere.[10]

We need to build new common ground. In a much-cited review of international studies of climate change perceptions, it was people's ideological beliefs, rather than just their economic circumstances, that, in the US at least, were found to be the most reliable predictor of whether or not they believed in climate change.[11] As philosopher Michael Sandel has commented,

> we cannot deliberate about common purposes and ends without a sense of belonging, without seeing ourselves as members of a community to which we are indebted. Only in so far as we . . . recognise our dependence [on others], do we have reason to appreciate their contributions to our collective well-being.[12]

Sandel is discussing material inequalities, but there is a cultural question too: does our current space of the world help us recognise our inter-dependence with each other, or hinder us? How can we today find 'resources for critique, vision and solidarity', as former Archibishop of Canterbury Rowan Williams put it?[13]

When Online Solidarity Works

Throughout history people have made the most of tools given them by the very systems they wanted to resist, for example capitalist media and market structures. And, even if they didn't want to resist the 'system', they have found uses for the system's tools that were never planned or foreseen by their designers and producers. Put simply, we find the world as it is; we won't change it if first we insist on reinventing everything in it. People have found ways of turning the market forces that shape social media to social and political ends that were not in the platforms' original gameplan. So let's celebrate online solidarity on today's commercial platforms where it occurs.

Sometimes, in resistant patterns of platform use, we glimpse what US tech commentator Ben Tarnoff calls 'other universalities'. Tarnoff is a fierce critic of the commercial platform world, but he is surely right to celebrate the 'moments of online life that elude or exceed market control. In such moments people relate to one another as people – not as eyeballs or clients or purchasing power or labor power'.[14] There is hope in such moments.

Alongside the pessimistic academic research discussed in Part 2, there is also research that draws more optimistic conclusions about social media. One paper used US survey data over an extended time period to show that people who said they used social media were more likely to participate in political action, both online and offline.[15] True, this survey was conducted in 2009–10, long before polarising processes came to be widely observed on social media. Other researchers have argued that social media platforms provide opportunities to express one's political opinion which may otherwise be lacking.[16] There is also some evidence that, provided you have prior experience of taking political action, using social media can lead to more such action (assuming also you believe that online action is effective). A positive feedback loop therefore around social media platforms *is* possible, alongside the negative feedback loops discussed in previous chapters.[17]

The Positive Difference Social Media Can Make

There are indeed many aspects of social media that, taken by themselves, are positive for political involvement. The hashtag function of platforms such as Twitter provides a means, largely under users' control, to gather people fast around a topic: the #MeToo movement was a clear example, and Black activism on Twitter has provided many more, especially #BlackLivesMatter.[18] Meanwhile the ease of circulating mobilising messages fast across multiple locations – and in view of each location – helped campaigns like Greta Thunberg's 'School Strike 4 Climate' that encouraged urgent action on a global scale, as in the coordinated school strikes of 15 March 2019.[19]

Indeed the mere existence of social media platforms can have major impact in breaking the silence of authoritarian regimes around key issues. In the profoundly unequal and controlled political space of Saudi Arabia, it mattered when in 2011 a tweeter named Mujtahidd began challenging royal power. In China, Weibo from 2015 played a major role in foregrounding environmental disasters that the Chinese government had previously preferred to keep quiet about.[20] The background communication context against which platform activity occurs plays a huge role here.[21]

Similar lessons have been learned in democratic systems, when obdurate power needs to be faced down. After the tragic Parkland School shooting in Florida on Valentine's Day 2018, US schoolkids protested against guns using Twitter and Facebook to gather support and then using social media to mobilise a March for Our Lives on Washington DC.[22] Platforms have played a positive role in workers' activism: the New York Taxi Workers Alliance campaign used social media and even SMS messages to force Uber to allow tips in 2017. They have helped expand the scope of civic activism too: consider the platform Ushahidi, which has become a crowd-based data platform, challenging entrenched power, for example by identifying corruption in elections across Africa.[23]

More generally, the affordances of social media platforms such as hashtags (Twitter, Instagram, TikTok) and sub-groups (Reddit) have made it easier and quicker for small specialist groups to form. It is clear, then, that when people are connected online in the powerful ways that social media offer, new possibilities of coordinated action can emerge. From the point of view of social outcomes, however, this phenomenon is more ambiguous. Everything depends on the goals of the group that comes together. Consider a group that forms on YouTube to watch and comment on videos of school shootings. Such anonymous 'communities of destruction' can form fast and 'almost instantly transcend the national level', according to Johanna Sumiala and Minttu Tikka, two Finnish researchers who have specialised in these gruesome communities that banalise violence.[24] Or think of the private online communities that swap and gloat over videos of male violence against women.[25] Yes, *sometimes*, when such disgraceful images go viral on wider social media, this can generate wider political protest, as when a privately taken video of gang rape in Manipur State, India in May 2023 went viral on social media two months later.[26] Indeed NGOs have tried to use social media as a site for re-educating men against taking pleasure in such violence.[27] But the ambiguity of social media communities can't be eliminated.

The Wider Question

Beneath these various examples, not all of them to be celebrated, there is a contradiction: commercially created platforms, intended purely to make money, can under certain circumstances have significant, even transformative, political effects, because of the ease and speed with which they bring people together around news topics. If we are to have the resources to combat climate change, we can hardly ignore these possibilities for transformation.

What is special about these online moments of solidarity? According to cultural theorist Jeremy Gilbert, they are best seen as moments of collective joy.[28] BlackLivesMatter was founded in 2013 and, through its eponymous hashtag, grew massively in July 2020 in response to the appalling police murder of George Floyd in Minneapolis, US. 'Joyful togetherness' is a term used to describe #BlackLivesMatter, even in the face of appalling injustice.[29] It fits the early stage of many online movements when people start to gather around a growing issue.[30]

But do these examples of transformative platform action provide a reason to celebrate commercial platforms more generally? Faced with the absolute need to challenge the oppression of the US's black population, Twitter's features were indeed a useful tool, creating the possibility, under particular circumstances, of a Black counter-public that rivalled the working class and other counter-publics from earlier points in history. But this work was not done by Twitter the platform. It only happened because of a huge amount of cultural work by

Black Twitter users, monitoring the boundaries of what speech was acceptable.

According to liberal commentators like Yascha Mounk, what matters most about social media is that they redistribute the tools of broadcasting to a much wider range of citizens, enabling new voices to be heard.[31] For sure, that was important in the case of Black Twitter: the democratising potential of social media as a format should never be discounted.[32] But perhaps it's *more* important to foreground the specificity of US black activism. Drawing on centuries of struggle, it used a capitalist platform to its own advantage. Recognising this does not mean ignoring the costs that flow from how platforms *generally* try to manage social experience that we've seen in earlier chapters.[33] As Sarah Jackson and colleagues comment towards the end of a book on Black Twitter, we must 'acknowledge the serious limitations of the technological platforms and corporate logics' within which 'racial justice and feminist narratives evolve'.[34]

Just as in authoritarian societies, so too in a hierarchical white-dominated society/media like the US, Black attempts to carve out a distinctive Black space of action and expression mattered, because they brought people together around a single cause. As André Brock puts it, the mere fact of 'millions of Black people interacting through networked devices . . . at once separate and conjoined' is enormously significant.[35] Significant too are the dynamics of how Black Twitter and the US's Black podcasting community worked: the interaction of a platform feature – hashtags – with high-volume platform consumers and a lot of cultural work by users to mark the boundaries of that special public sphere.[36]

Yet in the debate about the significance of Black digital activism, important questions started to emerge. When discussing the mass protests that developed in response to the police murder of Michael Brown in Ferguson, Missouri, Keeanga-Yamatta Taylor writes that 'it is impossible to imagine any of this happening only online'.[37] Or, as Meredith Clark reflected when Black users started to leave Twitter after Elon Musk's takeover in October 2022, 'to ask about what comes "after Black Twitter", as though Black communication practices somehow begin and end with the social networking age' is a profound misunderstanding.[38] Those practices had an integrity that in no way depended on Twitter, the format.

It is essential therefore not to reduce what was achieved in Black Twitter to the platform itself. Other values were involved which far transcended Twitter's mechanisms as an interface. Christopher Lebron, historian of the early Black Lives Matter, has written of its special community of 'unfragmented compassion'.[39] Its socially oriented value of *care* was completely odds with commercial social media platforms and how they normally drive shallow community. Perhaps such counter-values can, in time, be shifted to other architectures of social media, to a different space of the world that we might build in the future.

When Solidarity Does Not *Win Out Online*

Solidarity is not a simple phenomenon. This has led some theorists to dismiss it as too fuzzy to be worth analysing.[40] But, as we have seen, when solidarity happens, it is transformative. All the more important, then, to understand what happens when processes of apparent solidarity go wrong.

Is Connecting Enough?

There is a great temptation to believe that social media have changed life so fundamentally that older understandings of solidarity as collective identity no longer matter. Political scientists Lance Bennett and Alexandra Segerberg asked: what if *connective* action on online platforms becomes our new form of collective action, bypassing the need for a collective identity outside our actions on platforms?[41] Certainly actions on social media that point towards politics can produce a real sense of meaningful practical involvement.[42] But, as we saw with Black Lives Matter, a movement's power is not just based in networking: it is built on an identity that goes far beyond the flux of retweets and likes.

Let's not fall into the trap, under the influence of Big Tech's self-promoting narratives, of believing that just because many of us do things on Facebook, Twitter, Instagram or TikTok, it is those actions themselves that drive wider consequences, such as increased political engagement.

If we look at the mountain of research done into the links between young people's social media activity and politics, we find that the vast majority of studies did not even test for causal effects: at most they looked for correlations, which, of course, can always go either way. Consider a meta-study of 106 survey-based papers on young people's digital media use.[43] True, those studies didn't show any negative effect between social media use and political engagement but, when causal effects *were* tested, they tended to reverse what researchers had assumed: indicating that *offline political actions caused increased social media use* (an 'overspill effect'), rather than social media use generating increased political involvement (the often assumed 'gateway effect').[44] This changes completely where we focus when reforming the political environment: maybe we need to start *offline*, not online, in looking for solutions.[45]

A decade of reflection on social media movements strongly supports this. Ever since hopes of political change faded from the 2011 Arab Spring, there has been an intense debate about how much weight to put on the undoubted mobilising power of contemporary social media. For one thing, the state communications infrastructure in Arab countries that, before social media, had dominated authoritarian societies did not disappear; indeed it adapted well to social media, benefitting from the greater surveillance opportunities for the state that flowed from ordinary citizens' visibility on social media. Today, over a decade later, social media platforms are working well to give authoritarian regimes such as the Saudi royal family the appearance of legitimacy, while sustaining the highest level of citizen surveillance. Snapchat is used by 20 million Saudis, including 90 per cent of those under thirty-four. A base for citizen solidarity perhaps, but also an 'extension of the [kingdom's] social fabric', as noted by an executive at Snap Inc., Snapchat's owner. A leading Saudi dissident, Khalid Aljabri, sees it differently: 'Snapchat's popularity makes it an ideal tool for a repressive regime that exploits Snapchat in the dissemination of state propaganda, character assassination of detractors, and surveillance of activists and influencers.'[46]

Meanwhile solidarity on social media may amount only to superficial 'slacktivism', which gets in the way of serious organising. A well-known example was the black square symbol on Instagram, used initially in response to the murder of George Floyd, which became, many felt, purely gestural, detached from any actions that could lead communities to change.[47] Similarly, when isolated Filipino platform workers used social media to connect to each other, researchers found few real outcomes that actually challenged the power of the Big Tech for whom they worked.[48]

Social media certainly enable people to mobilise weak social ties to generate bridges to others they don't know,[49] but those bridges may be as thin as a line in a database. Acting online is performed individually, but in full view of others and in view of those with real power, and this creates pressures *against* taking collective risks.[50] In the Arab Spring social media did not encourage the resource-building from which positive political programmes could be developed and defended,[51] even if they enabled remarkable demonstrations to come together at lightning speed in Tahrir Square and elsewhere.

What is often missing in social media, argues Gal Beckerman, drawing on interviews with activists involved in the Arab Spring, is a space for conversation and reflection: 'a space for theorising, for allowing in complexity, for working toward action'. Instead what commercial social media, especially Facebook, provides, alongside speed, is 'an incessant rejectionism'.[52] Social media provide a space for saying no, but not a space for building a coherent and sustainable yes.

This is why some activists have moved away from reliance on social media, for example, in a controversial areas like migrant rights, fearing that social media's demands – the constant need to keep busy, to keep posting, while guarding against harassment and surveillance – may distract from the main task of developing policy and building organisational resources.[53] No less than Pope Francis warned against this danger in his worldwide encyclical on solidarity, *Fratelli Tutti*: 'digital connectivity is not enough to build bridges'.[54] If the goal is sustaining solidarity for the long term, then online platforms and digital spaces cannot be sufficient. Whatever role they may play in future politics, this will be more effective accompanying, rather than replacing, the face-to-face.

Solidarity face-to-face

One of the most remarkable cases of effective political solidarity in recent years was the large-scale Korean protests against President Park Geun-hye in 2016–17. Those protests challenged her corruption and demanded her impeachment. In a political context that at the start was highly polarised, reinforced by a polarised media system, a near-unanimous popular campaign developed. Although social media continued to offer opportunities to polarise audiences for the President's right-wing defenders, the core of the movement was the physical rituals of candlelit protest in the centre of South Korea's capital Seoul, which on the night of 3 December 2016 involved 2.3 million citizens. Although Korea has had very high online connectivity for longer than most, a decisive factor in the protests' success, according to their leading researcher Hyunjin Seo, was not social media, but the long history of popular protest in the centre of Seoul that started with the battles to end dictatorship in the late 1980s.[55]

The act of physically gathering together – in view of media including social media, but also in view of each other – is crucial in generating solidarity and sharing in the act of directly challenging power. Standing, sitting or walking together can be, in the words of philosopher Judith Butler, 'a form of social solidarity both mournful and joyful', a 'gathering' that 'signifies persistence and resistance' in the face of silence or rejection.[56]

Wherever we start its modern history – from the civil rights march across a bridge in Selma, Alabama in 1965 or the silent protests in front of the Presidential Palace of the Madres del Plaza de Maio in Buenos Aires from 1977 – we know that gathering physically at key symbolic sites unleashes a wave of collective reflection. A more recent example would be the Euromaidan revolution in Ukraine in 2013, where continued protests in the centre of Kyiv built a revolution against excessive Russian influence on Ukrainian politics. Gathering together in a common place can bring, in the words of Argentinian feminist Verónica Gago, 'a collective evaluation to strength, and the ability to evaluate possibilities that did not pre-exist the assembly as a space of encounter'.[57] In other words, the context not just to act, but to debate, reflect and think together.

Is this the root of what Jeremy Gilbert calls the collective joy of collective protest? Gilbert's example was the social media campaigns around the British general election of 2017, an election that, like all British elections, revolved around a whole network of physical sites and meetings in electoral constituencies. In the important Polish election of October 2023, which ended an authoritarian government, it was the hours spent queuing up to vote together that, according to some witnesses, generated a sense of solidarity.[58] Gal Beckerman gives a vivid example from English political history: the working class chartist movement in the late 1830s, faced with overwhelming rejection from the English political elites, responded by collecting a vast signed petition to present to parliament and demand voting rights. Its lead organiser, Feargus O'Connor, saw importance, as Beckerman puts it, 'in the actual, physical work of gathering the signatures – the need to go door-to-door, to convince others, to mark one's ink in allegiance to a cause'.[59] Indeed it was the physical gatherings for the Occupy encampments in London, New York and elsewhere in late 2011 that even the theorists of 'connective action' acknowledge was their 'unifying focal point'.[60]

Perhaps it is time to ask: what sort of solidarity is it that we are looking for in confronting the world's challenges?

What Is Solidarity Really?

There is no democratic politics without solidarity of some sort. Solidarity can be imagined on many levels, from the family and street, to large societal groupings and whole nations. We have seen how the platformed space of the world undermines the bases of solidarity in multiple ways, whether at the level of individual or group experience (Chapter 3), information flow and trust (Chapter 4) or the polarisation of feelings (Chapter 5), even if sometimes it appears to spark it. So how do we counter those effects and begin the renewal of solidarity that humanity desperately needs?

Affective Solidarity

One starting-point might be to revisit the view of politics based in the unseen compulsion of economic and social forces that Hobbes calls Leviathan. The past forty years have seen neoliberalism massively reinforce market forces at every level of social organisation.[61] Those market forces, with all their fine-tuning of our individual desires and plans, can *seem* to offer something like solidarity, a reliable way of individually acting-together towards larger goals and consequences. Consider influencers on Instagram or TikTok: individuals who are rewarded by the market for doing exactly what the market wants of them, while encouraging us to follow their example. The risk is that, when one influencer disappears, after leading this or that campaign, individuals are left unchanged: just an uninvolved consumer, sceptically waiting for the next influencer to come along.[62]

The risk of mistaking market-simulated solidarity for the real thing has led some theorists to reject mere 'calculative solidarity' in contrast with what they call 'affective solidarity'.[63] Affective solidarity requires much more from us than just competing with each other to send signals, as the platform expects. It involves the acts of care that help sustain families and friendships, but which are also needed in institutional settings such as health, education and welfare.[64]

Affective solidarity is when we act together in an appreciation of our interdependence with each other and the sense of commonality that comes from recognising that. This deeper solidarity, based in *care* both for each other and for what we share, must be protected against the affective costs of our platformed space of the world. Affective solidarity, if we can achieve it, can be a response to the growth of affective polarisation in politics and across platforms in so many countries.

Philosophers and social theorists have been reflecting for a long time on the conditions for this deeper form of solidarity. We can look back to Karl Marx in the nineteenth century, or psychologist Erich Fromm and philosophers Hannah Arendt and Simone Weil in the twentieth century.[65] But one thing they did not need to factor into their theorising was the vast expansion of global communications in the late twentieth century. Here, reflecting back critically on that tradition, is American social theorist Craig Calhoun:

> The idea that people need 'naturally' to feel at home in . . . an internally homogeneous community contends with . . . cultural fields too large and differentiated to be organized as communities. Within such larger settings, it is not an adequate response to human differences to allow each person to find the group within which they feel at home. It is crucial to create public space within which people may engage each other in discourse . . .[66]

In 1999, Calhoun's hope was still that the internet could provide that space of expanded solidarity. But that was then – before a fully commercialised interest and commercial social media. Now we must rebuild solidarity amid the ruins of social media that have relied on overstimulating group formation and shallow community.

Escaping the Deadlock?

But aren't there many other forces undermining solidarity in the contemporary world apart from social media? There are. We mentioned growing inequality at the start of the chapter; there are fundamental and widening differences of religious worldview, for example, between Islamic and Christian fundamentalism. There are the geopolitical rifts that reflect the violent legacies of European and North American colonialism. And more generally there is the fact that, in modern highly differentiated societies and economies, solidarity always feels diffuse and uncertain: as the philosopher Michael Walzer once remarked, 'people experience solidarity separately and differently. This is . . . [a] fact about modern life.'[67] Worse than that, civil society institutions that once invested in building bridges between people across class and racial difference have become, over many decades, increasingly like lobbying organisations and PR agencies with ever less basis in actual solidarity on the ground,[68] while trade unions almost everywhere have declined in the face of the hostile labour markets and legal environments characteristic of neoliberalism.

Yet the challenge for institutions seeking to build solidarity has never been greater. If we ignore the risks that our space of the world poses to the basic conditions of solidarity, we risk being locked into an unending Prisoners' Dilemma in which, as the sociologist Diego Gambetta pointedly put it, no one any more can 'trust trust'.[69]

Two other points, one positive and one negative, may help us clarify the challenge here.

Starting with the negative, it is likely that the networked decision-space of social media is reducing our chances of *seeing together* the facts that could encourage us to feel solidarity to 'care for our common home'.[70] Some biologists recently conducted an experiment to model how decisions get taken in networks. They identified the possibility of what they called 'information gerrymandering'. By this they mean a situation where small numbers of people within networks have the greatest impact on how decisions get taken. The reason is that people want to act not only in accordance with their perceived self-interest, but also 'to coordinate their vote with their entire group', an echo of the pressures towards polarisation identified by Social Identity Theory (see Chapter 5). Zealots who loudly proclaim their views and why others should follow them can have outsize influence: and zealots can perfectly well be simulated by bots.[71]

What follows? In a situation where two groups are competing, the group with more zealots (human or artificial) is likely to have more disciplined voting and so more success in political or civic competition, what the authors call 'influence assortment'. Where both groups are configured so as to have significant numbers of zealots, the wider population 'loses its ability to reach consensus and remains trapped in deadlock'. The result: 'a group level social dilemma' or Prisoners' Dilemma writ large.[72] Social media platforms in their current form seem designed to achieve exactly this sort of outcome: either a one-sided outcome that favours zealots or a deadlock with no way out.

At the same time, and more positively, the reality in which today we have to make decisions about the planet may lift us out of the narrow constraints of Game Theory. Game Theory generates its terrifying dilemmas only through a process of abstraction, ignoring actual experience and knowledge, and focusing exclusively on calculations within the narrow space of what economists call 'bounded rationality'.[73] But what if we now, the majority of us, increasingly, *share* the experience of climate change effects and the new knowledge that flows from that? Then our preferences might change, lifting us out of the deadlock of the social media zero-sum game.[74]

The only catch is that, first, the digital space of the world must allow us to start seeing this possibility in mutual awareness of others. As Naomi Klein writes, 'change requires collaboration and coalition, even (especially) uncomfortable coalition'.[75] And this, surely, requires us to be ready to listen to each other and think about what might be at stake in acting together.

Conclusion: Being Realistic about Solidarity

We need therefore to be realistic about solidarity, which doesn't mean giving up on it.

Important figures like the late James Lovelock have insisted that to confront climate change we need some temporary curbs on democracy, perhaps even authoritarianism.[76] More recently Gaia Vince has argued that representative politics is less helpful for combatting climate change than science-led action.[77] But, surely, as one reviewer of Vince noted, to confront climate change 'we need more politics, not less'.[78]

Why would people accept the trade-off of democracy for combatting climate change unless first they felt they had reached an inclusive decision about this, which surely requires more democracy? Ditching democratic process, others have warned, might be 'the ultimate derangement'.[79] Perhaps the real choice, as Jedediah Purdy puts it, is between a neoliberal Anthropocene which doubles down on all the inequalities of the neoliberal era and a democratic Anthropocene that addresses both the climate emergency *and* the intensified inequalities that climate extremes will inevitably cause.[80] Take the anti-democratic fork, and we may just guarantee our wider collective failure.

It will not, after all, be enough to rely on the actions of those already on the side of combatting climate change. More people, not fewer, need to take action. But how can consensus around the need for more action develop? Leading climate change scientist Michael Mann fears the rise of 'inactivism': a very active lobbying effort by oil companies and others to convince us that climate change is the result of individual actions and so it is only individuals who can act – and yet, because climate change is too big and too costly for individuals to affect, nothing can be done . . . so why not do less, not more?[81]

In response to these siren calls – abandon democracy to 'get more done', or simply do nothing – the answer is not to give up on democratic politics or building greater solidarity. But we need some pragmatism.

There are currently few more polarised countries politically than the US, which makes it a good place to consider a different approach to communicating the message about climate change. After all, US views about climate change are profoundly polarised, with a recent poll showing that 78 per cent of Democrats, but just 23 per cent of Republicans, view climate change as a 'major threat to the country's wellbeing'.[82]

But one Republican pollster has explored the possibility of posing questions about climate change to Republican voters in terms not of global or national action, but in terms of local specifics: what's good for the family, neighbourhood, indeed for the individual herself. Everyone rightly cares first about their own health and safety, and they *do* care a lot about the health and safety of, say, their kids and grandkids; they care about the world they are passing on to them. The pollster doing this research, Frank Luntz, is no angel: he advised George W. Bush two decades ago to campaign against climate change action by emphasising the uncertainty of the evidence, but now he has repented and appears serious in shifting Republican minds on climate change.[83]

Such an approach is realistic about the underlying drivers of political engagement at a time when there are few common beliefs shared across the US spectrum. Underlying this apparently eccentric choice of tactics is a deeper point. The goal is not solidarity for its own sake, but for all of us to change our lives in parallel with each other. Why should this require us agreeing on exactly what we want to do and why? What matters is that my actions *resonate* sufficiently with yours and others', and by resonating build a larger pattern of positive behavioural change. For this, it may be enough that each of us is broadly oriented to certain important facts that we accept as the common facts that affect us all, whatever our feelings towards each other.

Alberto Melucci, one of the first to make sense of the new social movements around identity, culture and politics that emerged in the 1980s, once asked a crucial question: 'through what processes do individuals recognise that they share certain orientations in common and on that basis decide to act together?'[84] Underlying this is the even more basic question: what does it mean to 'act *together*'? We always assume this means literally acting in concert – in direct coordination – with each other. But there is another possibility. Yes, as Melucci says, people must recognise that they 'share certain orientations in common': no one wants to act entirely alone. But having that basic horizon in common doesn't mean we have to literally act in concert, let alone share the same motivation. It is enough that my actions practically *resonate* with and reinforce yours, rather than conflict with them. Resonance is compatible with quite a lot of disagreement about factual detail, feelings and even worldview.

I offer resonance as a way of starting to think about how action for social change may emerge in very large societies without relying on coordination, let alone on platforms that seek to manage and steer our behaviour. Could resonance be a way to think differently about the future of both our politics and our technology,[85] without relying on the assumption that it is only large managed platforms that can bring us together?

We'll stay with this idea in the final chapter, as we address a key question, unwelcome to the Big Tech industry but essential to addressing what's gone wrong with today's commercialised social media: the question of scale. As one of the sharpest observers of platform culture, Tarleton Gillespie, put it bluntly: what if 'some platforms are simply too big'?[86] What if all commercial platforms are?

CHAPTER 7

Rebuilding Social Media

'In designing tools we are designing ways of being.' (Terry Winograd and Fernando Flores)[1]

'Technology that mediates social relations (like, you know, the Internet) inherently *creates* institutions – the only choice is to do so deliberately, or haphazardly.' (Robin Berjon)[2]

A quarter of the way through the twenty-first century, and at the end of a major experiment with commercial social media, societies face a dilemma.

On the one hand, as human beings we need to connect. In the past thirty years particular humans – actually a very small elite – have built the most powerful technologies of connection in history. People everywhere have adapted their lives to fit those technologies and, through their creativity, they have developed new formats (whole genres) of social connection. To name a few: the asynchronous group-chat, direct messaging (phone to phone), the sharing of images, videos, news, links and commentary, the witnessing of events by pictures or video taken on our phone, small-scale publicity via social media post, payment on-the-move via social media . . . Things which many may find it hard to imagine giving up.

And yet, in the process, fundamental errors have been made. First, expanding the scale of human interaction without limit, but without considering the impact of this on the texture of social life. Second, turning over that massively expanded space to commercial forces, with barely any civic, public or social control over the possible consequences (ignoring the risks from the first error). Third, delegating to business the specific opportunity of designing living spaces in this new online world (ignoring the risks from the second error). Fourth, allowing platform businesses for years to operate without any need to consider public values, and under whatever business model and parameters of control they wished (ignoring the risks from the third error).

Four errors, stacked one on the top of the other, creating one giant error: the conversion of our space of the world, the space of almost all possible sites of social interaction, into a site of commercial exploitation. Earlier chapters reviewed the resulting social costs, and how they have undermined solidarity, just when humanity needs more solidarity. We have no choice but to try and reverse some of the ecological harms done.[3] But we know that major technological change, once embedded into daily life, cannot easily be reversed.

So how can we move forward?

A Dilemma That Is Personal

Each of us will feel this dilemma in personal terms.

I certainly don't want to give up WhatsApp. It's important in my family for sharing news, expressing affection and just keeping in touch. For me, it's not where I go for wider social or public interactions, it's where I stay in touch with those closest to me. And yet there is plenty of evidence that WhatsApp's functions have played a role in fuelling devastating public violence. In India in July 2018 videos were circulated on WhatsApp that appeared to show young children being abducted on motorbikes, leading to rumours of a child kidnapping network; in response, vengeful lynch mobs started murdering men who proved to be completely innocent. Yes, WhatsApp responded by limiting the ability to forward messages to five recipients, a restriction for India then rolled out globally,[4] but there are good reasons to doubt the effectiveness of this.[5] It is in any case paradoxical: the whole point of WhatsApp is sharing! So, even in this most private of social media, there is a problem of public consequences that platforms are barely addressing.

Others will feel a similar conflict about Instagram, Facebook, Twitter or TikTok. These are not just individual choices: the collective value of some platforms for social and political struggle was discussed in Chapter 6, and yet the social costs of social media platforms were laid out in previous chapters.

The dilemma we face shares a feature with all ecological problems: if there are costs to reversing problems in the environment with which we all interact, we must all pay them. Our dilemma is also part of something larger to which there are no clear solutions: the system of extractive capitalism, which cannot be understood except within the even longer time-frame of colonialism.[6] From that perspective, our dilemma might seem truly insoluble. So let's focus initially on a more specific malfunction that the Austrian philosopher and social theorist Ivan Illich already diagnosed in the 1970s.

Illich, who lived much of his life in Mexico, thought deeply about the right – and the wrong – relationship for humanity to have with its tools. The right relationship is when individuals and communities have control of their tools and can use them for their own ends. The wrong relationship comes when humans have no control over their tools, because larger power structures and economic forces exercise that control. For Illich, large-scale capitalist manufacturing production exemplified this dysfunctional relationship:

> Society can be destroyed when further growth of mass production renders the [social] milieu hostile . . . when it isolates people from each other and locks them into a manmade shell, when it undermines the texture of community by promoting extreme social polarization and splintering specialization, or when cancerous acceleration enforces social change.[7]

There are, of course, many differences between Illich's 1970s diagnosis of mass production's consequences and the world of capitalist social media today. But there are also striking similarities: not least risks of isolation, discussed in Chapter 3, and the risks of corrosive polarisation which undermine possibilities for solidarity, discussed in Chapter 5. Although social media corporations continually say they are about 'us', they are actually focused on rewarding corporate control: managing an environment from which corporations (and the extremely wealthy individuals at their heart) profit in the form of data extracted.

Social media, however convivial they seem, are the polar opposite of Illich's vision of a convivial society 'designed to allow all its members the most autonomous action by means of tools least controlled by others'.[8] The one thing we *don't* do with digital platforms is control them! Social media are among the least convivial tools in our lives, far less convivial than kettles, hammers or furniture, which we use and move around more or less at will.

And yet, there is no turning back. As a leading critic of commercial social media, Robert Gehl, has said, 'it is pointless to long for a time before social media'; nor can we pretend that the pleasures we get from social media, and their democratising potentials, don't exist.[9] Those pleasures and potentials are important, not just now but for the future. To the extent that we need to dismantle the current space of the world, we must also commit to *rebuilding* it to a new design.[10] A new design that is pro-social, not anti-social. That is the topic of this chapter.

Social Media's Growing Crisis

A sense of crisis is building around commercial social media. But, as one of the (sadly) most influential thinkers of the late twentieth century, Milton Friedman, the sage of neoliberalism, once said, 'only a crisis – actual or perceived – produces real change. When this crisis occurs, the actions that are taken depend on the ideas that are lying around.'[11] So a crisis is not necessarily a reason for despair, provided the right ideas are lying around. We will see shortly that they are. But first let's take the pulse of this crisis one last time.

A Pew Research Center study from May/June 2018 showed – after the Cambridge Analytica revelations, but before Zuboff's best-selling book on surveillance capitalism and the whistleblower revelations of Frances Haugen and Sophie Zhang – that, while most US adults (74 per cent) felt they personally benefited from social media, a significant minority thought social media negative for society (36 per cent). Only 28 per cent trusted Big Tech 'to do what is right' most of the time, and roughly half (51 per cent) felt social media platforms should be regulated more than they were.[12]

Less than three years later, a leading economist, Robert Frank, was arguing that social media platforms' advertising business model posed 'a profound threat to the nation's political and social stability'.[13] One year later, a leading *New York Times* opinion writer was asking 'how do we want to be shaped [by social media]? What do we want to become?' What if, he asked, social media are a toxic ecology, particularly for children: 'a mold we should not want our children to pass through'?[14]

By 2023, even leading outlets of the tech press were saying the game was up for social media. Consider some article titles from *Wired*: 'Social Media Has Run Out of Fresh Ideas', 'Super-Apps Are Terrible for People – and Great for Companies'.[15] Major politicians caught a similar mood. In March 2023, US President Biden wrote in the *Wall Street Journal* that 'the risks Big Tech poses for ordinary Americans are clear'. Just a few weeks later, former New Zealand Prime Minister Jacina Ardern became an international envoy for the Christchurch Call, a project to combat the spread of violence on social media that she herself set up in 2019.[16] A year later, calls were emerging from UK parents for the banning of social media for under-16s.[17]

There is, then, a growing sense of crisis, in the US, where commercial social media platforms have their main base, and in the UK, notwithstanding loud claims by social media leaders to have resolved the issues of toxic content through intensive use of AI.[18]

Certainly social media platforms have had success stories in controlling content: for example, Reddit's efforts to control right-wing extremism in discussion groups.[19] And Big Tech's claims to be managing the crisis caused by their platforms grow ever more insistent, for example, Instagram's 'Family Center', which from 2023 has offered 'helpful . . . tools for a safer online experience for your family'.[20] But social media platforms, such as Telegram, that once offered a positive challenge to Big Tech giants have become a haven for extreme figures such as Brazil's ex-President Jair Bolsonaro.[21] Scepticism abounds about the success of mainstream platforms' containment strategies,[22] and it is not going away. As this book was completed, Lotte Rubaek, a Danish psychologist resigned as an official adviser to Facebook on mental health issues in protest at its continued failures, and research conducted for the UK regulator Ofcom concluded that violent online content is now unavoidable for young children.[23] Meanwhile Tucker Carlson, once one of Fox News's most extreme voices, after falling out with them, got his own channel on the 'free-speech'-celebrating platform 'X' of Elon Musk.

Indeed Elon Musk's takeover of Twitter in late 2022 crystallised many people's sense that a different set of values was needed for social media. Many left Twitter not because Twitter was inconvenient – on the contrary, it was very convenient – but because they were uncomfortable with the values its new owner represented. Further decision-points emerged in 2023: when leading voices on climate change left Twitter in protest at its hosting of climate deniers[24] and during the intensification of the Israel–Hamas war in October 2023, when the inadequacies of X's new model for 'fact-checking' and its reliance on 'blue tick' authentication (obtainable for a fee that secures algorithmic boosting) became all too clear.[25]

So, if a sense of crisis is emerging around commercial social media, how can we make it a basis for change? The answer lies in building new rules of engagement.

Social Media: Towards New Rules Of Engagement

What might these new rules look like?

What We Don't Need

As we redesign social media, we must think differently about what we mean by social media: we must 'socialise social media'.[26] Yet we are exposed to more bad stuff *because* we have massively expanded the scale of human interaction, prioritising scalability over any consideration of risk.[27] Our social spaces are vulnerable to toxic content *because* platforms have increasingly commercialised the spaces of everyday life. Everyday life is riven by perverse incentives *because* we allowed commercial business models to manage how social space functions. As a result, our priority must be to design counter-weights that work against those inherent risks, turning vicious circles into virtuous circles: the exact opposite of what commercial social media have done to date.

Thinking seriously about the inherent risks of digital space means, first, limiting, rather than relentlessly expanding, the scale of social media platforms except where scale is socially necessary. So, just as a national emergency-calling service needs a national phone network formed of local hubs but not a network on an international scale, so too there is a certain scale required for family messaging services, or for friends to message each other, or for a community to discuss common issue. Exactly what that scale should be for each case is a difficult question, but one generally ignored in the stampede to generate the best numbers for Big Tech's investors. Commercially desirable doesn't mean socially necessary, so the default rule must be: *build social media always to the smallest scale needed!*

A corrective design for social media would also involve outlawing business models that introduce the wrong incentives to social life. For example:

- People will always want to be liked, but we don't need, and most of us don't want, a social world where people are automatically incentivised to compete over how much they are liked and followed.[28]
- There will always be patterns in what people are engaged by, but we don't need a social world where businesses profit from skewing communication flows, just so their measures of 'engagement' are maximised.
- People will often want influence, but we don't need a social world where they are pushed to compete over who can produce the content most likely to go viral (TikTok is the extreme case, but such competition has been implicit in commercial platforms ever since platform feeds became algorithmic: to appear in someone's timeline, your post may need lots of engagement soon after you post it).[29]
- In market societies, advertising plays a necessary role as information, but there is no *social* argument for exposing people to advertising while socialising with friends or connecting with family (the fact that advertisers want this isn't a social rationale, and the fact that consumers appear to tolerate it is just evidence of the relentless pressure applied to them).[30] In addition, the argument for societies directing *any* advertising at children and young people under the age of eighteen has yet to be convincingly made.
- And if we do believe digital social media platforms have a role as supports for social life (this book has never denied that), why suppress *genuine* competition between them? Platforms' business models should not be based on locking people's socialising into their unique platform. Would anyone want a world where some café businesses became so powerful that they could prevent their customers meeting friends in another café if they felt like it?

All these points derive from business models that incentivise what we *don't* want in a healthy social world. Genuinely pro-social regulation would work to outlaw such business models.

Some Positive Principles

We need to build our online institutions 'deliberately', not 'haphazardly' (recalling Robin Berjon's quote at the chapter's start). A set of positive principles is required to balance the negative principles just outlined. Here I'm drawing on a decade of important work by designers and scholars around the world.[31]

First, there is *interoperability*: we just touched on it. If social media platforms are to work together for the greater social good, they must all, from a technical point of view, be interoperable in terms of their design, the formatting and data demands they make of users, the background information on which they run. Contrary to the neoliberal myth that unregulated markets help society function, unchecked competition currently *undermines* the market, incentivising Big Tech platforms to install incompatible systems that make it hard for businesses to work seamlessly across them.[32] If interoperability – across all platforms, not just within platforms under the same owner[33] – were imposed by regulators, we would have both a more robust communications ecology and a better-functioning market too.

The second principle, related to the first, is *transferability*: of contacts, archives and so on. The Solid project run by Tim Berners-Lee's company Inrupt has led the debate on this issue for nearly a decade.[34] Transferability is a key aspect of interoperability. As things stand, large platforms can lock in users artificially by making it difficult to transfer across their contacts to another platform, even if they hate the platform they're on. As Cory Doctorow has written, 'in the absence of adversarial inter-operability [i.e. rules which force interoperability on Big Tech], we're left trying to solve the impossible collective action problem of getting everyone to switch at once to alternative platforms'.[35] A redesigned social media needs more, not less, competition, and that is impossible without free transferability of user data.[36]

These first two principles require also that platforms' operating code is *open source*, openly available for copying and refashioning, rather than locked up in some corporate vault.[37] This is not to say that making every-thing open source will, itself, solve all our problems (the programme for Google's highly dominant Android phone operating system is largely open source!).[38]

In redesigning social media we must also insist on certain *norms of information production*. How these are implemented and distributed across opinion sites and information sites is a difficult problem. Norms of civil debate – and how they moderate for factuality, while allowing for the expression of opinion – will all require different answers, depending on context. But, whatever the scale, there is no avoiding the debate about how to source appropriate moderation. As elsewhere, the principle of 'subsidiarity' – devolving processes down to levels where they can most effectively be addressed by actual communities – is crucial.[39] That means giving significant autonomy to those groups.

Another key area is *norms of privacy and publicity.* Again, these depend on context. When people talk to friends or family, they need privacy, so encryption is a basic requirement. Encryption was introduced to social media by WhatsApp, while still independent, when it was Facebook's (not the US government's) surveillance of people's posts that was the issue. But then, when Facebook bought WhatsApp, it made encryption *its* USP for positioning itself against government regulators. So too has Apple, while getting into its own tangle about surveilling pornographic content on iPhones. Giving governments a backdoor into platforms' encrypted content (as the UK's new Online Safety Act requires) allows a government and police microphone to lurk in every private conversation space.[40] It is hard to see why any society which values freedom would want that.

Public discussion platforms are more complex. Sometimes account-ability for speaking in one's own name is an important guardrail against abuse, for example, in a large space where people can interact directly. But in other contexts, vulnerable people need to be able to speak anony-mously: women calling out sexual abuse, people under an oppressive regime pointing to injustices ignored by authorities, journalists and activists doing work that is critical of governments. Once again, detailed norms must be negotiated not top-down by corporations, but closer to those affected. The Latin American group Horizontal has created an app called Tella specifically for supporting anonymous reporting of this sort.[41]

Finally, if we no longer assume platform scale is automatically positive – why does everyone in the world need to be potentially connected to everyone else in order to ensure that those who do want to be networked to each other are so? – let's install appropriate frictions *against* circulation that limit virality within and between platforms.[42] To manage the risks that flow from the infinite openness of online space, we need firebreaks. This might seem like a negative principle, but in fact it's positive: it preserves the boundaries needed for healthy spaces of social interaction, boundaries systematically overridden when the internet was commercialised.

Resonance: a General Principle For Social Media

Is there a general principle that underpins these new rules of operation for the space of the world? Redesigning social media so they serve society means reimagining the role we *want* social media to play in social space. An idea that helps us is resonance, introduced at the end of Chapter 6.

Resonance is a term borrowed from physics. It is a feature of how sound, indeed vibrations of any sort, moves across space. By analogy, it can offer us insight into better ways of information and communication flowing through our space of the world.

Under the current dominant approach to social media, designers, without any idea of the social space in which they were intervening, have skewed the space in which individuals interacted. But why manage the relations between information space and social space in this manipulative way?

Resonance in physics derives from the fact that every object has a natural frequency: this principle applies all the way down to the quantum level.[43] When an external source (a sound or other vibration) reaches the object, the object picks out its natural frequency from the many frequencies in the external source and begins vibrating in that frequency. When we put two tuning forks near to each other and strike one, the fork which has not been hit, excited by the airwaves around it, starts vibrating on that frequency.[44] Resonance occurs, however large the space and however many objects in it.

How might this apply to the social media case? Remember that, for resonance to happen, objects filter out everything in the external input which is not at *their* natural frequency. No question here of a filter bubble situation where the external source is limited to one frequency. Resonance combines agency at the level of receivers and complexity at the level of the environment. It can serve as a metaphor for a space of the world in which positive, not negative, side-effects are sustained.[45]

True, sending sounds at an object's natural frequency to excess can break it apart. But for that you would need to go on applying the external frequency without stopping, right up until it broke.[46] Why would you do that, if your goal was to avoid negative effects?

Resonance is a scale effect that builds *from* the natural features of the entities affected. By contrast, today's space of the world is designed *against* the natural features of the people it affects: recall Meta CTO Andrew Bosworth's admission that 'the natural state of the world is not connected'. Engineers have optimised for their corporations' goals, but under the principle of resonance, we can design the space of the world without optimising for any external goal.[47]

The idea of resonance refocuses our priorities back onto social life itself, which, after all, should be run by us, social actors. As Robin Berjon puts it, 'global . . . does not entail either centralized or unified under a single institution'.[48] We need social media that operate as carefully scaled *resonance chambers*, not society-wide echo chambers.[49]

And there is one final but crucial point, that resonance helps us see. We no longer need to maximise for *any* particular output (including resonance: doing that, remember, would destroy the resonating object). If so, why not redesign the online world in a way that recognises the complementary importance of *face-to-face* interactions? As we saw in Chapter 6, there's a strong argument for saying that face-to-face contexts are generally better for the deep thinking and organising that all movements for social change need. So, why not build a space of the world whose incentives point towards more engagement with the world offline, not less?

Towards a New Deal for Young People from Social Media

Let's test out the implications of resonance as a principle in relation to one of the thorniest issues raised by social media, its psychological impacts on young people. This issue reached fever-pitch in the UK by February 2024 as I completed this book, with calls from parents to ban social media for the under-16s and claims by the National Police Chiefs' Council that social media were fuelling an alarming rise in sexual assaults on children *by other children.*[50] The credibility of social media platforms had already been damaged in the UK when, in spite of TikTok's loud protestations to the contrary and its official age-limit of thirteen, UK regulators reported that children under five were using TikTok.[51] The case for a radical change of policy in relation to the manifest risks that commercial social media have for children and young adults is growing.

By building social media on the smallest scale needed and dropping the idea that a platform's purpose is to maximise our time on the platform, we have a way forward. Why not challenge the assumption that we need large-scale spaces for young people's interactions, just so advertising can be directed at them at scale? Surely it is protecting young people's offline social context from which we should start. The debate about how best to do this has barely begun: attempts to ban social media for children without parental consent or during the night, as the US state of Utah's governor did in March 2023,[52] seem barely practicable. What is needed is a much more serious debate about *when if at all and on what scale* social media are likely to benefit children as they mature and how to *redesign* social media spaces that actually achieve those benefits at an appropriate scale. But this is just one example of how, from different principles, we can rebuild social media.

An Alternative Model

Where can we put these new principles into practice? There are multiple models for rebuilding social media. Let's start with one of the most intensely debated: federation.

A New Type of Social Media

There already exists a whole family of platforms not run for profit, with no advertising, no data extraction from users and no algorithms that push content at users to shape their attention. These platforms challenge the configuration of digital space more fundamentally, because they are federated.

What is meant by federation? The principle of federation addresses the difficulty with not just social media but the internet generally: that it creates connection on a scale that, without careful safeguards, may not be liveable. Federated platforms cannot override the internet's openness as a space, but they *counterbalance* it through a very different approach to scale.[53]

Instead of building one huge single platform, governed top-down by one set of managers who control everything, federated platforms achieve scale by networking, or 'federating', a set of smaller 'instances', each built, managed and moderated by an individual or community. Each instance is independent in its operations, but also an instantiation (an 'instance') of the open-source software and protocols which apply across the whole platform which allows users to move between instances, as they wish, taking their content with them.[54] As Ben Tarnoff writes, 'decentralization is not the same as fragmentation'.[55]

Federation imposes barriers on unconstrained content flow. Not only *is* there no platform centre, but, if a particular instance does not *want* to see content from another instance, then it can independently choose to block it. This ability was tested when the extreme right-wing platform Gab adopted the Mastodon open source protocol after being outlawed by Big Tech companies. At first Gab tried to federate like any other Mastodon instance and find ways of connecting to the whole network. But Mastodon's community succeeded in isolating Gab's content when the vast majority of instances blocked it.[56] This was a crucial test, because when extremists are de-platformed by the mainstream, they *will* try to find homes with smaller competitors, and why not federated ones? [57] The open source nature of Mastodon's software cannot, in principle, prevent bad actors from adopting it and so becoming what designers call a 'fork' in the network. But when this occurs, defence is possible by mobilising community values. This is made easier, not harder, by federation.

A federated network gives autonomy to small, socially meaningful communities (or at least their administrators) who can be clear about their values. When it comes to moderation, that does require each instance to commit enough resources to this, but at least the almost impossible problem of moderation (for top-down large-scale platforms) has been transposed to a scale that is potentially manageable.[58] Why shouldn't social media tools be under the control of the communities who use them, not their corporate makers?[59] That said, there is scope to devise interfaces that would enable federated instances to cooperate more easily when they do face shared difficulties, as in the Gab case.[60]

Mastodon is the best-known federated platform: it is a comment platform, broadly like X. There are others, covering many of the same genres as commercial platforms: Pixelfed for image or photo-sharing (like Instagram), PeerTube for video sharing (like YouTube), Lemmy for thematic discussion groups (like Reddit) and so on.[61] There are currently well over 100 federated platforms: together they form the Fediverse, which claims more than 13 million users, with Mastodon being the largest platform at over 1.6 million users and over 9,700 servers.[62]

A key reason that these non-profit platforms can interoperate and allow transfer of data between them is that they are all built on an underlying open source protocol, called ActivityPub, developed by the World Wide Web Consortium (W3C), which Tim Berners-Lee founded.[63] This underlying protocol ensures the compatibility of data stored on one platform with that stored on others, facilitating data transfer and interactions. Even Meta's would-be Twitter rival Threads plans to use ActivityPub,[64] though another Twitter rival, Bluesky, founded by ex-Twitter CEO Jack Dorsey, is built on the different AT protocol.

Federated platforms have learned from the evidence gathered in earlier chapters. They rely for their funding not on commercial profit, but on premium fees paid by some users, charitable funding or crowdsourcing from users, which means they don't need to adopt consumer-tracking and engagement-driven business models.[65] They make explicit their shared values through codes of conduct, which seek to exclude racism and other discrimination and affirm an expectation of socially responsible moderation.[66] Mastodon's approach is far from an 'anything goes' libertarianism, and they have introduced nudges to discourage risky behaviour that borrow from the best practice occasionally developed by commercial platforms like Twitter.[67] The result, as the Gab incident showed, is a space based on broadly shared norms, very different from the individualised relations each of us has with the commercial platforms we use.[68]

But there remain issues to be resolved.

First, functionality. There's no reason why every function from corporate social media should be adopted. Hashtags may be important to support content flow, but, as we saw in Chapter 5, even the simple 'like' or 'forward' is potentially the starting-point of pressures towards polarisation. So why do Pixelfed and Mastodon have 'likes' (Mastodon also enables you to 'boost', rather like a 'retweet')? Those features need to be closely monitored for their social consequences. Why not experiment? One platform for testing public opinion, Pol.is,[69] used in Singapore and elsewhere, reduced polarising pressures by preventing direct replies to people's opinion statements (instead votes of approval were counted, leading to useful visualisations of how opinion was forming). It remains to be seen how innovative Mastodon and other Fediverse platforms will be over the longer term.

A related point is personalisation. Mastodon does not offer personalisation of newsfeeds, but some apps for accessing Mastodon do (such as Mammoth); Bluesky also does.[70] Can personalisation be done without re-creating the rabbit-hole risks noted in Chapter 4? As yet, behaviour on alternative platforms is under-researched,[71] so we must beware of making wrong choices now that store up problems for the future.[72]

One area where federated platforms are currently at a disadvantage compared with commercial social media is encryption, whose importance we discussed earlier. While not technically impossible on federated platforms, it would be costly and complex to implement and so has not yet been done.[73] While this may matter less on public comment platforms like Mastodon, it matters more on private-feeling platforms, especially given that Meta's message functions are now standardly encrypted.

Given Mastodon's relative success, a final point is its future relation to commercial social media. What if Threads seeks to federate with Mastodon? So far Mastodon has made it clear it rejects external commercial funding and many instance operators have confirmed they want no relation to Threads, but whether this holds remains to be seen.

Supporting Conditions

Various factors, however, hold back this alternative universe of non-profit platforms.

The first is the platform interface. Mastodon is currently not easy to use, yet, as designer Darius Kazemi put it, we need a way of 'having fun on this decentralized web'.[74] Here's the problem: in a federated social media network, not just users, but their archived posts, and the servers needed for search functions, are *distributed* across the network. This creates technical problems for designers, since users, trained on non-federated platforms, expect features that make continual demands on *centralised* memory. So how can users, housed on particular instances, interact with content users on other instances? Until recently, when you liked content posted on a different instance from you, you had to search for it from your own instance before you could comment on it. A new Mastodon operating system (OS 4.2) addressed this by prompting users that they needed to reconnect with such content from their instance first, before they could comment.[75] Just one example, but it illustrates the adjustments that will continue to be needed.

Another thing holding back federated social media is the lack of robust regulation of commercial platforms. It might seem that robust regulation, at least in Europe, is now in place: the European Commission's GDPR, Digital Services Act and Digital Markets Act, and the UK's Online Safety Act.[76] But onerous as they are proving for platforms such as Meta,[77] in terms of increased moderation responsibilities and limits on unwanted data extraction, and TikTok[78] (now under investigation by the European Union for inadequate safeguards for child users), they still fall short of addressing the roots of the problem.

There are many unexplored regulatory possibilities (recall the principles outlined earlier): outlawing certain business models; requiring platforms to systematise their current occasional requirements to dampen, not boost, virality; imposing interoperability between all platforms. Outlawing should mean outlawing for real: in March 2019, Facebook claimed to have pivoted to being a 'privacy-focussed platform'. Yet even in 2023, it still made its money from targeting ads sold to third-party advertisers; its encrypted services (Instagram, even WhatsApp) are key sources of advertising income. Why? Because its business model hasn't been fundamentally challenged, even though recently the pressure of threatened EU legal action has led Meta to propose a paid-for ad-free service as an alternative source of income.[79]

The case of transferability of user data and contacts illustrates the importance of robust regulation. Right now, it is not possible to transfer your Twitter followers across to competitor platforms, holding back Mastodon. Without transferability the social media market operates in a monopolistic way. Regulators' existing anti-trust agendas should be used to address this.

Along the way, users have an important role to play, helping each other cope with the costs of shifting networks. In the past year, tech commentators have begun talking openly about changing their social media habits. Devin Coldewey wrote in the magazine *TechCrunch* that 'there is no "next Twitter" and that's ok', because this is 'a moment when the very nature of social media platforms . . . [is] up in the air'.[80] Not that Coldewey spoke for everyone: around the same time, Johnathan Flowers argued strongly for the dangers of a mass migration from Twitter that would undermine Black Twitter and the Twitter space of disabled people.[81] The debate continues.

The key factor, which we can't just wish into existence, is *cultural will*: the cultural will to make the change, in other words, solidarity. This sounds like a vicious circle: we need a better space of the world to grow solidarity again, but we need more solidarity to start that growth. But the circle is only vicious if we remain locked in the individualised mindset that commercial social media encourage. Under commercial social media, our online moments of collective joy or fury are, for most of us, experienced alone on an individual device.[82] Maybe that intense individualisation – fuelled by commercial social media, but more deeply based in the neoliberal turn in market societies since the early 1980s – is part of the problem.[83]

So, why not turn the problem on its head? What if, instead of imagining that individuals can all at once shift over to alternative social media, we looked for real contexts in which *existing communities* can help each other adopt federated platforms to gain more control? This is the insight that sociologist Gordon Gow is pursuing in ongoing work with communities in the Canadian state of Alberta.[84] Meanwhile in Oakland, California, a decade-long project called Dynamicland is building new ways of computing based in face-to-face creation and sharing, overturning our habit of interacting with our devices alone:[85] 'the computer of the future', they say, 'is not a project, but a place'. In Mexico the Sursiendo collective for digital human rights is a leading participant on Mastodon.[86] Consider also the concept of 'movement technology' that has emerged amongst Black abolitionist activists in the US, concerned to challenge fundamentally the legacy of racism in US institutions such as the police and prison system.[87]

What seems missing so far is a bridge between activism around federated platforms and the world, say, of Black Twitter. There is real force in the claim of Black academic Johnathan Flowers that Mastodon is white.[88] This needs to change. If Mastodon is white, it is not because of a lack of computing skills in Black communities: there has been a long, if neglected, history of Black computer activism since early in the computer age, as Charlton McIlwain has shown.[89] Nor is it because of Mastodon's overall Code of Conduct, which refuses to publicise instances that breach its principles of rejecting racism and other forms of discriminatory speech.[90] But the raced (and gendered) history of computing casts a long shadow. The way forward must be through actual Black *and* feminist communities seeing benefits in the community-led, non-commercial norms of the Fediverse and working directly to change its balance, as happened with Black Twitter and Black Lives Matter discussed in Chapter 6. Roland Pulliam, who set up the first Black Mastodon instance, is currently developing a toolkit to help all instances block those who represent a threat to them.[91] In line with feminist thinking for decades, Fediverse communities can become communities of care: caring for their common infrastructure.[92] A decentralised Fediverse is an ideal space for community experiment.

But the current technical complexities of alternative social media raise a further question of power. The skills needed to run an instance of Mastodon are not trivial, and they are unevenly distributed.[93] In addition, there are huge variations in size of Mastodon instances, which inevitably concentrate some power in the hands of those who run them. Managing those power differentials means addressing a problem that goes far beyond the Fediverse: the problem of hierarchies in computing practice. Our commercialised world of computing assumes that computers are resources requiring highly specialised skills, without which you are excluded from discussion about how things should get done. But when computers become the tool to redesign *our* space of the world (remember Ivan Illich), this exclusionary principle becomes both unnecessary and unjust. In a more inclusive digital world, those with high computer skills need to work in solidarity with those who lack them, sharing skills and teaching them.[94]

We are just at the beginnings of articulating these alternative visions that offer to 'plant the seeds of a humane future', indeed to 'humanise our machines'.[95] At their heart is a willingness to face a key question of our times: 'who decides who decides?'[96] Why should corporate elites be the ones who decide on the design of the spaces that bring us together? We'll come back to vision at the chapter's close.

Broader Conditions of Change

Assume for a moment that the will to migrate away from commercial social media platforms builds, migration gets under way, and the desire for an internet after commercial social media grows.[97] Will this be enough to give us the solidarity we need to combat climate change? Of course not.

This book's argument has never been that redesigning our digital space of the world is *in itself* enough sufficient to change how we address the climate emergency. The argument has been that social media platforms – and the commercialised design of the space of the world – are amplifying *existing* social trends that undermine solidarity, exactly when we cannot afford this to happen. It follows that many other actions must fall into place if deep reforms in social media are, long-term, to bear fruit in a better politics.

The first is to combat rising inequality. A world that is growing ever more unequal, in both absolute and relative terms, is always likely to be more polarised. We should never ignore that as a background force, especially when inequality is rising to extreme levels.[98] We should particularly not ignore this, given that climate change is likely to intensify the global struggles that are the legacy of centuries of capitalism and colonialism.[99] We discussed the interaction between inequality and solidarity in Chapter 6.

The difficult context of rising inequality is not entirely a reason for despair. Yes, deep inequalities drive political divisions, and rightly so: just telling people to be less polarised is like telling someone who has suffered a deep injustice not to express anger against their oppressors. But this does not mean that, against the background of those divisions, *new* solidarities cannot emerge, that draw in others in large numbers who are supportive of social change. Consider working-class movements in the UK and their role in the emergence of a welfare state in the nineteenth and early to mid-twentieth centuries; consider the US civil rights movement in the late twentieth century; or the anti-colonial struggles of the second half of the twentieth century in Africa and Asia and early nineteenth century in Latin America. All those movements represented not just polarisation, but also an *expanding* solidarity that included those less severely affected by the underlying injustices, but willing to help build a wider movement to right them.

The second broader action needed is to reverse the declining quality of information production in twenty-first-century societies. There is no simple 'objective' measure of quality information production, but particular processes have unquestionably undermined average quality: lack of investment in journalists and news production; changing norms of truth-seeking among media management that put profit before accuracy; and the increasing dominance in the US and elsewhere of partisan media.[100]

To which we must add another dangerous consequence of today's digital space of the world: the profound changes in the economics of news audiences caused by social media as spaces where people can circulate news-links effortlessly and for free. While traditional media have adapted to the symbiotic relationship with social media forced on them, the tensions are showing.[101]

Local press is struggling in many countries, because its advertising market collapsed when most local advertisers shifted to Facebook and Google.[102] Meanwhile platforms' impact on how we consume and circulate news seems irreversible. Consider that in 2022, of the top seven online news sources for UK adults (16+), three were owned by Meta (Facebook, Instagram and WhatsApp), two by Alphabet (Google News and YouTube), one was Twitter, one was the BBC, and none was a newspaper.[103] The result is that the largest Big Tech corporations, such as Meta and Google, have immense power over the terms on which news producers operate.[104] But that doesn't mean an independent press is unsalvageable.

Governments have attempted to impose charges on Big Tech for circulating newslinks to help subsidise struggling journalism, but with mixed success. While Germany and Spain quickly backed off from this, Australia, after an uncomfortable stand-off with Facebook and Google, saw its threat to use new arbitration powers to impose charges prompt Facebook and Google into private fee deals with the largest Australian media; the potential for benefiting news providers of all sizes was, however, lost.[105] In Canada, the government faces an ongoing news withdrawal by Facebook in response to its draft code, and the situation is unresolved, with Facebook usage in Canada apparently unaffected.[106]

When they act singly, governments allow Big Tech to pick them off and withdraw permission for news circulation in each nation, perfectly illustrating the unaccountable social power we have delegated to platforms. *But what if many governments acted together?* That would be much harder for Big Tech to handle.

Admittedly, social media's disruption of news production has been in some respects so deep that it seems beyond repair, with new AI-driven chatbot search only intensifying the harm of overriding original news content. The way forward must lie in direct national strategies for supporting civic news production, and here public financial support must have a role.[107] The success of those potential 'supply-side' changes will depend on a major renewal in news demand. But, as the need for local *and* national responses to the climate emergency grows, an increased demand for better news sources, more closely attuned to practical needs and global imperatives, may well emerge.

This leads to a final factor needed for real change: adequate funding to sustain the alternative platform infrastructure that is emerging. Alternative platforms are non-profit and depend on private funding, including donations and premium subscribers. This funding must grow substantially if the potentially large numbers migrating to these platforms are to be satisfied. This challenge cannot be resolved just through volunteers donating their labour, as now.

As the cultural will to move towards a better social media grows, there may well be more crowdfunding in the short term, but it is very unlikely to be sufficient in size or regularity, to meet the demand.[108] There is a role for philanthropists to be sure, but also the state, at least in richer countries. The state's role cannot be to own new or existing federated platforms: fears of censorship would be too strong. Something closer to sponsorship – sponsoring an infrastructure that helps a range of non-commercial social media to flourish – is needed. In return for support, new social media platforms would need to agree pro-social norms and rules of operation, rather like those set out earlier in the chapter.[109]

I can't offer a blueprint of what that subsidy scheme would look like, but what matters at this early stage is to avoid a counsel of despair. There is, especially in Europe, strong inherited support for public service values in media.[110] From this, ideas can be built for application elsewhere. Why assume, amidst the ruins of neoliberal capitalism, that only bad things can emerge?[111]

The Wider Knowledge Landscape

Any reform of social media, however ambitious, will take place in the infinite informational space of the internet, from which toxicity can never fully be excluded. This leads to another issue that must be addressed if we are really to transform our space of the world: search engines.

Towards a Public-value Search Engine?

As signalled at the start, this book has focused principally on social media platforms. While issues with Google's video platform YouTube have surfaced at times, I have discussed less often concerns with Google's primary product, its search engine, which remains by far the world's dominant search engine with nearly 92 per cent of global market share.[112]

The critiques of Google are numerous.[113] Some (its distortion of various information markets, its extraction of data from user behaviour) don't relate directly to questions of solidarity, while other critiques of the inherent biases of the search engine are extremely important, but not always directly connected to the undermining of solidarity.[114] Google as a search engine is undeniably useful – writing this book has relied upon it, I don't hide that – but the main worry for us here is more subtle: that, because of Google's overwhelming dominance in the production of everyday knowledge, its ongoing biases, defaults and steers may have outsize consequences for public debates, for example about climate change.

So, it matters, as we saw in Chapter 5, that Google's normal functioning makes extremist sources (that may well oppose climate action) more visible than they would otherwise be.[115] As Swedish scholars Jutta Haider and Malte Rödl note, 'the assumptions, contexts and histories that underlie [Google's] judgements and their results melt into the background', *because* we are regularly so reliant upon it. And it really matters when a simple Google search result for travel or food information subtly highlights, for example, air travel or convenience food options which are less environmentally sustainable.[116] Could Google, Haider and Rödl ask, be as much involved in the production of our *ignorance* as our knowledge in relation to climate change?

That this is a real possibility emerges from an important recent study of those across many countries who avoid news, rather than seeking it out. Many of them justified dispensing with regular news consumption by saying 'they preferred googling information periodically . . . because the search engine gave them greater control over their own news exposure' and allowed them to be more selective about the sources they used'.[117] More in control maybe (at least until ChatGPT-inspired composite search answers take over), but also more dependent on Google with all its faults.

A broader debate is needed about whether it can ever be in the interests of democratic health for one corporation, focused on generating profit, to have such an overwhelming dominance over knowledge production.

The everyday practice we call search is complex. It involves three elements: a 'crawler' or bot that seeks out pages online, and then places them in an 'index', which, in turn, is searched by a 'search engine'. Google has by far the world's largest index (with only Microsoft's Bing offering a real alternative: even Yahoo, Google's original rival, no longer compiles one); it has the most powerful search engine, and a crawler to which many websites give default access (which they don't give to most crawlers, because it is Google traffic that generates most hits for them).[118] Independents, by contrast, may not have their own index or crawlers, let alone a search engine.

Yet, over two decades, concerns about Google's treatment of privacy have prompted attempts to build alternative search engines, not based on the tracking of users. The leading privacy-based search engine is DuckDuckGo, established in 2008 and now with 0.58 per cent of the global search market and more than 100 million searches daily by 2022.[119] It does have its own crawler and index, but it relies for much of its results on Microsoft's Bing.[120] There are other alternative search engines, some more independent than DuckDuckGo and all offering user privacy (for example, Mojeek in the UK, founded four years before DuckDuckGo, Qwant in France, which the French government requires for its internal use, and the German search engine Ecosia), but none has made inroads.[121] The German and Spanish governments in the 2000s attempted and failed to build public search engines, and Australia's Green party revived the idea in 2021 when Google threatened to pull out of Australia, but it wasn't pursued.

This brief history of Google's would-be rivals indicates the *extreme* rigidity of the search engine market. This was confirmed when in February 2023 Microsoft announced that its search engine Bing would incorporate advanced AI via ChatGPT (itself the product of Open AI, in which Microsoft is a major investor). Would this eye-catching innovation increase Bing's market share? Six months later, in spite of ChatGPT's popularity, Bing's and Google's shares of the global search market had still not changed![122]

Three factors lock in Google's dominant market share. First, people's habits. Google is the only search engine whose name has entered the English language. Second, Google's installation of itself as our search default on our phones, with Google Chrome the default web browser for all the world's Android phones and, through an agreement with Apple, all the world's iPhones (Chrome unsurprisingly sets Google search engine as its default). Although Apple represents itself as Big Tech's leading privacy advocate, it receives a significant percentage of its annual income from this agreement with Google.[123] A third factor is that, in relation to search (unlike social media), scale really *is* a necessity: when we search, we do want to search across the whole universe of material online. Such huge scale require lots of time and investment.

But the vision of a public-service alternative to Google continues, particularly in Europe, with the Open Search Foundation being a leading force.[124] For sure, it would require building a complete new infrastructure: not just a search engine, but the index on which it runs, and the crawler bots that generate that index.[125] But multiple projects are working on this, inspired by a vision of a more trustworthy public knowledge and their rejection of a world in which, as one developer put it, 'it's as if a private vendor would own the streets'.[126]

Why not help those groups by having regulators impose on Google the obligation to be more transparent about the operation of its search algorithm and how it presents search results, to ensure these fit with relevant public values? Why not impose a tax on Google to support rival search engines and introduce some competition into the search engine market?

Towards an Overarching Vision

Federated platforms and alternative search engines remain rather technical. You might therefore be wondering: even if we can imagine a space of the world differently configured from the commercial model, what are we building this *for*? What is the vision that guides this?

There is no need for one single dominant vision. After all, the federated alternatives to the dominant commercial platforms *may not* quickly succeed in gaining significant market share: if the dominance of Google is extremely hard to shift without drastic regulatory action, the incumbent power of Meta is not much less entrenched. Fortunately there are other alternatives to the dominant platforms: for example, the not-for-profit messaging platform, Signal, and the not-for-profit email platform Protonmail, or local group chat sites like Front Porch Forum.[127] Given the various public relations debacles that have affected Facebook's and Meta's standing, there are also emerging commercial chat platforms such as Discord which emerged from the online gaming world, but now has more than 350 million users.[128]

Once we look at the wider range of alternative platforms, it becomes clear that just building alternative platforms cannot, by itself, protect democracy, or even solidarity. Large-scale digital platforms are compatible with both democracy *and* authoritarianism. When journalists in October 2023 lamented the collapse of Twitter as a source for what was happening on the ground in the Israel–Hamas war, this demonstrated why authoritarian governments (China and Russia, for example) really *like* social media: as a means to keep their enemies under continuous surveillance.[129]

But the possibility of designing our space of the world cannot now be put back in the bottle. When engineers write code, they are designing institutions: as Winograd and Flores wrote nearly four decades ago (the chapter's opening quote), 'in designing tools we are designing ways of being'. Are we really happy to leave our whole *way of being* for markets and their elites to design? Surely there are some things too important, too large, to be put under the control of exclusive private interests,[130] and the design of our space of the world is one of them. We need, as I noted earlier, to rethink who *decides* on who decides.

That means thinking seriously and positively about what values we *do* want to guide the social institutions we build when we design our digital platforms. I use the term 'institutions' deliberately. Robert Wuthnow, a sociologist who studied the cultures of the book in the eighteenth and nineteenth centuries, showed that social change is about much more than technologies in isolation. It is about how 'producers and their audiences come together', based on what sort of 'environmental resources' and what feedback loops and 'concrete communities of discourse' emerge.[131] Technologies' consequences, in short, have a social history in which values play a crucial role.

We need a new value that will help us recover the space of the world for humanity as a whole. This value must be publicly oriented, based in processes that are accountable and available for participation by all.[132] Rather than profit, we need to be motivated by care for the infrastructures we share.[133]

What form can we give to this public value?

Public Values for Social Media

Federated platforms are not the only answer to our needs, but they clearly express a public value: rejecting the tyranny of pure markets, they assert a principle of community, devolving much of their governance down to smaller scales where actual communities can operate, groups of people who have reason to know and trust each other and act in a common interest.

Another approach, which may be useful while commercial social media remain powerful, is to introduce something like *community governance* into commercial platforms themselves. This was largely how things were done in the early years of online communities on bulletin boards, multi-user domains and the like. Right now, there are examples within commercial platforms, such as the 'subreddit' groups within Reddit, to which are delegated at least the moderation of their discussions. In the short run, this might be a way of shoring up the 'crisis of legitimacy' in large platforms,[134] but the risk is that in the long run those platforms would refuse to make more fundamental changes in their business models, while happily free-riding on the community efforts of their users.

A third proposal goes further: to build a *new public infrastructure* for social media and indeed for other forms of online organising, alongside commercial platforms and federated alternatives. This 'intentionally digital public infrastructure',[135] as Ethan Zuckerman puts it, would be publicly supported and non-commercial. An infrastructure that supports existing communities, including civil society organisations, to meet, talk and organise online. In the US, campaigning organisations are now emerging to signal this new direction, such as New Public (led by Eli Pariser, mentioned in Chapter 5) and the Center for Humane Technology, founded by former Google psychologist, Tristan Harris.[136]

Consider also the PublicSpaces collective of Dutch organisations. This is currently building spaces such as PubHubs, where people can talk within a secure larger space that is not for profit, designed to support civic values and solidarity.[137] PublicSpaces operates on a federated principle, devolving the management of discussions and activities down to particular communities on the network. But, unlike federated social platforms, it does not have any plans to scale globally beyond its Dutch setting.[138] It is intended, however, as a complement to the Fediverse.[139] In size, it is significant: it links thirty-five Dutch civic social and arts organisations, so reaching potentially more than 70 per cent of the Dutch population.[140] Meanwhile, in Mexico and the US, the MayFirst Movement Technology group securely hosts thousands of activist websites and email accounts so they no longer need to depend on commercial platforms.[141]

PublicSpaces and the MayFirst Movement Technology are funded with public seed-money or membership fees, but there are other funding possibilities. Why don't national governments raise taxes on the commercial social media platforms, targeted at their revenues from extractive business models?[142] Why shouldn't national governments, when commercial platforms blatantly distort market competition, use their leverage to extract from them resources that can fund more publicly oriented ways of running social media?[143]

Supporting community platforms could be a very useful way of addressing two important problems. One may be temporary, but it is still serious. There are many groups in society, particularly vulnerable groups like forced migrants with few resources and even less political voice, who rely on the free infrastructure of Big Tech platforms.[144] A priority for new public infrastructures should be to build resources for vulnerable groups for whom federated platforms may not right now be helpful. There is an important role here to be played by platform cooperatives that bring individual workers together, based on 'communal ownership and democratic governance'.[145] Why not reconnect with the positive visions of computer-based sharing from earlier eras that were overwhelmed by the drive to commercialise the internet?[146]

The other problem is how to rethink the appropriate scale and context for social media for children and young adults, a debate that, as we saw, has barely begun. Just as any community would want a say in how its young people are educated, so it should want a say in the spaces where they can interact and learn social skills. Public community initiatives may be the best starting-point for this debate. Commercial platforms have shown that they cannot be trusted to perform this role.

To sum up the vision so far: instead of gambling everything on building federated competitors to today's commercial social giants, we can complement them by encouraging existing communities to pursue principles and spaces beyond the commercial options. Why not build from the communities that exist around our public institutions, such as schools, colleges, community centres? If this feels strange, that's the legacy of thirty years of relentlessly commercialised computing. Maybe it's time to renew what historian Joy Lisi Rankin calls the 'people's history of computing'.[147]

Of course, this will not resolve everything. In particular, there will remain the difficulty of toxic groups looking for a home somewhere online, a problem that exists in society generally. This problem is not, ultimately, resolvable by single platforms: it's a problem for the ecology of the whole internet (everything from domain names to cloud services).[148] Meanwhile choosing open-source architecture does, by definition, allow anyone to adopt it (as Donald Trump's Truth Social adopted Mastodon's protocol). But effective solutions will always have their basis in the values defended by particular communities.[149] Here federated platforms, whose members are real communities, have an advantage over commercial platforms driven by abstract business measures and shareholders looking for a return.[150]

Contrast Mastodon's success as a comment platform in isolating Gab's offensive content, discussed earlier, which came from the actions of the people who run its instances, with how the alternative commercial chat platform Discord handled similar problems. Discord is a closed-source platform that is centralised, not federated, although it devolves moderation down to its groups on the basis of some powerful shared moderation tools. It is home to many very large groups (called confusingly 'servers') and also many very small ones. Some smaller Discord servers became notorious for being populated by alt-right extremists, including those who planned the white nationalist march in Charlottesville, USA in August 2017.

Although Discord made efforts centrally to expunge those groups, two US researchers (Daniel Heslep and P. S. Berge) have shown how the problem persists. If you want to find groups on Discord, there is a platform search engine, but this only covers large public groups. However, a third-party service called Disboard, endorsed by Discord, can help you search for smaller groups which otherwise would be invisible. This is where the offensive groups can be found.[151] As those researchers say, Discord can advocate as many intensive moderation standards as it likes, and delete as many groups as it likes, but, given its size, this 'is not unlike a prairie fire: fertilizing the ground after every attempted burn'.[152]

Underlying all these difficulties is the permanent problem of protecting our common resources of social life, a problem that Silicon Valley engineers have ignored. The insights of Nobel Prize-winning economist Elinor Ostrom are enduring here: that the commons is best protected from erosion and misuse by a set of rules, which include clearly defined group boundaries and respect the right of communities to adapt and implement their own version of those rules.[153] Put more directly, platforms designed for communities are much more likely to hold to social values than platforms built for profit: after all, it is communities that are directly affected by what platforms do and so are most likely to care about getting solutions right.[154]

What about state ownership of commercially social media? For sure, the need to reject the corporate elite who own our space of the world has never been clearer. Take the debacle at Twitter in late 2022. US communications scholar Victor Pickard spoke for many: 'we can't let billionaires control major communications platforms'.[155] The ex-CEO of Twitter and founder of Twitter rival BlueSky, Jack Dorsey had already said back in 2022: 'I don't believe any individual or institutions should own social media.'[156]

Is the answer as simple as nationalising commercial social media?[157] Many left-wing critics argued this before the alternatives just discussed emerged more clearly. But nationalisation has two downsides. First, it is too optimistic about how democratic control can be asserted over today's huge commercial platforms: how can that be done without unprecedented regulatory force? And what would democratic control mean for the longer term? Can every aspect of platform management be opened up to democratic deliberation?[158] Second, it ignores the wider consequences of platform scale: what if many of the problems in today's space of the world flow not just from the capitalist drive to extract profit from social life, but from the *sheer scale* at which they operate (itself, of course, motivated by the lust for global expansion)? It is this second problem – of scale – that federated platforms meet head on, returning 'democratic control' *down* to a scale where it can be meaningfully exercised, while maintaining overall technical oversight of the platform.

The way forward then depends not on ownership – nationalising commercial platforms – but on collective values and how those values are woven into social media designs. Let's encourage a wealth of non-commercial alternatives to grow around Big Tech platforms in an inclusive process whereby commercial giants are weakened and, over time, lose their relevance.

Finally, consider the most radical alternative of all: the Small World model of computing proposed by Aral Balkan and Laura Kalbag, which proposes dispensing not only with large distant platforms, but even distant computer servers, with all our computer needs (including new versions of social media interfaces) being met by each person having their own small server.[159] This alternative vision of the internet's basic infrastructure launches in 2024 and, if it inspires developers to work with it, might offer a completely new starting-point for a public-value-driven internet, a connected space of the world beyond even the Fediverse.

We must wait and see how fast these visionary ideas develop.

Conclusion: Towards a Better Space of the World

Suppose cultural will builds to transform fundamentally the digital space of the world, away from profit and towards social ends. Suppose this connects with the forms of cooperation and solidarity in which people are already engaged outside of platforms.

For sure, this won't happen everywhere at once. As we saw in earlier chapters, there are many parts of the world where weak social and communications infrastructure or the oppression of authoritarian regimes makes it impossible right now to divert energy from commercial social media platforms to support alternatives (take the case of Iran, for example). But in other places the balance will be different, and change may occur.

Such change could be a first step towards reorganising our social and economic life to reprioritise for human creativity and collaboration. This transformation might even be one form that socialism in the twenty-first century takes.[160] True, the proposals I have outlined do not challenge capitalism as a whole: all would use market products, whether app stores, or cloud services, or software developed somewhere in market economies. And they avoid the ambition of building *one* overarching (state-driven or other) structure to govern all these new spaces: indeed the principle of resonance doesn't require this.

But maybe *total* system transformation is not the form that socialism now must, or even can, take. Maybe confronting the decades-long neoliberal entrenchment of capitalist forces into every recess of daily life – of which our digital space of the world is a clear example – requires something initially more modest. Modest, but still very bold: turning, as UK cultural theorist Jeremy Gilbert puts it, 'people's desire for connection into real social and cooperative action for the greater good'.[161] Solidarity, seen as an inclusive goal and oriented to shared decision-making,[162] has always been part of socialism, though neoliberalism capitalism has in the past four decades tried to crush it. If reversing that damage constitutes the first stage towards a wider socialist transformation, then so be it.

For now, given the huge risks created by capitalist-driven technological and institutional change, let's hold onto the more modest principle of resonance and start transforming our space of the world in ways that are bottom-up, not top-down. The will to do so will resonate, as more people select for those aspects of our digital world that, as Raymond Williams put it, 'contain the seeds of life within them',[163] rather than 'the seeds of death'. Ever more radical possibilities for doing so are now opening up. The future, while uncertain, remains hopeful.

As more of us gain control over our digital tools and platforms, we may find ourselves learning what it means to design a better way of being. That, after all, was the vision computer scientists had in the 1980s before the wave of optimism in a commercialised internet drowned out their voices. A way of being that helps, not hinders, us in addressing together the true existential challenges of our time.

Acknowledgements

The original idea for this book emerged half a decade ago, but much of it has come together under considerable time pressure over the past year.

The title came to me and I did some early research for Chapter 2 in January 2019, while I was on sabbatical (thanks to the Department of Media and Communications at LSE for making that possible). Then for two and a half years work on the separate but related project of understanding the wider forces of data colonialism as well as life circumstances during the pandemic absorbed me. I only returned to my sketch in the autumn of 2021, when I began to think about a trilogy of books of which this would be the first. For much of 2022, I worked closely with my wonderful and extraordinarily resourceful research assistant at LSE, Louise Hurel, on preparing the research background for Part 2 of the book and managed to sketch out the shape of most of the chapters, before another huge wave of work (Ulises Mejias's and my second book on data colonialism) took over, delaying this book further. The book was largely completed during a very intense period between July and November 2023, and reached its final form in March 2024.

For the fact that this book was possible at all I have a number of people to thank:

First, Mary Savigar, my editor at Polity Press, whose vision, support and sound editorial advice when I was bringing together the proposal and then at crucial points in the final year of writing was absolutely crucial. Thanks as ever to the whole team at Polity for excellent support, including Stephanie Homer and Maddie Tyler. Thanks to David Watson for his skilled copy-editing.

Second, my research assistant Louise Hurel who has been remarkably adaptable in pursuing my sometimes vague guidance and providing a wide research base from which I could build the book's arguments, particularly Part 2. I benefited also from her careful reading of most chapters near completion and for the design of Figure 1.1. I am hugely grateful to her.

I also want to thank friends and colleagues who were willing to read parts of the book (or related material) at short notice as I pulled the argument together: Rob Gehl, Gordon Gow, Bob Hariman, Sonia Livingstone and Bruce Schneier. Thanks also to Aral Balkan, Joanne Cheung, Judith Donath, José Van Dijck, Ethan Zuckerman and the attendees of the iWORD 1 and 2 conferences at the Harvard Kennedy School in December 2022 and 2023, for some important conversations. And huge thanks to Polity's two anonymous reviewers for their comments and advice, again at relatively short notice, which were important in helping me finalise the manuscript.

I dedicate this book to my wife, Louise Edwards: in deep gratitude for the love and support she has given me over more than three decades and with profound admiration for her indomitable strength, in particular in facing the multiple challenges that the past five years have brought.

Nick Couldry
Islip, near Oxford
March 2024

Further Reading Suggestions

Each chapter draws on a wide range of academic, journalism and policy sources for its argument, which are set out in the detailed notes. I will not try to summarise those sources here. Instead, I have compiled a small number of texts that could be useful starting-points for reading beyond each chapter.

Introduction

Naomi Klein, *Doppelganger* (Allen Lane, 2023) (on the broader consequences of toxic platform culture on political activism).

Milagros Miceli, Adrienne Williams and Timnit Gebru, 'The Exploited Labor Behind Artificial Intelligence', *Noema* (October 2022), https://www.noemamag.com/the-exploited-labor-behind-artificial-intelligence/ (on why Artificial Intelligence is not really artificial but depends on exploited human labour).

Hannah Murphy, 'The Rising Threat to Democracy of AI-powered Disinformation', *Financial Times* (11 January 2024), https://www.ft.com/content/16f23c01-fa51-408e-acf5-0d30a5a1ebf2 (useful summary of fears of democratic risks from AI).

Jose Van Dijck, Thomas Poell and Martijn de Waal, *The Platform Society* (Oxford University Press, 2018) (analyses the broader consequences of platform culture on social and public values).

Finally, both Mariana Mazzucato, *The Value of Everything* (Allen Lane, 2018) and Michael Sandel, *What Money Can't Buy: The Moral Limits of Markets* (Allen Lane, 2012) explain the importance of thinking about social change from perspectives not limited to narrow market logics.

Chapter 1

Julie Cohen, *Between Truth and Power* (Oxford University Press, 2019), especially Chapter 2 (on the dangers of platform power for economy and society).

Kevin Driscoll, *The Modem World: A Prehistory of Social Media* (Yale University Press, 2022) (gives a vivid picture of how the internet might have taken a different form and almost did).

Robin Mansell, *Imagining the Internet* (Oxford University Press, 2012) (pioneering critique of the divergence of internet design from social values).

Ulises Mejias and Nick Couldry, *Data Grab: The New Colonialism of Big Tech and How to Resist It* (WH Allen, 2024) (explains how the internet's development fits within the longer history of colonialism).

Tamar Sharon and Raphael Gellert, 'Regulating Big Tech Expansionism? Sphere Transgressions and the Limits of Europe's Digital Regulatory Strategy', *Information Communication & Society* (2023), https://doi.org/10.1080/1369118X.2023.2246526 (fundamental critique of the limits of platform regulation).

Ben Tarnoff, *Internet for the People* (Verso, 2022) (an engaging account of the internet we have lost).

Ethan Zuckerman, 'The Internet's Original Sin', *The Atlantic* (14 August 2014), https://www.theatlantic.com/technology/archive/2014/08/advertising-is-the-internets-original-sin/376041/ (an early critique of the wrong turn taken in internet development).

Chapter 2

After reading this chapter, you could explore the history of political theory, on which this chapter lightly draws. Useful contemporary entry-points are:

Jens Bartelson, *Visions of World Community* (Cambridge University Press, 2009).

Jeremy Gilbert, *Common Ground: Democracy and Collectivity in an Age of Individualism* (Pluto Press, 2014).

Pierre Rosanvallon, *Democratic Legitimacy: Legitimacy, Reflexivity, Proximity* (Princeton University Press, 2011).

David Runciman, *How Democracy Ends* (Profile Books, 2018).

Tomer Shadmy, 'The New Social Contract: Facebook's Community and Our Rights', *Boston University International Law Journal* 39 (2019): 307–54, available from https://www.bu.edu/ilj/files/2020/04/Shadmy.pdf.

Chapter 3

Marshall Van Alstyne and Erik Brynjolfsson, 'Global Village or Cyber-Balkans? Modeling and Measuring the Integration of Electronic Communities', *Management Science* 51/6 (2005), 818–68 (early study on the potentially polarising features of the internet).

Joan Donovan, Emily Dreyfuss and Brian Friedberg, *Meme Wars* (Bloomsbury, 2022) (definitive study of the role of social media platforms in the growth of the US alt right).

Amy Orben, Andrew Przybylski, Sarah-Jayne Blakemore and Rogier Kievit, 'Windows of Developmental Sensitivity to Social Media', *Nature Communications* 13 (2022): 1649, https://doi.org/10.1038/s41467-022-29296-3 (important scientific paper on young people's psychological sensitivity to social media harms).

Jamie Smyth and Hannah Murphy, 'The Teen Mental Health Crisis: A Reckoning for Big Tech', *Financial Times* (26 March 2023), https://www.ft.com/content/77d06d3e-2b9f-4d46-814f-da2646fea60c (useful entry-point to the debate among psychologists about social media's impact on young people's mental health).

Zeynep Tufekci, 'YouTube the Great Radicaliser', *New York Times* (10 March 2018), https://www.nytimes.com/2018/03/10/opinion/sunday/youtube-politics-radical.html (on the radicalising impact of YouTube's algorithm).

Georgia Wells, Jeff Horwitz and Deepa Seetharanam, 'Facebook Knows Instagram Is Toxic for Teen Girls, Company Documents Show', *Wall Street Journal* (14 September 2021) and Karen Hao, 'How Facebook and Google fund Global Misinformation', *MIT Tech Review* (20 November 2021), https://www.technologyreview.com/2021/11/20/1039076/facebook-google-disinformation-clickbait/ offer useful overviews of Frances Haugen's revelations about Instagram in 2021.

Chapter 4

Sarah Banet-Weiser and Kat Higgins, *Believability* (Polity, 2023) (fundamental reassessment of how the social media environment shapes who is and who is not believed).

Renee DiResta, 'The Supply of Disinformation Will Soon Be Infinite', *The Atlantic* (20 September 2020), https://www.theatlantic.com/ideas /archive/2020/09/future-propaganda-will-be-computer-generated /616400/ (pessimistic survey of impact of social media on the quality of public information).

Henry Farrell and Bruce Schneier, 'Common Knowledge Attacks on Democracy' (October 2018), available from https://papers.ssrn.com /sol3/papers.cfm?abstract_id=3273111 (important paper on the impacts on democracy of damage to shared information).

Keith Hampton, Lee Raine, Weizi Lu, Maria Dwyer, Inyoung Shin and Kristen Purcell, 'Social Media and the "Spiral of Silence"', Pew Research Center (2014), https://www.pewresearch.org/internet/2014 /08/26/social-media-and-the-spiral-of-silence/ (on the likelihood of spirals of silence emerging online).

Philip Howard, *Lie Machines* (Yale University Press, 2020) (on bad actors in public information flows).

Alice Marwick and Rebecca Lewis, 'Media Manipulation and Disinformation Online', *Data & Society* (May 2017), https:// datasociety.net/library/media-manipulation-and-disinfo-online/ (on the key role played by mainstream social media in right-wing political ecologies).

Russell Muirhead and Nancy Rosenblum, *A Lot of People Are Saying* (Princeton University Press, 2020) (useful study by political scientists of the dynamics of political misinformation).

Jonathan Ong and Jason Cabañes, 'Architects of Networked Disinformation: Behind the Scenes of Troll Accounts and Fake News Production in the Philippines' (2018), https://scholarworks.umass .edu/communication_faculty_pubs/74/ (excellent study of dynamics of misinformation in one country).

Soroush Vosoughi, Deb Roy and Sinan Aral, 'The Spread of True and False News Online', *Science* 359 (2018): 1146–51 (fundamental scientific paper on why false claims tend to spread online faster than truths).

Bernard Williams, *Truth and Truthfulness* (Harvard University Press, 2002) (fundamental philosophical perspective on how societies cannot function without a commitment to truthfulness).

Chapter 5

Shakuntala Banaji and Ramnath Bhat, *Social Media and Hate* (Routledge, 2022) (analysis of the complex dynamics of online hate in India).

Shanto Iyengar, Gaurav Sood and Yphtach Lelkes, 'Affect, not Ideology: A Social Identity Perspective on Polarization', *The Public Opinion Quarterly* 76(3) (2012): 405–31 (key scientific paper on affective polarisation).

Arvind Narayanan, 'Understanding Social Media Recommendation Algorithms', Knight First Amendment Institute (9 March 2023), https://knightcolumbia.org/content/understanding-social-media-recommendation-algorithms (very useful explanation of the evolution of social media business models and how they were reflected in platform functions).

Whitney Phillips, *Why We Can't Have Nice Things: Mapping the Relationship Between Online Trolling and Mainstream Culture* (MIT Press, 2015) (pioneering book on the roots of toxic online culture).

Aaron Smith, Laura Silver, Courtney Johnson and Jingjing Jiang, 'Publics in Emerging Economies Worry Social Media Sow Division', Pew Research Center (13 May 2019), https://www.pewresearch.org/internet/2019/05/13/publics-in-emerging-economies-worry-social-media-sow-division-even-as-they-offer-new-chances-for-political-engagement/ (international survey showing widespread concern about social media's impact on political division).

John Turner and Penelope Oakes, 'The Significance of the Social Identity Concept for Social Psychology with Reference to Individualism, Interactionism, and Social Influence', *British Journal of Social Psychology* 25 (1986): 237–52 (for those interested in the original version of Social Identity Theory).

Kerrie Unsworth and Kelly Fielding, 'It's Political: How the Salience of One's Political Identity Changes Climate Change Beliefs and Policy Support', *Global Environmental Change* 27 (2014): 131–7 (on the link between political polarisation and climate change opinion).

Siva Vaidhyanathan, *Anti-Social Media* (New York University Press, 2018) (early critique of Facebook's business model and its social impacts).

Chapter 6

Gal Beckerman, *The Quiet Before* (Penguin, 2022) (interesting book on the continuing importance of face-to-face interactions in long-term political change).

Judith Butler, *Notes toward a Performative Theory of Assembly* (Harvard University Press, 2015) (a philosopher's perspective on the importance of the face-to-face).

Lilie Chouliaraki, *The Ironic Spectator* (Polity, 2013) (strong critique of the limitations of online solidarity).

Pope Francis, *Fratelli Tutti* (March 2020), https://www.vatican.va/content/francesco/en/encyclicals/documents/papa-francesco_20201003_enciclica-fratelli-tutti.html (Pope Francis' perspective on the threat to human solidarity).

Verónica Gago, *Feminist International: How to Change Everything,* (Verso, 2020) (Latin American feminist perspective on solidarity and protest).

Catherine Knight Steele, *Digital Black Feminism* (New York University Press, 2021) (Black feminist perspective on the usefulness and limits of social media).

Chapter 7

Robin Berjon, 'The Internet Transition' (13 January 2023), https://berjon.com/internet-transition/ (bold reinterpretation of the internet's evolution).

Geert-Jan Bogaerts, Jose van Dijck and Ethan Zuckerman, 'Creating PublicSpaces: Centering Public Values in Digital Infrastructures', *Digital Government: Research and Practice* 4/2 (2023): 1–13 (Dutch perspective on how to build digital infrastructure through community support).

Cory Doctorow, *The Internet Con: How to Seize the Means of Communication* (Verso, 2023) (lively critique of the internet's dominant business models and their dependence on social lock-in).

Robert Gehl, *Move Slowly and Build Bridges: Mastodon, the Fediverse, and the Struggle for Ethical Social Media* (Oxford University Press, 2024) (visionary book by leading expert on federated social platforms).

Jeremy Gilbert, *Twenty First Century Socialism* (Polity, 2020) (a bold rethinking of socialism for the twenty-first century which offers a broader context for this chapter's ideas).

Ellen Goodman, 'Digital Fidelity and Friction', *Nevada Law Journal* 21 (2021): 623–53, https://scholars.law.unlv.edu/nlj/vol21/iss2/6/ (rare call to limit the circulation of posts across social media platforms).

Ivan Illich, *Tools for Conviviality* (Fontana, 1975) (pioneering book on the dangers that flow when capitalism takes control of our social tools).

Victor Pickard, *Democracy without Journalism?* (Oxford University Press, 2022) (study of the damaging impacts of social media on journalism and public information).

Alison Powell, *Undoing Optimisation* (Yale University Press, 2021) (a vision of how to challenge corporate platform logics through community projects).

Nathan Schneider and Amy Hasinoff, 'Mastodon Isn't Just a Replacement for Twitter', *Noema* (29 November 2022), https://www.noemamag.com/mastodon-isnt-just-a-replacement-for-twitter/ (on the long-term importance of federated social media).

Nathan Schneider, *Governable Spaces: Democratic Design for Online Life* (University of California Press, 2024) (a vision of online governance that complements this book's argument).

Ethan Zuckerman, *What Is Digital Public Infrastructure?*, Center for Journalism and Liberty (November 2020), https://www.journalismliberty.org/publications/what-is-digital-public-infrastructure (a vision for new forms of community-based digital infrastructure).

Notes

These notes give the book's detailed sources. For simplicity, last access dates to web sources have only been given where the source is likely to be subject to change, for example personal blogs, organisational websites or statistical databases.

Preface to Humanising the Future *Trilogy*

1 Mike Hulme, *Why We Disagree About Climate Change* (Cambridge University Press, 2009), 361.

2 Joanna Zylinska, *Minimal Ethics for the Anthropocene* (Open Humanities Press, 2014), 93, emphasis removed.

Introduction

1 Quoted Ryan Mac, Charlie Warzel and Alex Kantrowitz 'Growth at Any Costs: Top Facebook Executive Defended Data Collection in 2016 Memo – and Warned that Facebook Could Get People Killed', *BuzzFeed* (29 March 2018), https://www.buzzfeednews.com/article/ryanmac/growth-at-any-cost-top-facebook-executive-defended-data.

2 Onora O'Neill, *Towards Justice and Virtue* (Cambridge University Press, 1996), 192.

3 The difference between physical architecture and the design of online spaces is fundamental, but rarely commented upon. But see Judith Donath, *The Social Machine* (MIT Press, 2014), 13.

4 Kari Paul, 'Families Sue Tiktok After Girls Died While Trying "Black Out Challenge"', *Guardian* (6 July 2022), https://www.theguardian.com/technology/2022/jul/05/tiktok-girls-dead-blackout-challenge. The UK parliament in September 2023 passed legislation to restrict online access to such stunts for those under eighteen (the Online Safety Act).

5 Haroon Siddique, '"It's Heartbreaking: Mother of Archie Battersbee Says He Was Bullied Online', *Guardian* (2 February 2023), https://www.theguardian.com/society/2023/feb/02/mother-of-archie-battersbee-says-he-was-bullied-online.

6 Richard Adams and Sally Weale, 'Revealed: UK Children Being Ensnared

by Far-Right Ecosystem Online', *Guardian* (4 August 2022), https://www.theguardian.com/politics/2022/aug/03/revealed-uk-children-ensnared-far-right-ecosystem-online; Katie McQue and Mei-Long McNamara, 'How Facebook and Instagram Became Marketplaces for Child Sex Trafficking', *Guardian* (27 April 2023), https://www.theguardian.com/news/2023/apr/27/how-facebook-and-instagram-became-marketplaces-for-child-sex-trafficking.

7 Hannah Murphy and Joe Miller, 'Meta's Platforms Were "Prime Locations for Predators", Lawsuit Alleges', *Financial Times* (6 December 2023), https://www.ft.com/content/69f9d6dc-9521-4cfb-b790-88d05cf21698.

8 Hudson Lockett, Ryan McMorrow and Sun Yu, 'China's Tencent Imposes Controls to Tackle Gaming Addiction Among Children', *Financial Times* (3 August 2021), https://www.ft.com/content/1ee4f40b-cad8-45f7-b8dd-de25b89736d3.

9 Kalyeena Makortoff, 'Social Media Serve as a Gateway for Scammers, Says City Watchdog', *Guardian* (28 September 2021), https://www.theguardian.com/money/2021/sep/28/social-media-giants-serve-as-gateway-for-scams-warns-finance-watchdog#:~:text=Social%20media%20sites%20such%20as,tougher%20action%20on%20financial%20scams.

10 Jim Pickard, Emma Dunkley and Cristina Criddle, 'Meta Singled Out by UK Financial Lobby Group Over Digital Scams', *Financial Times* (8 July 2023), https://www.ft.com/content/d0215c7c-90e5-4e53-b5ea-a19140730b21; Rupert Jones, 'Social Media Sites Are Wild West for Online Shopping Fraud', *Guardian* (29 May 2023), https://www.theguardian.com/money/2023/may/28/social-media-sites-wild-west-shopping-uk-bank-facebook-instagram.

11 Constance Malleret, Dan Milmo and Alex Hern, 'Pro-Bolsonaro Violence: Experts Highlight Role of Social Media Platforms', *Guardian* (9 January 2023), https://www.theguardian.com/world/2023/jan/09/pro-bolsonaro-violence-social-media-platforms.

12 For Germany, see Karsten Müller and Carlo Schwarz, 'Fanning the Flames of Hate: Social Media and Hate Crime', *Journal of the European Economic Association* 19(4) (2021): 2131–67; for Turkey, see Ozge Ozduden, Umut Kokut and Cansu Ozduden, '"Refugees Are Not Welcome": Digital Racism, Online Place-making and the Evolving Categorization of Syrians in Turkey', *New Media & Society* 23(11) (2021): 3349–69.

13 Annie Njanja, 'Facebook Risks Ban in Kenya for Failing to Stop Hate Speech', *TechCrunch* (29 July 2022), https://techcrunch.com/2022/07/29/facebook-risks-ban-in-kenya-for-failing-to-stop-hate-speech/.

14 Beena Pallical, quoted International Dalit Solidarity Network, *Caste-Hate Speech* (2021), https://idsn.org/wp-content/uploads/2021/03/Caste-hate-speech-report-IDSN-2021.pdf, 20 (accessed 26 July 2023).

15 Jeff Horwitz and Deepa Seetharaman, 'Facebook Executives Shut Down

Efforts to Make the Site Less Divisive', *Wall Street Journal* (26 May 2020), https://www.wsj.com/articles/facebook-knows-it-encourages-division-top -executives-nixed-solutions-11590507499, citing an internal memo from 2016. See generally on Myanmar, Karen Hao, 'How Facebook and Google Fund Global Misinformation', *MIT Tech Review* (20 November 2021), https://www.technologyreview.com/2021/11/20/1039076/facebook-google -disinformation-clickbait/#:~:text=An%20MIT%20Technology%20Review %20investigation,information%20ecosystems%20around%20the%20world.

16 M. Falkenberg et al. (eleven authors), 'Growing Polarization Around Climate Change on Social Media', *Nature* (24 November 2022), https://www.nature .com/articles/s41558-022-01527-x.

17 I discuss in Chapter 3 the hotly debated topic of the rising mental health crisis among young people in many countries and its possible direct links to social media use.

18 Jose Van Dijck, Thomas Poell and Martijn de Waal, *The Platform Society* (Oxford University Press, 2018).

19 Tech Transparency Project, 'A Year Later, Christchurch Attack Videos Still on Facebook' (22 March 2020), https:// www.techtransparencyproject.org/articles/broken-promises-year-later- christchurch-attack-videos-still-on-facebook; Tess Owen, 'Mass Shooter in Louisville Livestreamed His Attack on Instagram', *Vice* (10 April 2023), https://www.vice.com/en/article/wxj8vm/mass-shooting-louisville.

20 Siva Vaidhyanathan, *The Googlization of Everything* (University of California Press, 2011)*;* Bernhard Rieder and Guillaume Sire, 'Conflicts of Interest and Incentives to Bias: A Microeconomic Critique of Google's Tangled Position on the Web', *New Media & Society* 16(2) (2014): 195–211.

21 Naver (https://www.naver.com/) was founded in 1999 as a web portal with search engine, and has become the main way most South Koreans access web information and services.

22 Jedediah Purdy, *After Nature* (Harvard University Press, 2015), 3.

23 Naomi Klein, *Doppelganger* (Allen Lane, 2023), 329, added emphasis.

24 World Economic Forum, *Global Risks Report 2024* (January 2024), 11, https://www.weforum.org/publications/global-risks-report-2024/.

25 Carolyn Marvin, *When Old Technologies Were New* (Oxford University Press, 1990).

26 Ian Watt, *The Rise of the Novel* (Chatto and Windus, 1987) (o.p. 1957).

27 Claude Fischer, *America Calling* (Yale University Press, 1987).

28 Stanley Cohen and Laurie Taylor, *Folk Devils and Moral Panics* (Harper Collins, 1973).

29 Yascha Mounck, *The People Versus Democracy* (Harvard University Press, 2018), 139; David Weinberger, *Too Big to Know* (Basic Books, 2011), 45

('traditional knowledge has been an accident of paper'); Jonathan Rauch, *The Constitution of Knowledge* (Brookings Institute, 2021), 121–2. For more detail on historical comparisons, see Nick Couldry and Andreas Hepp, *The Mediated Construction of Reality* (Polity, 2016), Chapter 3.

30 This is the process of 'deep mediatization' that I have written about elsewhere: see ibid.; cf. Andreas Hepp, *Deep Mediatization* (Polity, 2020).

31 R. Wike et al. (six other authors), 'Social Media Seen as Mostly Good for Democracy Among Many Nations, but US a Major Outlier', Pew Research Center (6 December 2022), https://www.pewresearch.org/global/2022 /12/06/social-media-seen-as-mostly-good-for-democracy-across-many -nations-but-u-s-is-a-major-outlier/.

32 Ibid.

33 Safiya Noble, *Algorithms of Oppression* (New York University Press, 2018); Ruha Benjamin, *Race after Technology* (Polity, 2019); Catherine d'Ignazio and Lauren Klein, *Data Feminism* (MIT Press, 2020).

34 Julia Carrie Wong, 'Facebook Overhauls News Feed in Favour of "Meaningful Social Interactions"', *Guardian* (12 January 2018), https://www.theguardian .com/technology/2018/jan/11/facebook-news-feed-algorithm-overhaul-mark -zuckerberg.

35 Hannah Murphy, 'The Rising Threat to Democracy of AI-Powered Disinformation', *Financial Times* (11 January 2024), https://www.ft.com /content/16f23c01-fa51-408e-acf5-0d30a5a1ebf2.

36 American Psychological Association, 'Health Advisory on Social Media Use in Adolescence' (10 May 2023), https://www.apa.org/topics/social-media -internet/health-advisory-adolescent-social-media-use (accessed 23 August 2023).

37 Robert Booth, '"Social Media Is Like Driving With No Speed Limits": The US Surgeon General Fighting For Young Persons' Happiness', *Guardian* (20 March 2024), https://www.theguardian.com/media/2024/mar/20/vivek -murthy-us-surgeon-general-social-media-youth-happiness.

38 Karen Hao, 'The Facebook Whistleblower Says Its Algorithms Are Dangerous. Here's Why', *MIT Tech Review* (5 October 2021), https:// www.technologyreview.com/2021/10/05/1036519/facebook-whistleblower -frances-haugen-algorithms/.

39 European Commission, 'Code of Practice on Disinformation: New Reports Available in the Transparency Centre' (26 September 2023), https://digital -strategy.ec.europa.eu/en/news/code-practice-disinformation-new-reports -available-transparency-centre. And see European External Action Service, *2nd EEAS Report on Foreign Information and Interference Threats* (23 January 2024), https://www.eeas.europa.eu/sites/default/files/documents/2024/EEAS -2nd-Report%20on%20FIMI%20Threats-January-2024_0.pdf.

40 Sarah Roberts, *Behind the Screen* (Yale University Press, 2021); Milagros Miceli, Adrienne Williams and Timnit Gebru, 'The Exploited Labor Behind Artificial Intelligence', *Noema,* (October 2022), https://www.noemamag .com/the-exploited-labor-behind-artificial-intelligence/; David Pilling and Madhumita Murgia, '"You Can't Unsee It": The Content Moderators Taking on Facebook', *Financial Times* (18 May 2023), https://www.ft.com/content /afeb56f2-9ba5-4103-890d-91291aea4caa.

41 Purdy, *After Nature*, 21.

42 Mariana Mazzucatto, *The Entrepreneurial State* (Anthem Press, 2014).

43 Mark Zuckerberg, statement, 5 October 2021, https://www.facebook.com /zuck/posts/10113961365418581 (accessed 15 November 2023).

44 Both quoted in Hannah Murphy, Antoine Gara and James Fontanella-Khan, 'Twitter Accepts Elon Musk's $44 bn Takeover', *Financial Times* (26 April 2022), https://www.ft.com/content/79e3bc48-96ef-4e62-b30b-d3ddb45d7a2f.

45 Dan Milmo, 'Twitter Admits Bias in Algorithm for Right Wing Politicians and News Outlets', *Guardian* (22 October 2021), https:// www.theguardian.com/technology/2021/oct/22/twitter-admits-bias-in- algorithm-for-rightwing-politicians-and-news-outlets.

46 See, for example, Pablo Boczkowski, *Abundance* (Oxford University Press, 2021); Ignacio Siles, *Living with Algorithms: Agency and User Culture in Costa Rica* (MIT Press, 2017); Dariusz Jemelniek and Aleksandra Przeyelinska, *Collaborative Society* (MIT Press, 2020).

47 For example, Council on Foreign Relations report, *Confronting Reality in Cyberspace* (New York, 2022), https://www.cfr.org/report/confronting-reality -in-cyberspace.

48 'A Declaration for the Future of the Internet' (April 2022), https://www .whitehouse.gov/wp-content/uploads/2022/04/Declaration-for-the-Future -for-the-Internet_Launch-Event-Signing-Version_FINAL.pdf.

49 Byron Tan and Dustin Volz, 'US State-Government Websites Use TikTok Trackers, Review Finds', *Washington Post* (21 March 2023), https://www .wsj.com/articles/tiktok-trackers-embedded-in-u-s-state-government-websites -review-finds-a2589f0.

50 Michael Sandel, *What Money Can't Buy: The Moral Limits of Markets* (Allen Lane, 2012); Robin Mansell, *Imagining the Internet* (Oxford University Press, 2012); Mariana Mazzucatto, *The Value of Everything* (Allen Lane, 2018). Compare Joseph Stiglitz, 'Facebook Does Not Understand the Marketplace of Ideas', *Financial Times* (17 January 2020), https://www.ft.com/content /d4419bd8-3860-11ea-ac3c-f68c10993b04.

51 Francis Fukuyama, 'Putin's War on the Liberal Order', *Financial Times* (4 August 2022), https://www.ft.com/content/d0331b51-5d0e-4132-9f97 -c3f41c7d75b3.

52 Compare Niels ten Oever, '5G and the Notion of Network Ideology, or the Limitations of Sociotechnical Imaginaries' (forthcoming), *Telecommunications Policy*, 47(5) (2023), https://doi.org/10.1016/j.telpol.2022.102442.

53 As noted recently by Lawrence Lessig in Nilay Patel, 'Harvard Professor Lawrence Lessig on Why AI and Social Media Are Causing a Free Speech Crisis for the Internet', *The Verge* (24 October 2023), https://www.theverge.com/23929233/lawrence-lessig-free-speech-first-amendment-ai-content-moderation-decoder-interview.

54 Judy O'Neill (1990) 'An Interview with Vinton Cerf', April 1990, Charles Babbage Institute, available from https://conservancy.umn.edu/handle/11299/107214 (accessed 24 March 2024).

55 Vint Cerf, 'In 2018 We Will Tackle the Internet's Dark Side', *Wired* (6 January 2018), https://www.wired.co.uk/article/vint-cerf-internet-free-speech-censorship-fake-news.

56 Tim Berners-Lee, *Weaving the Web* (Harper Business, 2001), 36.

57 The signs, however, were already there, as Stanford historian Fred Turner shows in his investigation of how, already in the 1940s, 1950s and 1960s, imaginations of public space were, in the USA at least, entirely dependent on seeing it as a space committed to market values rather than public values: Fred Turner, *The Democratic Surround* (MIT Press, 2011). On the lack of public platform values, see Van Dijck et al., *The Platform Society*.

58 Julien Mailland and Kevin Driscoll, *Minitel: Welcome to the Internet* (MIT Press, 2017).

59 Kevin Driscoll, *The Modem World: A Prehistory of Social Media* (Yale University Press, 2022); Charlton McIlwain, *Black Software* (Oxford University Press, 2020), Chapter 4.

60 Joy Lisi Rankin, *A People's History of Computing in the US* (Harvard University Press, 2018).

Chapter 1: Redesigning the Social World as if by Accident

1 From 'On My Philosophy', quoted by Amanda Lagerkvist, *Existential Media* (Oxford University Press, 2022), 99.

2 Nicholas Negroponte, *Being Digital* (MIT, 1996); Stewart Brand, *The Media Lab: Inventing the Future at M.I.T.* (Penguin, 1988), 38.

3 The Web's protocols had been announced by Tim Berners-Lee in 1991, but the innovation did not start to be more widely taken up until 1993, when commercial browsers became available: see the history at https://home.cern/science/computing/birth-web/short-history-web#:~:text=Tim%20Berners%2DLee%2C%20a%20British,and%20institutes%20around%20the%20world (accessed 7 August 2023).

4   I am thinking here of Robin Berjon's discussion of the internet as the social equivalent of the 'evolutionary major transitions' in the early history of life on earth in 'The Internet Transition' (13 January 2023), https://berjon.com /internet-transition/ (accessed 23 August 2023).

5   Ramesh Srinivasan, *Beyond the Valley* (MIT Press, 2020), 314.

6   The first scholar to see where things were heading was probably Philip Agre, 'Surveillance and Capture: Two Models of Privacy', *The Information Society* 10(2) (1994): 101–27.

7   Janet Abbate, 'How the Internet Lost Its Soul', *Washington Post* (1 November 2019), https://www.washingtonpost.com/outlook/2019/11/01/how-internet -lost-its-soul/.

8   Benjamin Bratton, *The Stack: On Software and Sovereignty* (MIT Press, 2015).

9   Helen Thomas, 'Threats to Undersea Cables Should Worry World Business as Well as Government', *Financial Times* (26 April 2023), https://www.ft.com /content/1addaf05-49d9-4172-8eff-eabb2ac01a16/.

10 Daniel Greene, 'Landlords of the Internet: Big Data and Big Real Estate', *Social Studies of Science* 52(6) (2022): 904–27.

11 Ben Tarnoff, *Internet for the People* (Verso, 2022), xiii, 45.

12 https://www.eff.org/cyberspace-independence.

13 Joseph Turow, *The Daily You* (Yale University Press, 2011).

14 Nick Couldry and Ulises Mejias, *The Costs of Connection: How Data Is Colonizing Human Life and Appropriating it for Capitalism* (Stanford University Press, 2019); Ulises Mejias and Nick Couldry, *Data Grab* (WH Allen, 2024).

15 Shoshana Zuboff, *The Age of Surveillance Capitalism* (Profile Books, 2019), 92.

16 As leading algorithm expert Arvind Narayanan puts it, 'the primary objective of almost every recommendation algorithm on social media platforms is to rank the available content according to how likely it is that the user in question will engage with it': 'Understanding Social Media Recommendation Algorithms', Knight First Amendment Institute (9 March 2023), https:// knightcolumbia.org/content/understanding-social-media-recommendation -algorithms, 13.

17 Driscoll, *The Modem World*, 22, 185, 213n85.

18 Jesse Daniels, *CyberRacism: White Supremacy Online and the New Attack on Civil Rights* (Rowman and Littlefield, 2009), 168.

19 Bernhard Rieder, '"What Is in Page Rank?", A Historical and Conceptual Investigation of Recursive Search Data', *Computational Culture* 6 (2012): 1–28.

20 In the course of this Google also acquired YouTube in 2006.

21 As Ethan Zuckerman pointed out, it was this reorganising of platforms around attempts to get personalised attention that mattered, not whether it actually succeeded, which many marketers still doubt: 'The Internet's Original

Sin', *The Atlantic* (14 August 2014), https://www.theatlantic.com/technology/archive/2014/08/advertising-is-the-internets-original-sin/376041/.

22 Mark Andrejevic, *Infoglut: How Too Much Information is Changing the Way We Think and Know* (Routledge 2013); Julie Cohen, *Between Truth and Power: The Legal Constructions of Informational Capitalism* (Oxford University Press, 2019); Christian Fuchs, *Social Media: A Critical Introduction* (Sage, 2014); Robin Mansell, *Imagining the Internet* (Oxford University Press, 2012); Siva Vaidhyanathan, *Anti-Social Media* (New York University Press, 2018); Zuboff, *The Age of Surveillance Capitalism*. See also the succinct account of internet growth in Tarnoff, *Internet for the People*, Part I.

23 Driscoll, *The Modem World*, 8, 195.

24 In *Data Grab* (Chapter 1), Mejias and I explain this through the concept of data territories.

25 Abbate, 'When the Internet Lost Its Soul'. See for an argument for a more radical version of telecommunications policy, Dwayne Winseck, 'Vampire Squids, "the Broken Internet", and Platform Regulation', *Journal of Digital Media & Policy* 11 (2020): 241–82.

26 For a vivid account of one version of that alternative, early world of connection, see Driscoll, *The Modem World*.

27 Rankin, *People's History of Computing*, 241.

28 Rana Faroohar, 'Techlash: The Year in a Word', *Financial Times* (16 December 2018), https://www.ft.com/content/76578fba-fca1-11e8-ac00-57a2a826423e.

29 On capitalism and the imposition of abstract space, see Henri Lefebvre, *The Production of Space* (Blackwell, 1974), and for the connection between this and the digital world, Robert Prey, 'Henri Lefebvre and the Production of Music Streaming Spaces', *Sociologica* 3 (2015), https://www.doi.org/10.2383/82481.

30 On the close relations between capitalism and colonialism, see Mejias and Couldry, *Data Grab*, chapter 1.

31 Kate Losse, 'I Was Zuckerberg's Speechwriter. "Companies Over Countries" Was His Early Motto', *Vox* (16 April 2018), https://www.vox.com/first-person/2018/4/11/17221344/mark-zuckerberg-facebook-cambridge-analytica.

32 On the concept from the philosophy of justice of 'sphere transgressions', see Tamar Sharon and Raphael Gellert, 'Regulating Big Tech Expansionism? Sphere Transgressions and the Limits of Europe's Digital Regulatory Strategy', *Information Communication & Society* (2023), https://doi.org/10.1080/1369118X.2023.2246526, drawing on Michael Walzer, *Spheres of Justice* (Blackwell, 1983). On colonial aspects of extraction, see Couldry and Mejias, *Costs of Connection*.

33 From 'On My Philosophy'; see note 1 above.

34 5.2 billion smartphones in the world in 2023, rising to estimated 6.1 billion

in 2028, against world population (2023) of 8 billion: figure retrieved from Statista, 'Number of Smartphone Users Worldwide from 2013 to 2028' (2023), https://www.statista.com/forecasts/1143723/smartphone-users -in-the-world. The percentage stated in the text may be a little overstated, given that there are a few countries where people have on average more than one smartphone per person (e.g. Brazil, average 1.2): Fundação Getulio Vargas, Brazil, https://portal.fgv.br/noticias/uso-ti-brasil-pais-tem-mais-dois -dispositivos-digitais-habitante-revela-pesquisa.

35 Mailland and Driscoll, *Minitel* (on France); Yu Hong, *Networking China: The Digital Transformation of the Chinese Economy* (University of Illinois Press, 2017); Evan Feigenbaum and Michael Nelson (eds.), *The Korean Way with Data* (Carnegie Foundation, August 2021), https://carnegieendowment .org/files/202108-KoreanWayWithData_final5.pdf; Evgeny Morozov, 'Project Cybersyn: and the Origins of the Big Data Nation', *New Yorker* (6 October 2014), https://www.newyorker.com/magazine/2014/10/13/planning -machine (on Chile).

36 I am adapting here the phrasing of Eli Pariser, who said in a TED Talk (2019), available from https://www.youtube.com/watch?v=bWA1gvA5lxU: 'Sometimes it feels like this whole project of wiring up a civilization and getting billions of people to come into contact with each other, is just impossible.' Cited by Berjon, 'The Internet Transition', 3.

37 Michele Lamont and Virag Molnar, 'The Study of Boundaries in Social Sciences', *Annual Review of Sociology* 28 (2002): 167–95.

38 Ellen Goodman, 'Digital Fidelity and Friction', *Nevada Law Journal* 21(2) (2021), 632–53, at 648.

39 Alice Marwick and danah boyd, 'I Tweet Honestly, I Tweet Passionately: Twitter Users, Context Collapse and the Imagined Audience', *New Media & Society* 13(1) (2010): 114–33.

40 For a rare exception, see Donath, *The Social Machine*, Chapter 7.

41 Robinson Meyer, 'Everything We Know About Facebook's Secret Mood-Manipulation Experiment', *The Atlantic* (28 June 2014), https://www .theatlantic.com/technology/archive/2014/06/everything-we-know-about -facebooks-secret-mood-manipulation-experiment/373648/.

42 Maria Ressa, *How to Stand Up to a Dictator: The Fight for Our Future* (WH Allen, 2022), 140.

43 'Global Gross Domestic Product (GDP) at Current Prices from 1985 to 2028', Statista (2023), https://www-statista-com.gate3.library.lse.ac.uk /statistics/268750/global-gross-domestic-product-gdp/.

44 For classic diagnoses of the deep flaws and violences in neoliberal thinking, see Michel Foucault, *The Birth of Biopolitics* (Palgrave, 2008); and Wendy Brown, *Undoing the Demos* (Zone Books, 2013).

45 Howard Rheingold, *The Virtual Community* (Secker and Warburg, 1994).

46 Yochai Benkler, *The Wealth of Networks* (Yale University Press, 2006).

47 Charles Leadbeater, *We-think* (Penguin, 2008).

48 Alberto Melucci, 'The Process of Collective Identity', in H. Johnston and B. Klandermans (eds.), *Social Movements and Culture* (UCL Press, 1995), 41–63, at 41.

49 For a typical example, see John Palfrey and Urs Gasser, *Born Digital* (Basic Books, 2008), especially 294.

50 David Weinberger, *Too Big to Know* (Basic Books, 2011), xiii.

51 Ibid., 77, 81ff, discussing the work of Carl Sunstein on echo chambers.

52 Ibid., 181, 193–4.

53 Associated Press, 'Number of Active Users at Facebook Over the Years', *Yahoo!news* (23 October 2023), https://finance.yahoo.com/news/number -active-users-facebook-over-years-214600186--finance.html. See also 'Number of Monthly Active Facebook Users Worldwide as of 1st quarter 2023', Statista (April 2023), https://www.statista.com/statistics/264810/number-of-monthly -active-facebook-users-worldwide/.

54 W. Russell Neuman, *The Digital Difference* (Harvard University Press, 2016), e.g. 15, 201.

55 Ibid., 201. For a more complex view of network space, see Tiziana Terranova, *Network Culture* (Pluto, 2004).

56 Mohamed Zayani, *Networked Publics and Digital Contention* (Oxford University Press, 2014).

57 Ibid., 195.

58 Manuel Castells, *The Rise of the Network Society* (Blackwell, 1996), 477.

59 The first authors to isolate the problem of 'context collapse' online were Marwick and boyd: '"I Tweet Honestly, I Tweet Passionately"'. For a classic earlier account of this issue, see Joshua Meyrowitz, *No Sense of Place* (Oxford University Press, 1985).

60 For the older idea of a computer world which is a model that can picture the world's complexities, see David Gelernter, *Mirror Worlds* (Oxford University Press, 1991). For an excellent account of how platforms do not just model but directly shape our interactions with them, see Julie Cohen, *Between Truth and Power* (Oxford University Press, 2019), Chapter 2.

61 Ulrich Beck, *The Metamorphosis of the World* (Polity, 2016), 137; Arjun Appadurai, *Fear of Small Numbers* (Duke University Press, 2006), 25.

62 *Metamorphosis*, 138. Cf Sabine Selchow, *Negotiations of the 'New World'*, (Transcript, 2017).

63 Cohen, *Between Truth and Power*; Zuboff, *The Age of Surveillance*.

64 For emergent properties, see Anders Malm, *The Progress of this Storm* (Verso, 2020), 67. On platforms' emergent properties as complex systems,

see Narayanan, 'Understanding Social Media Platforms' Recommendation Algorithms', 3.

65 Rogers Brubaker, *Hyperconnectivity and Its Discontents* (Polity, 2022).

66 Paul Virilio, *Open Sky* (Verso, 1997), 51.

67 Julian Borger, Jennifer Rankin, Kate Lyons, 'The Rise and Rise of International Diplomacy by WhatsApp', *Guardian* (4 November 2016), https://www.theguardian.com/technology/2016/nov/04/why-do-diplomats-use-this-alien-whatsapp-emoji-for-vladimir-putin; Peter Walker, '"I can't keep track": Numerous Tory MP Factions Spawn on WhatsApp', *Guardian* (8 January 2022), https://www.theguardian.com/politics/2022/jan/08/erg-out-crg-tory-factions-boris-johnson-struggling-appease (headline taken from hard copy edition).

68 'The Need Behind the Need of Médecins sans Frontières', recorded conversation between Cris Villar, Landbot Head of Customer, and Nick Scott of MSF, no date, https://landbot.io/customer-stories/medecins-sans-frontieres (accessed 9 November 2023).

69 Ian Bogost, 'The Age of Social Media is Ending: It Should Never Have Begun', *The Atlantic* (10 November 2022), https://www.theatlantic.com/technology/archive/2022/11/twitter-facebook-social-media-decline/672074/. See also Adrienne LaFrance, 'Facebook Is a Doomsday Machine', *The Atlantic* (15 December 2020), https://www.theatlantic.com/technology/archive/2020/12/facebook-doomsday-machine/617384/.

70 Hannah Murphy, 'Meta's Revenue Growth Boosts Shares as It Touts AI Progress', *Financial Times* (27 April 2023), https://www.ft.com/content/3cccff6e-7589-4db0-9cfc-637fc3dd682c; John Keegan, 'Each Facebook User Is Monitored by Thousands of Companies', *The Verge* (17 January 2023), https://themarkup.org/privacy/2024/01/17/each-facebook-user-is-monitored-by-thousands-of-companies-study-indicates.

71 Kate Klonick, 'The New Governors: The People, Rules and Processes Governing Online Speech', *Harvard Law Review* (2018): 1598–1679.

72 For an early warning about the ambiguity of internet freedom, see Tamara Shepherd and Normand Lewis, 'Technology Design and Power: Freedom and Control in Communication Networks', *International Journal of Media and Cultural Politics* 9(3) (2013): 259–75.

73 https://www.statista.com/statistics/273018/number-of-internet-users-worldwide/ (accessed 4 August 2023).

74 https://ec.europa.eu/eurostat/web/products-eurostat-news/w/ddn-20230714-1 (accessed 7 August 2023).

75 Ministry of the Economy and National Institute for Statistics and Census, Argentina, *Acceso y uso de tecnologías de la información y comunicación* (2020, fourth quarter), https://www.indec.gob.ar/uploads/informesdeprensa

/mautic_05_213B13B3593A.pdf; J. Paz, 'Older People in Argentina: Various Disadvantages in the Face of the Coronavirus Pandemic', UNDP (30 June 2020), https://www.undp.org/latin-america/blog/older-people-argentina-various-disadvantages-face-coronavirus-pandemic; Telecommunications Subsecretariat of Chile, *Encuesta de Acceso y Usos de Internet* (2017), https://www.subtel.gob.cl/wp-content/uploads/2018/07/Informe_Final_IX_Encuesta_Acceso_y_Usos_Internet_2017.pdf, 47 (all accessed 7 August 2023).

76 Eurobarometer, *Special Report on Online Platforms* (April 2016), https://webgate.ec.europa.eu/ebsm/api/public/deliverable/download?doc=true&deliverableId=59695.

77 Peter Stalker, Sonia Livingstone, Daniel Kardefeldt-Winther and Marium Saeed, *Growing Up in a Connected World* (2019), https://www.unicef-irc.org/publications/1060-growing-up-in-a-connected-world.html, 10.

78 'Internet Usage Rate in Brazil from 2015 to 2023, by Access Device', Statista (19 December 2023), https://www.statista.com/statistics/1000103/brazil-internet-user-penetration-device/#:~:text=Approximately%2099%20percent%20of%20internet,the%20internet%20on%20a%20computer (accessed 28 July 2023).

79 Comscore statistics quoted by Ofcom, *Online Nation 2021 Report* (June 2021), https://www.ofcom.org.uk/__data/assets/pdf_file/0013/220414/online-nation-2021-report.pdf.

80 See Ofcom, *Online Nation* (2021), 11, for UK statistics, but the same phenomenon was reported globally.

81 Ofcom, *Online Nation 2022 Report* (June 2022), https://www.ofcom.org.uk/__data/assets/pdf_file/0023/238361/online-nation-2022-report.pdf, 61.

82 Nic Newman, Richard Fletcher, Kirsten Eddy, Craig T. Robertson and Rasmus Kleis Nielsen, *Reuters Institute Digital News Report 2023*, Reuters Institute for the Study of Journalism (2023), https://reutersinstitute.politics.ox.ac.uk/sites/default/files/2023-06/Digital_News_Report_2023.pdf.

83 Ian Johnston, 'TikTok Censured for Misusing Children's Data', *Financial Times* (4 April 2023), https://www.ft.com/content/36ac09ac-1066-4695-925d-d15525ea6d9b; Hibaq Farah and Dan Milmo, 'TikTok Allowing Under-13s to Keep Accounts, Evidence Suggests', *Guardian* (20 December 2023), https://www.theguardian.com/technology/2023/dec/19/tiktok-allowing-under-13s-to-keep-accounts-evidence-suggests#:~:text=TikTok%20faces%20questions%20over%20safeguards,parents%20were%20overseeing%20their%20accounts.

84 Emily Vogel, Risa Gelles-Watnick and Navid Massart, 'Teens, Social Media and Technology 2022' (2022) Pew Research Center, https://www.pewresearch.org/internet/2022/08/10/teens-social-media-and-technology-2022/.

85 Amanda Lenhart, *Teens, Technology and Friendships* (2015) Pew Research

Center, https://www.pewresearch.org/internet/2015/08/06/teens-technology-and-friendships/.

86 UNESCO/Ipsos, 'Survey on the Impact of Online Disinformation and Hate Speech' (September 2023), https://www.unesco.org/sites/default/files/medias/fichiers/2023/11/unesco_ipsos_survey.pdf.

87 Pew Research Center, 'Social Media and News Factsheet' (15 November 2023), https://www.pewresearch.org/journalism/fact-sheet/social-media-and-news-fact-sheet/.

88 Newman et al., *Reuters Institute Digital News Report 2023*. Reuters' figures show 'online including social media' and 'social media' separately: for most countries, the former figure (but not the latter) is larger than television as a news source, but this mode of presentation makes it hard to identify the exact role of social media as a news source.

89 Nic Newman, Richard Fletcher, Anne Schulz, Simge Andı, Craig T. Robertson and Rasmus Kleis Nielsen, *Reuters Institute Digital News Report 2021*, Reuters Institute for the Study of Journalism (2021), https://reutersinstitute.politics.ox.ac.uk/sites/default/files/2021-06/Digital_News_Report_2021_FINAL.pdf, 53–4.

90 Ibid., 53.

91 Meng Liang, 'The End of Social Media? How Data Attraction Model in the Algorithmic Media Reshapes the Attention Economy', *Media Culture & Society* 44(6) (2022): 1110–31.

92 Cristina Criddle and Arjun Alim, 'TikTok Undercuts Social Media Rivals with Cheap Ads in Battle for Growth', *Financial Times* (9 January 2023), https://www.ft.com/content/2e62de44-7877-4ec3-8eec-68dd7788b9dc; Mark Sweney, 'The Rise of TikTok: Why Facebook Is Worried about the Booming Social App', *Guardian* (9 April 2022), https://www.theguardian.com/technology/2022/apr/09/rise-of-tiktok-why-facebook-is-worried-booming-social-app.

93 Alex Hern, 'TechScape: Suspicious of TikTok? You're Not Alone', *Guardian* (20 July 2022), https://www.theguardian.com/technology/2022/jul/20/tiktoks-privacy-problem-isnt-what-you-think; Julian McAuley, quoted in Ben Smith, 'How TikTok Reads Your Mind', *New York Times* (5 December 2021), https://www.nytimes.com/2021/12/05/business/media/tiktok-algorithm.html.

94 Jon Henley, 'Young People More Likely to Doubt Merits of Democracy', *Guardian* (12 September 2023), https://www.theguardian.com/world/2023/sep/11/younger-people-more-relaxed-alternatives-democracy-survey.

95 Andrea Geraci, Mattia Nardotto, Tommaso Reggiano and Fabio Sabatini, 'Broadband Internet and Social Capital', *Journal of Public Economics* 206 (2022) 104578, https://www.sciencedirect.com/science/article/abs/pii/S0047272721002140.

96 An important question after all is the continued importance of traditional media. According to a major 2021 report (Eurobarometer, *Climate Change*, available from https://webgate.ec.europa.eu/ebsm/api/public/deliverable/download?doc =true&deliverableId=75838), although for the first time climate change has become recognised as the most serious problem 'facing the world', only 18 per cent believe this (there are so many competing alternatives). For those who think this, *television* is the main news source, even though Facebook is the most important source for news on climate change among younger people.

97 Asking ecological questions about media has a long history, but a key anticipation was Roger Silverstone, *Media and Morality* (Polity 2007), vi, 13.

98 Driscoll, *The Modem World*, 199.

Chapter 2: When Political Theory Gets Bypassed

1 David Runciman, *How Democracy Ends* (Profile Books, 2018), 139.

2 Thomas Hobbes, *Leviathan* (Penguin, 1985), 185.

3 Engagement is the core goal that, aside from all the details, drives all major platforms' algorithms, according to algorithm analyst Arvind Narayanan: Narayanan, 'Understanding Social Media Recommendation Algorithms', 13.

4 For interesting reflections on this long-term legacy of four decades of neoliberal economic and social policy, see Klein, *Doppelganger*. See also Liesbet Van Zoonen, 'I-pistemology: Changing Truth Claims in Popular and Political Culture', *European Journal of Communication* 27(1) (2012): 56–67 for a pioneering commentary on similar issues.

5 Purdy, *After Nature*, 267.

6 Aristotle, *The Politics* (Penguin, 1992), 59.

7 Ibid.

8 Ibid., 60.

9 Ibid., 404–5.

10 Ibid., 404.

11 Jean-Jacques Rousseau, *The Social Contract and Discourses* (Everyman's Library, 1973), 192.

12 Pierre Rosanvallon, *Democratic Legitimacy: Impartiality, Reflexivity, Proximity* (Princeton University Press, 2011), 128.

13 Ibid., 70, 132, 215.

14 Ibid., 188.

15 James Bohman, *Democracy Across Borders: From Demos to Demoi* (MIT Press, 2007); cf. Craig Calhoun, 'Nationalism, Political Community and the Representation of Society: Or, Why Feeling at Home Is Not a Substitute for Public Space', *European Journal of Social Theory* 2(2) (1999): 217–31.

16 Bohman, *Democracy Across Borders*, 91.

17 Ibid., 63.

18 danah boyd, 'Social Network Sites as Networked Publics: Affordances, Dynamics and Implications', in Z. Papacharissi (ed.), *Networked Self* (Routledge, 2011), 39–58; Manuel Castells, *Networks of Outrage and Hope* (Polity, 2012).

19 In particular, the work of Vico, *The First New Science* (Cambridge University Press, 2002) (o.p. 1725); and Montesquieu, *The Spirit of Laws* (Cosimo Classics, 2011) (o.p. 1748).

20 Edmund Burke, *Reflections on the Revolution in France* (Oxford University Press, 1993) (o.p. 1790), especially 95–9.

21 Alexis de Tocqueville, *Democracy in America* (Bantam, 2002) (o.p. 1835), 186–7.

22 Above all the US federalists such as James Madison, in Clinton Rossiter (ed.), *The Federalist Papers* (Penguin, 2003), 76–9, 95–6. See for an earlier notion of confederation: Montesquieu, *Spirit of Laws*, 126–7.

23 Hannah Arendt, *The Human Condition* (Chicago University Press, 1958), 199.

24 Ibid., 199.

25 Will Kymlicka, 'Citizenship in an Era of Globalisation: Commentary on Held', in I. Shapiro and C. Hacker-Cordón (eds.), *Democracy's Edges* (Cambridge University Press, 1999), 112–26, at 119–25.

26 Philip Pettit, *Republicanism: A Theory of Freedom and Government* (Oxford University Press, 1997), 241ff.

27 Ibid., 249.

28 Ibid., 252.

29 Ibid., 253.

30 Berjon, 'Internet Transition', 6.

31 Marquis de Condorcet, *Selected Writings*, ed. Keith Michael Baker (Bobbs Merrill, 1976), 221.

32 Hobbes, *Leviathan*, 192, 188.

33 John Locke, 'An Essay Concerning the True Original Extent and End of Civil Government', in E. Barker (ed.), *Social Contract* (Oxford University Press, 1960), 1–143.

34 Jeremy Gilbert, *Common Ground: Democracy and Collectivity in an Age of Individualism*, (Pluto Press, 2014), 50.

35 Ibid., Chapter 3, especially 59–60.

36 Axel Honneth, *Struggle for Recognition* (Polity, 1995); Bruno Campanella, *Recognition in the Age of Social Media* (Polity, 2023), Chapter 1.

37 Pascal Konig, 'Dissecting the Algorithmic Leviathan: On the Socio-Political Anatomy of Algorithmic Governance', *Philosophy and Technology* 33 (2020):

467–85; Iyad Rahman, 'Society-in-the-loop: Programming the Algorithmic Social Contract', *Ethics & Information Technology* 20 (2018): 5–14; and, more critically, Kathleen Creel and Deborah Hellman, 'The Algorithmic Leviathan: Arbitrariness, Fairness, and Opportunity in Algorithmic Decision-making Systems', *Canadian Journal of Philosophy* 52(1) (2022): 26–43. See most recently Paul Gowder, *The Networked Leviathan* (Cambridge University Press, 2023).

38 For an interesting discussion of this image, see Quentin Skinner, 'A Bridge Between Art and Philosophy: The Case of Thomas Hobbes', *European Review* 30(5) (2022): 627–38. Thanks to Göran Bolin for this reference.

39 Comment by Republican Chair of the US House of Representatives Financial Services Committee, quoted Georgia Wells and Alexa Corse, 'Social-media Postings Amplify Anxiety Over SVB Collapse', *Wall Street Journal* (14 March 2023), https://www.wsj.com/articles/social-media-postings-amplify-anxiety-over-svb-collapse-860d8f30.

40 Hobbes, *Leviathan*, 369.

41 'In our days we receive three different or contrary educations, namely of our parents, of our masters, and of the world. What we lean in the latter effaces all the ideas of the former': Montesquieu, *Spirit of Laws*, 33.

42 Ibid., 328.

43 Tomer Shadmy, 'The New Social Contract: Facebook's Community and Our Rights', *Boston University International Law Journal* 39 (2019): 307–54, available from https://www.bu.edu/ilj/files/2020/04/Shadmy.pdf.

44 Ibid., 314.

45 The classic text on this is Lawrence Lessig, *Code and Other Laws of Cyberspace* (Basic Books, 1999); Manuel Castells, *Communication Power* (Oxford University Press, 2009), 55.

46 Shadmy, 'New Social Contract', 334–40.

47 Ibid., 341.

48 For a parallel argument, see João Magalhães and Jun Yu, 'Social Media, Social Unfreedom', *Communications* 47(4) (2022), 553–71, especially 567–8.

49 Center for Countering Digital Hate, *Hidden Hate: How Instagram Fails to Act on 9 in 10 Reports of Misogyny in DMs* (6 April 2022), https://counterhate.com/research/hidden-hate/.

50 Wendy Brown, *Undoing the Demos: Neoliberalism's Stealth Revolution* (Zone Books, 2015); Colin Crouch, *The Strange Non-Death of Neoliberalism* (Polity, 2011).

51 Ibid., 173. In this passage, Brown is actually discussing, as an example of neoliberalism, the US *Citizens United* Supreme Court case (2010) which gave the constitutional right of free speech to corporations: https://en.wikipedia.org/wiki/Citizens_United_v._FEC (accessed 21 August 2023). This is exactly the sort of freedom on which platforms seek increasingly to rely.

52 Saskia Sassen, *Territory Authority Rights* (Princeton University Press, 2006), 422.

53 Saskia Sassen, *Expulsions* (Harvard University Press, 2016), 221.

54 Ricardo Mendonca, Virgilio Almeida and Fernando Filgueiras, *Algorithmic Institutionalism* (Oxford University Press, 2023).

55 For concern about the impacts of platform power on liberal law and ethics in particular, see Sebastian Benthall and Jake Goldenfein, 'Data Science and the Decline of Liberal Law and Ethics' (2020), available from https://ssrn .com/abstract=3632577. For broader concerns, see Cohen, *Between Truth and Power*; and Mireille Hildebrandt, *Smart Technologies and the End(s) of Law* (Edward Elgar, 2015).

56 Martha Nussbaum, *The Monarchy of Fear* (Oxford University Press, 2018), 238.

57 Jedediah Britton-Purdy, David Singh Grewal, Amy Kapczynski and K. Sabeel Rahman, 'Building a Law-and-Political-Economy Framework: Beyond the Twentieth-Century Synthesis', *Yale Law Journal* 129 (2020): 1784–1835, at 1831.

58 Roberto Unger, *Democracy Realized: The Progressive Alternative* (Verso, 1998), 5, 24.

59 Jens Bartelson, *Visions of World Community* (Cambridge University Press, 2009), 9. Sincere thanks to my friend Kristina Riegert for the gift in 2013 that alerted me to Bartelson's fascinating work.

60 Ibid., 181.

Chapter 3: The World at My Fingertips?

1 Quoted Luke O'Brien, 'The Far-Right Helped Create the World's Most Powerful Facial Recognition Technology', *The Huffington Post* (7 April 2020), https://www.huffpost.com/entry/clearview-ai-facial-recognition-alt-right _n_5e7d028bc5b6cb08a92a5c48?6p8.

2 See, for example, Mary Gray, *Out in the Country* (New York University Press 2009), 126.

3 On how technologies shape and mould our behaviour without determining it, see Couldry and Hepp, *Mediated Construction of Reality*, 32–3. There is no contradiction between this approach to media's long-term consequences in large populations and the common, but more narrowly focused, idea that each technology has particular 'affordances' which encourage a certain spectrum of interaction.

4 Marshall Van Alstyne and Erik Brynjolfsson, 'Global Village or Cyber-Balkans? Modeling and Measuring the Integration of Electronic Communities', *Management Science*, 51(6) (2005), 818–68.

5 For timing of Facebook's creation, see https://en.wikipedia.org/wiki/History _of_Facebook.

6 Marshall Van Alstyne and Erik Brynjolfsson, 'Could the Internet Balkanize Science?', *Science* 274 (1996): 1479–80.

7 Driscoll, *The Modem World*.

8 Van Alstyne and Brynjolfsson, 'Global Village', 852.

9 Ibid., 866, added emphasis.

10 Thomas Schelling, 'Dynamic Models of Segregation', *Journal of Mathematical Sociology,* 9(2) (1971): 143–86; Cass Sunstein, 'The Law of Group Polarization', *Journal of Political Philosophy* 10 (2002), 175–95.

11 Nicholas Carr, 'Tribes of the Internet', *Rough Type*, blog (December 2005), https://www.roughtype.com/?m=200512 (accessed 12 July 2023). A few years later, a book by Silicon Valley executive William Davidoff picked up on Carr's blog and developed the systems theory argument that, above a certain level of complexity, *all* open systems (such as the internet) become unstable: William Davidow, *Overconnected* (Headline Publishing, 2011), especially 157.

12 On shallow communities, see Joan Donovan, Emily Dreyfuss and Brian Friedberg, *Meme Wars* (Bloomsbury, 2022), 51; Philip Agre, 'Toward a Critical Technical Practice: Lessons Learned in Trying to Reform AI', in G. Bowker, L. Gasser, S. Leigh Star and W. Turner (eds.), *Bridging the Great Divide* (Lawrence Erlbaum, 1997).

13 Paul DiMaggio and Eszther Hargittai, 'From the "Digital Divide" to "Digital Inequality": Studying Internet Use as Penetration Increases', working paper, Center for Arts and Cultural Policy Studies, Princeton University (July 2001), https://culturalpolicy.princeton.edu/sites/cultural policy/files/wp15_ dimaggio_hargittai.pdf (accessed 6 July 2023); Ellen Helsper, *The Digital Disconnect* (Sage, 2021).

14 Dave Winer, quoted Adam Hodgkin, *Following Searle on Twitter* (Chicago University Press, 2017), 123.

15 UNICEF, *Perils and Possibilities Growing Up Online* (June 2016), https://www .unicef.org/eap/reports/perils-and-possibilities-growing-online, 4.

16 Stalker et al., *Growing up in a Connected World*, 45.

17 Lenhart, *Teens, Technology and Friendships* (2015).

18 Monica Anderson, Emily Vogels, Andrew Perrin and Lee Rainie, 'Connection, Creativity and Drama: Teen Life on Social Media in 2022', Pew Research Center (16 November 2022), https://www.pewresearch.org/internet/2022/11 /16/connection-creativity-and-drama-teen-life-on-social-media-in-2022/.

19 Ofcom, *Adults' Media Use and Attitudes* (2017), https://www.ofcom.org.uk/ __data/assets/pdf_file/0020/102755/adults-media-use-attitudes-2017.pdf.

20 Jin Ha Lee, Liz Pritchard and Chris Hubbles, 'Can We Listen to It Together? Factors Influencing Reception of Music Recommendations and

Post-Recommendation Behavior', 20th International Society for Music Information Retrieval Conference (ISMIR 2019), https://cpb-us-e1.wpmucdn.com/sites.uw.edu/dist/2/3760/files/2019/09/CanWeListenTogether.pdf.

21 Alei Fan, Han Shen, Laurie Wu, Anna Mattila, Anil Bilgihan, 'Whom Do We Trust? Cultural Differences in Consumer Responses to Online Recommendations', *International Journal of Contemporary Hospitality Management* 30(3) (2018): 1508–25.

22 UNICEF, *Perils*, 3.

23 Livingstone et al., *Growing Up*, 23, 31.

24 Denise Cheng, 'Having Information vs Being Informed', *New York Times* (23 October 2012), https://www.nytimes.com/roomfordebate/2012/10/22/reading-more-but-learning-less/having-information-vs-or-being-informed#:~:text=If%2C%20in%20what%20we%20call,way%20news%20and%20information%20are.

25 For an excellent recent survey, see Luci Pangrazio and Neil Selwyn, *Critical Data Literacies* (MIT Press, 2023).

26 Robert Kraut, Michael Patterson, Vicki Lundmark, Sara Kiesler, Tridas Mukophadhay and William Scherlis, 'Internet Paradox: A Social Technology that Reduces Social Involvement and Psychological Well-being?', *American Psychologist* 55(9) (1998): 1017–31.

27 Robert Putnam, *Bowling Alone* (Simon and Schuster, 2000).

28 See, for summaries, Chiungjung Huang, 'A Meta-analysis of the Problematic Social Media Use and Mental Health', *International Journal of Social Psychiatry* 68(1) (2022): 12–33; Alfonso Pellegrino, Alessandro Stasi and Veera Bhatiasevi, 'Research Trends in Social Media Addiction and Problematic Social Media Use: A Bibliometric Analysis', *Frontiers in Psychiatry* (10 November 2022), https://www.ncbi.nlm.nih.gov/pmc/articles/PMC9707397/.

29 Cecilie Andreassen, Torbjørn Torsheim, Geir Brunborg and Ståle Pallesen, 'Development of a Facebook Addiction Scale', *Psychological Reports* 110(2) (2012): 501–17; Regina van den Eijnden, Jeroen Lemmens and Patti Valkenberg, 'The Social Media Disorder Scale', *Computers in Human Behavior* 61 (2016): 478–87.

30 See, for another comprehensive review, Raquel Lozano-Blasco, Alberto Quilez Robres and Alberto Soto Sanchez, 'Internet Addiction in Young Adults: A Meta-analysis and Systematic Review', *Computers in Human Behavior* 130 (2022): 107201.

31 Hunt Allcott, Matthew Gentzkow and Lena Song, 'Digital Addiction', *American Economic Review* 112(7) (2022): 2424–63.

32 Hannah Devlin, 'Revealed: Almost Half of UK Teenagers Feel Addicted to Social Media, Study Says', *Guardian* (2 January 2024), https://www.theguardian.com/lifeandstyle/2024/jan/02/social-media-addiction-teenagers-study-phones.

33 Rebecca Nowland, Elizabeth Necka and John Cacioppo, 'Loneliness and Social Internet Use: Pathways to Reconnection in a Digital World?', *Perspectives on Psychological Science* 13(1) (2018): 70–87. John Cacioppo has been for decades a leading authority on loneliness.

34 Holly Shakya and Nicholas Christakis, 'Association of Facebook Use With Compromised Well-Being: A Longitudinal Study', *American Journal of Epidemiology* 185(3) (2017): 201–11.

35 Jean Twenge, Jonathan Haidt, Andrew Blake, Cooper McAllister, Hannah Lemon and Astrid Le Roy, 'Worldwide Increases in Adolescent Loneliness', *Journal of Adolescence,* 93 (2021): 257–69.

36 Ibid., 267.

37 Rita Latikka, Aki Koivula, Reetta Oksa, Nina Savela and Atte Oksanen, 'Loneliness and Psychological Distress Before and During the COVID-19 Pandemic: Relationships with Social Media Identity Bubbles', *Social Science & Medicine* 293 (2022): 114674, https://www.sciencedirect.com/science/article/pii/S0277953621010066?via%3Dihub, 2.

38 Latikka et al., 'Loneliness and Psychological Distress' studied this for Finland.

39 Sonia Livingstone, 'Book Review: Igen: Why Today's Super-Connected Kids Are Growing Up Less Rebellious, More Tolerant, Less Happy – and Completely Unprepared for Adulthood', *Journal of Children and Media* 12(1) (2017): 118–23, reviewing a book by Jean Twenge. Twenge et al.'s article (note 35 above) is not the only suggestive contextual study on mental health issues: see Charmaine Lo, Jeffrey Bridge, Junxin Shi, Lorah Ludwig and Rachel Stanley, 'Children's Mental Health Emergency Department Visits: 2007–2016', *Pediatrics* 145(6) (2020): e20191536, https://publications.aap.org/pediatrics/article/145/6/e20191536/76929/Children-s-Mental-Health-Emergency-Department?autologincheck=redirected. This latter study indicates rises in children's psychologically caused emergency hospital admissions in the US for 2007–16, a period that fits less neatly with Twenge's narrative. For bold claims about the *causal* impact of the smartphone on children's mental health, see Jonathan Haidt, *The Anxious Generation* (Allen Lane, 2024).

40 Lozano-Blasco et al., 'Internet Addiction'.

41 Esma Aimeur and Zakaria Sahnoune, 'Privacy, Trust and Manipulation in Online Relationships', *Journal of Technology in Human Services* 38(2) (2020): 159–83.

42 Taina Bucher, 'The Friendship Assemblage: Investigating Programmed Sociality on Facebook', *Television & New Media* 14(6) (2012): 479–93; *If . . . Then* (Oxford University Press, 2018), 8–9, 12–14.

43 Ofcom, *Adults' Media Use and Attitudes* (2015), https://www.ofcom.org.uk/__data/assets/pdf_file/0014/82112/2015_adults_media_use_and_attitudes_report.pdf.

44 R. I. M. Dunbar 'Do Online Social Media Cut Through the Constraints That Limit the Size of Offline Social Networks?' *Royal Society Open Science* 3: 150292 (2016), https://royalsocietypublishing.org/doi/epdf/10.1098/rsos .150292.

45 Bucher, *If . . . Then.*

46 Brian Primack et al. (eight authors), 'Social Media Use and Perceived Social Isolation among Young Adults in the US', *American Journal of Preventive Medicine* 53(1) (2017): 1–8.

47 Doo-Hun Choi and Ghee-Young Noh, 'The Influence of Social Media Use on Attitude Toward Suicide Through Psychological Well-Being, Social Isolation, and Social Support', *Information, Communication & Society* 23(10) (2020): 1427–43.

48 Dar Meshi and Morgan Ellithorpe, 'Problematic Social Media Use and Social Support in Real-Life Versus on Social Media: Associations with Depression, Anxiety and Social Isolation', *Addictive Behaviors* 119 (2021): 106949.

49 Mike Yao and Zhi-Jin Zhong, 'Loneliness, Social Contacts and Internet Addiction: A Cross-lagged Panel Study', *Computers in Human Behavior* 30 (2014): 164–70.

50 Erin Vogel, Jason Rose, Bradley Okdie, Katheryn Eckles and Brittany Franz, 'Who Compares and Despairs? The Effect of Social Comparison Orientation on Social Media Use and Its Outcomes', *Personality and Individual Differences* 86 (2015): 239–56.

51 Hui-Tzu Grace Chou and Nicholas Edge, '"They are Happier and Having Better Lives than I Am": The Impact of Using Facebook on Perceptions of Others' Lives', *Cyberpsychology, Behavior and Social Networking* 15(2) (2012): 117–21.

52 Vogel et al., 'Who Compares and Despairs?'.

53 Valentina Boursier, Francesca Gioia, Alessandro Musetti and Adriano Schimmenti, 'Facing Loneliness and Anxiety During the Covid-19 Isolation: The Role of Excessive Social Media Use in a Sample of Italian Adults', *Frontiers in Psychiatry* 11 (2020): 586222.

54 Stephen Marche, 'Is Facebook Making Us Lonely?', *The Atlantic* (May 2012), https://www.theatlantic.com/magazine/archive/2012/05/is-facebook-making -us-lonely/308930/.

55 HM Coroner Andrew Walker, North London Coroner's Service, Regulation 28 Report to Prevent Future Deaths (13 October 2022), https://www.judiciary .uk/wp-content/uploads/2022/10/Molly-Russell-Prevention-of-future-deaths -report-2022-0315_Published.pdf (accessed 14 July 2023).

56 Quoted by Georgia Wells, Jeff Horwitz and Deepa Seetharanam, 'Facebook Knows Instagram Is Toxic for Teen Girls, Company Documents Show', *Wall Street Journal* (14 September 2021), https://www.wsj.com/articles

/facebook-knows-instagram-is-toxic-for-teen-girls-company-documents-show -11631620739, 1. For academic publications on this topic, see, for example, Ivanka Prichard, Eliza Kavanagh, Kate Mulgrew, Megan Lim and Marika Tiggemann, 'The Effect of Instagram #fitspiration Images on Young Women's Mood, Body Image, and Exercise Behaviour', *Body Image* 33 (2020): 1–6, https://www.sciencedirect.com/science/article/abs/pii/S1740144519302578.

57 Wells et al., 'Facebook Knows Instagram Is Toxic', 2, 9.

58 Georgia Wells and Jeff Horvitz, 'Facebook's Effort to Attract Preteens Goes Beyond Instagram Kids, Document Shows', *Wall Street Journal* (28 September 2021), quotes at 1, 5.

59 Ibid., quote at 8.

60 Dan Milmo and Clea Skopeliti,'Harmful Spiral: How Instagram Offers Users Impossible Dreams', *Guardian* (18 September 2021), quoting Baroness Kidron of 5Rights, https://www.theguardian.com/technology/2021/sep/18 /teenage-girls-body-image-and-instagrams-perfect-storm.

61 Quoted ibid., 'Harmful Spiral'.

62 Quoted Wells et al., 'Facebook Knows Instagram Is Toxic', 6.

63 Van den Eijnden et al., 'Social Media Disorder Scale', 485.

64 Maria d'Arienzo, Valentina Boursier and Mark Griffiths, 'Addiction to Social Media and Attachment Styles: A Systematic Literature Review', *International Journal of Mental Health and Addiction* 17 (2019): 1094–118.

65 Joshua Hart, Elizabeth Nailing, George Bizer and Caitlyn Collins, 'Attachment Theory as a Framework for Explaining Engagement with Facebook', *Personality and Individual Differences* 77 (2015): 33–40.

66 Amy Orben, Andrew Przybylski, Sarah-Jayne Blakemore, Rogier Kievit, 'Windows of Developmental Sensitivity to Social Media', *Nature Communications* 13 (2022): 1649, https://doi.org/10.1038/s41467-022 -29296-3.

67 For an overview, see Jonathan Haidt, Zach Rausch and Jean Twenge (ongoing), *Social Media and Mental Health: A Collaborative Review*, unpublished manuscript, New York University. Available from https://tinyurl.com /SocialMediaMentalHealthReview (accessed 16 August 2023).

68 Amy Orben, quoted Jamie Smyth and Hannah Murphy, 'The Teen Mental Health Crisis: A Reckoning for Big Tech', *Financial Times* (26 March 2023), https://www.ft.com/content/77d06d3e-2b9f-4d46-814f-da2646fea60c.

69 Amy Orben and Andrew Przybylski, 'The Association Between Adolescent Well-being and Digital Technology Use', *Nature Human Behavior* 3 (2019), 173–82.

70 Jean Twenge, Jonathan Haidt, Thomas Joiner and W. Keith Campbell, 'Underestimating Digital Media Harm', *Nature Human Behaviour* 4 (April 2020): 346–8; Amy Orben and Andrew Przybylski, 'Reply to: Understanding

Digital Media Harm', *Nature Human Behavior* 4 (April 2020): 349–51; Jon Haidt, 'Social Media Is a Major Cause of the Mental Illness Epidemic in Teen Girls. Here's the Evidence', blog (22 February 2023), https://jonathanhaidt .substack.com/p/social-media-mental-illness-epidemic (accessed 16 August 2023); Jean Twenge, Jonathan Haidt, Jimmy Lonzano and Kevin Cummins, 'Specification Curve Analysis Shows That Social Media Use Is Linked to Poor Mental Health, Especially Among Girls', *Acta Psychologica* 224 (2022): 103512; and for an interesting commentary on both Haidt/Twenge and Orben/Przybylski, see David Stein, 'Haidt: Social Media in O & P Paper', blog (22 August 2023), https://shoresofacademia.substack.com/p/haidt -social-media-in-o-and-p-paper?utm_source=substack&utm_medium=email (accessed 22 August 2023).

71 Yvonne Kelly, Afshin Zilanawal, Cara Boker and Amanda Sacker, 'Social Media Use and Adolescent Mental Health: Findings from the UK Millennium Cohort Study', *EClinical Medicine* 6 (2018): 59–68.

72 Compare for example Jeff Hancock, Sunny Xun Liu, Mufan Luo and Hannah Mieckowski, 'Psychological Well-Being and Social Media Use: A Meta-Analysis of Associations Between Social Media Use and Depression, Anxiety, Loneliness, Eudaimonic, Hedonic, and Social Well-Being', available from https://ssrn.com/abstract=4053961; and Jon Haidt, 'Why Some Researchers Think I'm Wrong about Social Media and Mental Illness', blog (17 April 2023), https://jonathanhaidt.substack.com/p/why-some-researchers -think-im-wrong#:~:text=Most%20of%20the%20studies%20cited,odds %20ratios%20are%20below%203 (accessed 16 August 2023), especially 12–13.

73 See, for example, Claire Cain Miller, 'Everyone Says Social Media Is Bad for Teens. Proving It Is Another Thing', *New York Times* (17 June 2023), https:// www.nytimes.com/2023/06/17/upshot/social-media-teen-mental-health .html, which cites in support of its sceptical position research by Common Sense Media: 'Teens and Mental Health: How Girls Really Feel About Social Media', https://www.commonsensemedia.org/research/teens-and-mental -health-how-girls-really-feel-about-social-media (accessed 16 August 2023).

74 I am therefore sceptical about how much we can draw from studies which look for such associations: e.g. Matti Vuorre and Andrew Przybylski, 'Estimating the Association Between Facebook Adoption and Well-being in 72 Countries', *Royal Society Open Science* 10 (2023): 221451.

75 Haidt, 'Social Media Is a Major Cause', 2.

76 Quoted by Josep Fita, 'La imagen corporal y las redes sociales: "Pueden ser muy destructivas"', *La Vanguardia* (15 April 2022), from Consorci Santarida Barcelona y Agencia de Salut Pública: https://www.lavanguardia.com/vida /20220415/8188208/imagen-corporal-redes-sociales-destructivas.html.

77 Chrissie Thompson and Mark Wood, 'A Media Archaeology of the Creepshot', *Feminist Media Studies* 18(4) (2018): 560–74.

78 Lily, 'The Trauma of Growing Up Online' (7 February 2021), https://lilyfu .substack.com/p/growinguponline (accessed 14 July 2023).

79 The phrase comes from an internal research paper presented to Instagram, quoted in Wells et al., 'Facebook Knows Instagram Is Toxic', 6.

80 Jack Bratich, *On Microfascism* (Common Notions Press, 2022), 59, echoing David Riesman's sociological classic *The Lonely Crowd*, from 1950.

81 Justin McCurry, 'Isolation Nation: Japan Tries to Draw Its Citizens Out of Post-Covid Seclusion', *Guardian* (13 May 2023), https://www.theguardian .com/world/2023/may/12/isolation-nation-one-in-50-japanese-living-in -seclusion-after-covid.

82 Gray, *Out in the Country*, especially 103–7.

83 Ibid., 107.

84 Ibid., 130.

85 Alex Chan, Jo Mayoh, Shijie Song, Cesar Escobar-Viera and Ruth Plackett, 'Social Media Use and Health and Well-being of Lesbian, Gay, Bisexual, Transgender and Queer Youth: Systematic Review', *Journal of Medical Internet Research* 24(9) (2022): e38449, https://www.ncbi.nlm.nih.gov/pmc/articles/PMC9536523/; Zachary Owen, 'Is It Facebook Official? Coming Out and Passing Strategies of Young Adult Gay Men on Social Media', *Journal of Homosexuality* 64(4) (2017): 431–49, https://doi.org/10.1080/00918369.2016.1194112; Catharine Talbot, Amelia Talbot, Danielle Roe and Pam Brigges, 'The Management of LGBTQ+ Identities on Social Media: A Student Perspective', *New Media & Society* 24(8) (2020): 1729–50, https://doi.org/10.1177/1461444820981009.

86 Taylor Hatmaker, 'TikTok Is Where Young LGBTQ People of Color Feel the Safest Online', *TechCrunch* (19 July 2023), https://techcrunch.com/2023/07 /19/trevor-project-tiktok-mental-health-survey-social-media/.

87 Taylor Lorenz, 'Meet the Woman Behind Libs of TikTok, Secretly Fuelling the Right's Outrage Machine', *Washington Post* (19 April 2022), https:// www.washingtonpost.com/technology/2022/04/19/libs-of-tiktok-right-wing -media/.

88 Balca Arda and Ayşegül Akdemir, 'Activist Communication Design on Social Media: The Case of Online Solidarity Against Forced Islamic Lifestyle', *Media Culture & Society* 43(6) (2021): 1078–94.

89 Maya Stewart and Ulrike Schultze, 'Producing Solidarity in Social Media Activism: The Case of My Stealthy Freedom', *Information and Organization* 29(3) (2019), https://doi.org/10.1016/j.infoandorg.2019.04.003.

90 Kenneth Gergen, *The Saturated Self* (Basic Books, 1992).

91 Sarah Banet-Weiser, *Empowered* (Duke University Press, 2018), 119. See also the case of the UK incel mass shooter: Ben Quinn, 'Plymouth Gunman's

Glorification By "Incels" Prompts Calls For Action', *Guardian* (3 January 2022), https://www.theguardian.com/uk-news/2022/jan/03/glorification -plymouth-shooter-incels-prompts-calls-for-action.

92 Daniel Krauss, 'The Networked Self in the Age of Identity Fundamentalism', in Z. Papacharissi (ed.), *A Networked Self and Platforms, Stories, Connections* (Routledge 2019), 12–28.

93 Arjun Appadurai, *Fear of Small Numbers* (Duke University Press, 2006), 7, added emphasis.

94 Zeynep Tufekci, 'YouTube the Great Radicaliser', *New York Times* (10 March 2018), https://www.nytimes.com/2018/03/10/opinion/sunday/youtube -politics-radical.html; Manoel Horta Ribeiro, Raphael Ottoni, Robert West, Virgilio Almeida and Wagner Meira Jr, 'Auditing Radicalization Pathways on YouTube', Woodstock '18 ACM Symposium on Neural Gaze Detection, (3–5 June 2018), https://doi.org/10.1145/1122445.1122456. For general arguments in favour of the benefits of personalised rabbit-holes for non-toxic content, see Cory Doctorow, *The Internet Con* (Verso, 2023), 146–7; Nick Seaver, *Computing Taste: Algorithms and the Makers of Music Recommendation* (Chicago University Press, 2022).

95 Maximilian Boeker and Aleksandra Urman, 'An Empirical Investigation of Personalization Factors on TikTok' (January 2022), https://doi.org/10.48550 /arXiv.2201.12271.

96 Presented at the Rights Con conference, Costa Rica (June 2023), drawing on Becca Ricks and Jesse McCrosky, 'Does This Button Work? On YouTube's Inadequate User Controls', (Mozilla, September 2022), https://assets .mofoprod.net/network/documents/Mozilla-Report-YouTube-User-Controls .pdf.

97 Miller McPherson, Lynn Smith-Lovin and James Cook, 'Birds of a Feather: Homophily in Social Networks', *Annual Review of Sociology* 27(1) (2011): 415–44, at 415, cited by Wendy Chun, *Discriminating Data* (MIT Press, 2019), 95.

98 Quoted Aparajita Bhandari and Sara Bimo, 'Why's Everyone on TikTok Now? The Algorithmized Self and the Future of Self-Making on Social Media', *Social Media & Society* (2022), https://doi.org/10.1177/20563051221086241, 6.

99 Andrei Boutylin and Robb Willer, 'The Social Structure of Political Echo Chambers: Variation in Ideological Homophily in Online Networks', *Political Psychology* 38(3) (2017): 551–69, quotation from 565–6.

100 Mackenzie Hart, Jacob Davey, Eisha Maharasingam-Shah, Ciaran O'Connor and Aoife Gallagher, *An Online Environmental Scan of Right-wing Extremism in Canada* (Institute for Strategic Dialogue, 2021), https://www.isdglobal .org/wp-content/uploads/2021/07/ISDs-An-Online-Environmental-Scan-of -Right-wing-Extremism-in-Canada.pdf.

101 Donovan et al., *Meme Wars*, 222–4.

102 As noted by Imran Ahmed, 'Buffalo Might Never Have Happened If Online Hate Had Been Tackled After Christchurch', *Guardian* (16 May 2022), https://www.theguardian.com/commentisfree/2022/may/16/racist-words-social-media-kill-buffalo-meta-twitter-google-radicalisation.

103 Johanna Sumiala, *Mediated Death* (Polity, 2022), 127.

104 Quoted Jonathan Haidt, 'Yes, Social Media Really Is Undermining Democracy', *The Atlantic* (28 July 2022), https://www.theatlantic.com/ideas/archive/2022/07/social-media-harm-facebook-meta-response/670975/, 7.

105 Narayanan, 'Understanding Social Media Recommendation Algorithms', 6–7.

106 Byron Reeves of Stanford University, quoted in Matt Richtel, 'A Teen's Journey into the Internet's Darkness and Back Again', *New York Times* (22 August 2022), https://www.nytimes.com/2022/08/22/health/adolescents-mental-health-technology.html.

107 Karl Mannheim, 'The Problem of Generations', in K. Mannheim, *Essays in the Sociology of Knowledge* (Routledge & Kegan Paul, 1952) (o.p. 1928), 276–320; Hartmut Rosa, *Social Acceleration* (Columbia University Press, 2013); Göran Bolin, *Media Generations: Experience, Identity and Mediatized Social Change* (Routledge, 2017), 128–32.

108 Hannah Arendt, *The Origins of Totalitarianism* (Schocken Books, 2004) (o.p. 1948), 612.

Chapter 4: When Trust Starts to Fail

1 Quoted *Guardian* (13 March 2021), https://www.theguardian.com/lifeandstyle/2021/mar/15/tim-berners-lee-we-need-social-networks-where-bad-things-happen-less. The epigraph is the article title from the printed copy of the *Guardian* that day, although in the interview itself Berners-Lee attributed this phrase to how he *imagined* many people thinking, a thought that he nonetheless endorsed.

2 Clea Skopeliti and Sammy Gecsoyler, '"Terrified for My Future": Climate Crisis Takes Heavy Toll on Young People's Mental Health', *Guardian* (31 March 2023), https://www.theguardian.com/environment/2023/mar/30/terrified-for-my-future-climate-crisis-takes-heavy-toll-on-young-peoples-mental-health.

3 World Health Organisation, 'Mental Health and Climate Change: Policy Brief' (3 June 2022), https://www.who.int/publications/i/item/9789240045125; Caroline Hickman et al. (eight other authors), 'Climate Anxiety in Children and Young People and Their Beliefs About Government Responses to Climate Change: A Global Survey', *Lancet Planet Health* (2021) 5: e863-73, https://www.thelancet.com/action/showPdf?pii=S2542-5196%2821%2900278-3.

4 Henry Farrell and Bruce Schneier, 'Common Knowledge Attacks on Democracy' (October 2018). Berkman Klein Center Research Publication No. 2018-7, available from https://papers.ssrn.com/sol3/papers.cfm?abstract_id=3273111. Quote at 2.

5 Anne Applebaum and Peter Pomerantzev, 'How to Put Out Democracy's Dumpster Fire', *The Atlantic* (April 2021), https://www.theatlantic.com/magazine/archive/2021/04/the-internet-doesnt-have-to-be-awful/618079/.

6 Bernard Williams, *Truth and Truthfulness* (Harvard University Press, 2002), 100.

7 Cited in Deen Freelon and Chris Wells, 'Disinformation as Political Communication', *Political Communication* 37(2) (2020): 145–56, at 145.

8 William Eveland and Kathryn Cooper, 'An Integrated Model of Communication Influence on Beliefs', *PNAS* 11(3) (2013): 14088–95.

9 Anatolly Gruzd and Philip Mai, 'Going Viral: How a Single Tweet Spawned a COVID-19 Conspiracy Theory on Twitter', *Big Data & Society* (2020), DOI: 10.1177/2053951720938405; Wasim Ahmed, Francecsc Popez Segui, Josep Vidal-Alaball and Matthew Katz, 'COVID-19 and the "Film Your Hospital" Conspiracy Theory: Social Network Analysis of Twitter Data', *Journal of Medical Internet Research* 22(10) (2020): e22374, https://www.ncbi.nlm.nih.gov/pmc/articles/PMC7537721/?report=printable.

10 Eurobarometer, 'Attitudes on Vaccination against COVID-19' (29 June 2021), https://webgate.ec.europa.eu/ebsm/api/public/deliverable/download?doc=true&deliverableId=76287.

11 See for Brazil, Caio Vieira Machado, João Guilherme Santos, Nina Santos and Luiza Bandeira, 'Scientific (Self) Isolation: International Trends in Misinformation and the Departure from Scientific Debate', Infected Democracy project, Centre for the Analysis of Liberty and Authoritarianism (November 2020), https://laut.org.br/wp-content/uploads/2020/11/Political-Self-Isolation-vF.pdf.

12 Ashley Fetters Malor and Will Oremus, 'Pregnancy Apps have Become a Battleground of Vaccine Misinformation', *Washington Post* (23 December 2021), https://www.washingtonpost.com/technology/2021/12/23/pregnancy-apps-covid-vaccine-misinformation/, quoting Sarah Levy from Miami.

13 See Farah Ennab et al. (six other authors), 'Implications of Social Media Misinformation on COVID-19 Vaccine Confidence Among Pregnant Women in Africa', *Clinical Epidemiology and Global Health* (2022) 14: 100981, https://www.sciencedirect.com/science/article/pii/S2213398422000215; World Health Organization 'Countering COVID-19 Misinformation in Africa', (23 July 2021), https://www.afro.who.int/news/countering-covid-19-misinformation-africa-continent-13-billion-people-who-and-partners-are. For the expansion of pregnancy apps in Asia, see Marija Butkovic, 'Amma Pregnancy Tracker Raises $2Million in Pre-Series A for its AI-Powered Ecosystem of Parenting Applications', *Forbes* (30 September 2021), https://

www.forbes.com/sites/marijabutkovic/2021/09/30/amma-pregnancy-tracker
-raises-2-million-in-pre-series-a-for-its-ai-powered-ecosystem-of-parenting
-applications/.

14 Malor and Oremus, 'Pregnancy Apps', quoting Harvard Law School lecturer,
Evelyn Douek.

15 Ibid, for example the quotations from Mashaya and Claire.

16 Ibid.

17 Brittany Seymour, Rebekah Getman, Avinash Saraf, Lily Shang and Elsbeth
Kalenderian, 'When Advocacy Obscures Accuracy Online: Digital Pandemics of
Public Health Misinformation Through an Antifluoride Case Study', *American
Journal of Public Health* 105(3) (2015): 517–23, at 522, added emphasis.

18 Seymour et al., 'When Advocacy Obscures', added emphasis.

19 Christopher Holzmann-Littig et al. (thirteen authors), 'COVID-19
Vaccination Acceptance and Hesitancy among Healthcare Workers in
Germany', *Vaccines* 9(7) (2021): 777–97.

20 Neha Puri, Eric Coomes, Hourmazd Haghbayan and Keith Gunaratne, 'Social
Media and Vaccine Hesitancy: New Updates for the Era Of COVID-19 and
Globalized Infectious Diseases', *Human Vaccines and Immunotherapeutics*
16(11) (2020): 2586–93; Steven Lloyd Wilson and Charles Wiusonge, 'Social
Media and Vaccine Hesitancy', *BMJ Global Health* 194 (2021): 245–51.

21 YouGov, results at https://yougov.co.uk/topics/health/trackers/do-brits-think
-vaccines-have-harmful-effects-which-are-not-being-disclosed (accessed 24
July 2023).

22 Rebekah Getman, Mohammad Helmi, Hal Roberts, Alfa Yansane, David
Cutler and Brittany Seymour, 'Vaccine Hesitancy and Online Information:
The Influence of Digital Networks', *Health Education and Behavior* 45(5)
(2018): 599–606.

23 Andrew Chadwick, Cristian Vaccari and Natalie-Anne Hall, 'COVID Vaccines
and Online Personal Messaging: The Challenge of Challenging Everyday
Misinformation', Public Report, Everyday Misinformation Project (2022),
https://www.lboro.ac.uk/media/media/research/o3c/pdf/Chadwick-Vaccari
-Hall-Covid-Vaccines-and-Online-Personal-Messaging-2022.pdf (accessed 21
July 2023).

24 Elizabeth Noelle-Neumann, 'The Spiral of Silence: A Theory of Public
Opinion', *Journal of Communication* 24 (1974): 43–51. For the argument
that this continues online, see Keith Hampton, Lee Raine, Weizi Lu, Maria
Dwyer, Inyoung Shin and Kristen Purcell, 'Social Media and the "Spiral of
Silence"', Pew Research Center (2014), https://www.pewresearch.org/internet
/2014/08/26/social-media-and-the-spiral-of-silence/. For a similar argument
regarding social media, see Jonathan Haidt, 'Why the Past 10 Years of
American Life Have Been Uniquely Stupid', *The Atlantic* (May 2022), https://

www.theatlantic.com/magazine/archive/2022/05/social-media-democracy-trust-babel/629369/.

25 Wilson and Wiusonge, 'Social Media and Vaccine Hesitancy'.

26 Soroush Vosoughi, Deb Roy and Sinan Aral, 'The Spread of True and False News Online', *Science* 359 (2018): 1146–51, at 1146. See generally Claire Wardle and Hossein Derakhshan, 'Thinking About "Information Disorder": Formats Of Misinformation, Disinformation and Mal-Information', in Cherilyn Ireton and Julie Posetti (eds.), *Journalism, 'Fake News' & Disinformation: Handbook for Journalism Education and Training* (UNESCO, 2018), https://en.unesco.org/sites/default/files/journalism_fake_news_disinformation_print_friendly_0.pdf.

27 Stephan Lewandowsky, Ullrich Ecker and John Cook, 'Beyond Misinformation: Understanding and Coping with the "Post-truth" Era', *Journal of Applied Research in Memory and Cognition* 6 (2017): 353–69.

28 For a careful review of the debate on 'post-truth', see Johan Farkas and Jannick Schou, *Post-Truth, Fake News and Democracy* (Routledge, 2024), 2nd edition.

29 L. Weng, A. Flammini, A. Vespignani and F. Menczer, 'Competition Among Memes in a World With Limited Attention', *Scientific Reports* 2 (2012), https://doi.org/10.1038/srep00335.

30 Vosoughi et al., 'Spread of True and False News', 1147.

31 Ibid., 1148.

32 Elizabeth Blankenship et al. (eight authors), 'Sentiment, Contents and Retweets: A Study of Two Vaccine-Related Twitter Datasets', *Permanente Journal* 22 (2018), https://doi.org/10.7812/TPP/17-138.

33 Vosoughi et al., 'Spread of True and False News', 1150.

34 Andrew Guess, Jonathan Nagler and Joshua Tucker, 'Less Than You Think: Prevalence and Predictors of Fake News Dissemination on Facebook', *Science Advances* 5 (2019), https://doi.org10.1126%2Fsciadv.aau4586; Nir Grinberg, Kenneth Joseph, Lisa Friedland, Briony Swire-Thompson and David Lazer, 'Fake News on Twitter During the 2016 U.S. Presidential Election', *Science* 363 (2019): 374–8.

35 Avaaz, 'Facebook's Climate of Deception: How Viral Misinformation Fuels the Climate Emergency' (May 2021): https://secure.avaaz.org/campaign/en/facebook_climate_misinformation/, a finding confirmed by a study later in 2021 by Center for Countering Digital Hate, 'The Toxic Ten: How Ten Fringe Publishers fuel 69% of Digital Climate Change Denial' (2 November 2021), 5–6, https://counterhate.com/research/the-toxic-ten/.

36 Grinberg et al., 'Fake News on Twitter'.

37 Guess et al., 'Less Than You Think'.

38 Gordon Pennycook, Tyrone Cannon and David Rand, 'Prior Exposure

Increases Perceived Accuracy of Fake News', *Journal of Experimental Psychology General* 147(12) (2018): 1865–80.

39 Steen Steensen, 'Journalism's Epistemic Crisis and Its Solution: Disinformation, Datafication and Source Criticism', *Journalism* 20(1) (2019): 185–99.

40 Nic Fildes, 'Meta Sued by Australian Regulator for Allegedly "Misleading" Crypto Ads', *Financial Times* (18 March 2022), https://www.ft.com/content /132c7877-bd74-4957-925b-414f12ec6aa4.

41 Julia Carrie Wong, 'How Facebook Let Fake Engagement Distort Global Politics: A Whistleblower's Account', *Guardian* (12 April 2021), https:// www.theguardian.com/technology/2021/apr/12/facebook-fake-engagement -whistleblower-sophie-zhang.

42 Wong, 'How Facebook Let Fake Engagement', 4.

43 Tom Simonite, 'Facebook Is Everywhere; Its Moderation Is Nowhere Close', *Wired* (25 October 2021), https://www.wired.com/story/facebooks-global -reach-exceeds-linguistic-grasp/#:~:text=Human%20reviewers%20and %20AI%20filters,nuances%20in%20different%20Arabic%20dialects.&text =Thousands%20of%20internal%20documents%20show,warnings%20about %20its%20deepest%20problems.

44 Linda Geddes, 'Joe Rogan's Covid Claims: What Does the Science Actually Say?' *Guardian* (31 January 2022), https://www.theguardian.com/culture /2022/jan/31/joe-rogan-covid-claims-what-does-the-science-actually-say.

45 Russell Muirhead and Nancy Rosenblum, *A Lot of People Are Saying* (Princeton University Press, 2020): 3, 118.

46 Ibid., 15. danah boyd had already forcibly warned of this problem in 2017: 'Did Media Literacy Backfire?', *Journal of Applied Youth Studies* 1(4) (2017): 83–9, available from https://search.informit.org/doi/10.3316/informit .607936397466888.

47 Eurobarometer, *Climate Change* (2021), https://webgate.ec.europa.eu/ebsm /api/public/deliverable/download?doc=true&deliverableId=75838.

48 Ibid.

49 See Ofcom, *Adults' Media Use and Attitudes Report 2023* (29 March 2023), https://www.ofcom.org.uk/__data/assets/pdf_file/0028/255844/adults -media-use-and-attitudes-report-2023.pdf; Ofcom, *Children and Parents: Media Use and Attitudes* (29 March 2023), https://www.ofcom.org.uk/__data /assets/pdf_file/0027/255852/childrens-media-use-and-attitudes-report-2023 .pdf.

50 For early research that has raised concerns about the reliability of sources in TikTok climate change videos, see Corey Basch, Bhavya Yalamanchili and Joseph Fera, '#Climate Change on TikTok: A Content Analysis of Videos', *Journal of Community Health* (2022) 47: 163–7.

51 Farrell and Schneier, 'Common Knowledge Attacks', 5.

52 Hunt Allcott and Matthew Gentzkow, 'Social Media and Fake News in the 2016 Election', *Journal of Economic Perspectives* 31(2) (2017): 211–36, at 227.

53 For example, Grinberg et al., 'Fake News on Twitter' (p. 374) found that 5 per cent of political news exposure was to false stories.

54 Fabian Zimmermann and Matthias Kohring, 'Mistrust, Disinforming News, and Vote Choice: A Panel Survey on the Origins and Consequences of Believing Disinformation in the 2017 German Parliamentary Election', *Political Communication* 37 (2020): 215–37.

55 Zimmermann and Kohring, 'Mistrust', 222.

56 Yochai Benkler, Rob Faris and Hal Roberts, *Network Propaganda* (Oxford University Press, 2018).

57 Benkler et al., *Network Propaganda,* 23.

58 For an excellent review, see Dipayan Ghosh, *Terms of Disservice: How Silicon Valley Is Destructive by Design* (Brookings Institution Press, 2020).

59 Benkler et al, *Network Propaganda,* 38.

60 Alice Marwick and Rebecca Lewis, 'Media Manipulation and Disinformation Online', *Data & Society* (May 2017), https://datasociety.net/library/media-manipulation-and-disinfo-online/ (accessed 21 July 2023], especially 38.

61 Marwick et al., 'Media Manipulation', 45–6.

62 Nico Grant and Steven Lee Myers, 'Google Promised to Defund Climate Lies, but the Ads Keep Coming', *New York Times* (2 May 2023), https://www.nytimes.com/2023/05/02/technology/google-youtube-disinformation-climate-change.html.

63 Samuel Wooley and Philip Howard, 'Political Communication, Computational Propaganda, and Autonomous Agents', *International Journal of Communication* 10 (2016): 4882–90; Jonathan Ong and Jason Cabañes, 'Architects of Networked Disinformation: Behind the Scenes of Troll Accounts and Fake News Production in the Philippines' (2018), https://scholarworks.umass.edu/communication_faculty_pubs/74/.

64 Lex column, 'Twitter & Facebook: Jack and Mark's Bogus Journey', *Financial Times* (28 November 2019), https://www.ft.com/content/4c6928b3-4029-468e-94f5-4f6717081f20; Dave Lee, '"Twitter Covered Up Security Flaws and Fake Accounts", Says Whistleblower', *Financial Times* (13 August 2022), https://www.ft.com/content/e6afbc0b-6356-48b9-922b-5ea28eafacc3.

65 Finn Brunton, *Spam: A Shadow History of the Internet* (MIT Press, 2013).

66 Quoted, Dan Milmo and Alex Hern, 'Elections in UK and US at Risk from AI-driven Disinformation, Say Experts', *Guardian* (20 May 2023), https://www.theguardian.com/technology/2023/may/20/elections-in-uk-and-us-at-risk-from-ai-driven-disinformation-say-experts.

67 Freedom House, *Freedom on the Net 2023* (Freedom House, October 2023),

https://freedomhouse.org/sites/default/files/2023-10/Freedom-on-the-net
-2023-DigitalBooklet.pdf, especially 8–12.

68 Kathrin Wesolowski, 'Fact Check: Russia's Influence on Africa', *Deutsche
    Welle* (27 July 2023), https://www.dw.com/en/fact-check-russias-influence-on
    -africa/a-66310017.

69 Ellen Barry, 'How Russian Trolls Helped Keep the Women's March Out of
    Lock Step', *New York Times* (18 September 2022), https://www.nytimes.com
    /2022/09/18/us/womens-march-russia-trump.html.

70 Luke Harding, Julian Borger and Dan Sabbagh, 'Kremlin Papers Appear to
    Show Putin's Plot to Put Trump in White House', *Guardian* (16 July 2021),
    https://www.theguardian.com/world/2021/jul/15/kremlin-papers-appear-to
    -show-putins-plot-to-put-trump-in-white-house.

71 For social media and the internet as a key site of contemporary warfare, see
    P. W. Singer and Emerson Brooking, *Like War: The Weaponization of Social
    Media* (Mariner Books, 2018), especially 18–19.

72 Jason Burke, 'Facebook Struggles as Russia Steps Up Presence in Unstable
    West Africa', *Guardian* (18 April 2022), https://www.theguardian.com/world
    /2022/apr/17/facebook-struggles-as-russia-steps-up-presence-in-unstable
    -west-africa; Gary King, Jennifer Pan and Margaret Roberts 'How the
    Chinese Government Fabricates Social Media Posts for Strategic Distraction,
    Not Engaged Argument', *American Political Science Review* 111 (2017):
    484–501; Stephanie Kirchgaessner, Manisha Ganguly, David Pegg, Carole
    Cadwalladr and Jason Burke, 'Revealed: the Hacking and Disinformation
    Team Meddling in Elections', *Guardian* (15 February 2023), https://www
    .theguardian.com/world/2023/feb/15/revealed-disinformation-team-jorge
    -claim-meddling-elections-tal-hanan; Nilesh Christopher, 'Right-wing
    Groups Are Exploiting OSINT to spread propaganda in India', *Rest of World*
    (22 August 2022), https://restofworld.org/2022/right-wing-osint-propaganda
    -in-india/; Christopher Till, 'Propaganda Through "Reflexive Control" and
    the Mediated Construction of Reality', *New Media & Society* 23(6) (2021):
    1362–78.

73 Farrell and Schneier, 'Common Knowledge Attacks', 11, 13.

74 'Facebook Usage Penetration in the United States from 2018 to 2027', Statista
    (14 December 2023), https://www.statista.com/statistics/183460/share-of-the
    -us-population-using-facebook/ (accessed 27 September 2023).

75 Karen Hao, 'Troll Farms Reached 140 Million Americans a Month on
    Facebook Before 2020 Election, Internal Report Shows', *MIT Tech Review* (16
    September 2021), https://www.technologyreview.com/2021/09/16/1035851
    /facebook-troll-farms-report-us-2020-election/, 6.

76 Chloe Colliver, Mackenzie Hart, Eisha Maharasingam-Shah and Daniel Maki,
    'Spin Cycle: Information Laundering on Facebook', *Institute for Strategic*

Dialogue (December 2020), https://www.isdglobal.org/isd-publications/spin-cycle-information-laundering-on-facebook/.

77 Karen Hao, 'How Facebook and Google Fund Global Misinformation', *MIT Tech Review* (20 November 2021), https://www.technologyreview.com/2021/11/20/1039076/facebook-google-disinformation-clickbait/.

78 Sarah Evanega, Mark Lynas, Jordan Adams and Karinne Smolenyak, 'Coronavirus Misinformation: Quantifying Sources and Themes in the COVID-19 "Infodemic"' (Cornell Alliance for Science, 2020), https://allianceforscience.org/wp-content/uploads/2020/09/Evanega-et-al-Coronavirus-misinformationFINAL.pdf (accessed 25 July 2023).

79 Renee DiResta, 'The Supply of Disinformation Will Soon Be Infinite', *The Atlantic* (20 September 2020), https://www.theatlantic.com/ideas/archive/2020/09/future-propaganda-will-be-computer-generated/616400/.

80 Nick Couldry, 'Trump, the Wannabe King Ruling by Twiat', *The Conversation* (6 February 2017), https://theconversation.com/trump-the-wannabe-king-ruling-by-twiat-72269. More generally, see Sharad Goel, Ashton Anderson, Jake Hofman and Duncan Watts, 'The Structural Virality of Online Diffusion', *Management Science* 62(1) (2015): 180–96.

81 Lance Bennett and Steven Livingston, 'A Brief History of the Disinformation Age: Information Wars and the Decline of Institutional Authority', in Lance Bennett and Steven Livingston (eds.), *The Disinformation Age* (Cambridge University Press, 2020), 3–40.

82 Danny Hayes and Jennifer Lawless, 'The Decline of Local News and Its Effects: New Evidence from Longitudinal Data', *The Journal of Politics* 80(1) (2017), https://doi.org/10.1086/694105; Meghan Rubado and Jay Jennings, 'Political Consequences of the Endangered Local Watchdog: Newspaper Decline and Mayoral Elections in the United States', *Urban Affairs Review* 56(5) (2020): 1327–56; Media Reform Coalition, 'Submission to Digital, Culture, Media and Sport [UK Parliament] Committee on the Future of Local Journalism', https://www.mediareform.org.uk/wp-content/uploads/2022/03/MRC-Sustainability-of-local-journalism-March-2022.pdf (accessed 25 July 2023).

83 Victor Pickard, *Democracy without Journalism?* (Oxford University Press, 2020).

84 Melissa Aronczyk and Maria Espinoza, *A Strategic Nature: Public Relations and the Politics of American Environmentalism* (Oxford University Press, 2022), 4.

85 Lance Bennett, *Communicating the Future: Solutions for Environment, Economy and Democracy* (Polity, 2021). On traditional media and climate change agendas, see Patrick Murphy, *The Media Commons: Globalization and Environmental Discourse* (University of Illinois Press, 2017).

86 Bruce Bimber and Homero Gil de Zúñiga, 'The Unedited Public Sphere', *New Media & Society* 22(4) (2020): 700–15.

87 Alessio Cornia, Annika Sehla, David Levy and Rasmus Kleis Nielsen, 'Private Sector News, Social Media Distribution, and Algorithm Change', Reuters Institute for the Study of Journalism, (September 2018), https://reutersinstitute.politics.ox.ac.uk/our-research/private-sector-news-social-media-distribution-and-algorithm-change (accessed 21 July 2023); Rasmus Kleis Nielsen and Sarah Ganter, *The Power of Platforms* (Oxford University Press, 2022).

88 Pickard, *Democracy without Journalism?*, 10.

89 Farrell and Schneier, 'Common Knowledge Attacks', 14.

90 Lance Bennett and Steven Livingston, 'The Disinformation Order: Disruptive Communication and the Decline of Democratic Institutions', *European Journal of Communication* 33(2) (2018): 122–39.

91 Thomas Haussler, 'Civil Society, the Media and the Internet: Changing Roles and Challenging Authorities in Digital Political Communication Ecologies', *Information Communication & Society* 24(9) (2019): 1265–82.

92 Edelman, 'Government and Media Fuel a Vicious Cycle of Distrust' (18 January 2022), summarising Edelman's 2022 twenty-eight-country Trust Barometer, available from https://www.edelman.com/trust/2022-trust-barometer. The 2023 survey did not ask this question: The 2023 Edelman Trust Barometer Global Report (2023), accessible from https://www.edelman.com/sites/g/files/aatuss191/files/2023-03/2023%20Edelman%20Trust%20Barometer%20Global%20Report%20FINAL.pdf.

93 Seventy-eight per cent, as reported in Europa's twenty-eight-country survey conducted in 2016: https://webgate.ec.europa.eu/ebsm/api/public/deliverable/download?doc=true&deliverableId=59695.

94 Edelman, 'Government and Media'. The twenty-seven-country 2023 survey asked a slightly different question (about trust in social media as a sector), but still showed it falling year-on-year (to 44 per cent): 2023 Edelman Trust Barometer, 46.

95 Edelman, 'Government and Media'.

96 The 2019 Eurobarometer survey, conducted after Brexit (the figure rose to 72 per cent when the UK was included): https://webgate.ec.europa.eu/ebsm/api/public/deliverable/download?doc=true&deliverableId=72615.

97 Edelman, 'Government and Media'; compare 2023 Edelman Trust Barometer, 10, which also talks of a 'cycle of distrust'.

98 Kate Starbird, 'Information Wars: A Window into the Alternative Media Ecosystem' (15 March 2017), https://medium.com/hci-design-at-uw/information-wars-a-window-into-the-alternative-media-ecosystem-a1347f32fd8f. On polarisation, see 2023 Edelman Trust Barometer, 15ff.

99 Zimmermann and Kohring, 'Mistrust, Disinforming News', 15; compare Richard Fletcher and Rasmus Kleis Neilsen, 'Generalised Scepticism: How People Navigate News on Social Media', *Information Communication & Society* 22(12) (2019): 1751–69.

100 Sarah Banet-Weiser and Kat Higgins, *Believability* (New York University Press 2023).

101 Marwick and Lewis, 'Media Manipulation', 39. See also Muirhead and Rosenblum, *A Lot of People Are Saying*.

102 Stephanie Angwin, 'Do Beliefs Yield to Evidence? Examining Belief Perseverance vs Change in Response to Congruent Empirical Findings', *Journal of Experimental Psychology* 82 (2019): 176–99; Neil Garrett, Ana González-Garzón, Lucy Foulkes, Liat Levita, and Tali Sharot, 'Updating Beliefs Under Perceived Threat', *Journal of Neuroscience* 38(36) (2018): 7901–11.

103 Emily Saks and Alec Tyson, 'Americans Report More Engagement with Science News than in 2017', Pew Research Center (November 2022), https://www.pewresearch.org/short-reads/2022/11/10/americans-report-more-engagement-with-science-news-than-in-2017/.

104 Ibid.

105 Brigitte Huber, Matthew Barnidge, Homero Gil de Zúñiga and James Liu, 'Fostering Public Trust in Science: The Role of Social Media', *Public Understanding of Science* 28(7) (2019): 759–77. The research was conducted in 2015, when using social media as a news source was a majority habit in some countries but not others.

106 The [UK] Royal Society, 'The Online Information Environment: Understanding How the Internet Shapes People's Engagement With Scientific Information' (January 2022), https://royalsociety.org/-/media/policy/projects/online-information-environment/the-online-information-environment.pdf?la=en-GB&hash=691F34A269075C0001A0E647C503DB8F, 10.

107 Thomas Safford, Emily Whitmore and Lawrence Hamilton, 'Questioning Scientific Practice: Linking Beliefs About Scientists, Science Agencies and Climate Change', *Environmental Sociology* 6(2) (2020): 194–206, at 199, 202.

108 Eurobarometer, 'Attitudes on Vaccination against COVID-19'.

109 For trust in government in the early pandemic, see OECD, 'Government at a Glance 2021', https://www.oecd-ilibrary.org/sites/52552e1e-en/index.html?itemId=/content/component/52552e1e-en; for the period 2021–2, showing a fall in trust in government in seventeen out of twenty-seven countries, see https://www.edelman.com/trust/2022-trust-barometer.

110 Pew Research Center, 'Feature: Public Trust in Government: 1958–2023' (19 September 2023), https://www.pewresearch.org/politics/2022/06/06/public-trust-in-government-1958-2022/.

111 Peter Pomerantsev, 'The Disinformation Age: A Revolution in Propaganda', *Guardian* (22 August 2022); Timothy Schneider, *The Road to Unfreedom: Russia, Europe, America* (Vintage, 2018), 228–30, 250–51.

112 Katherine Ognyanova, David Lazer, Ronald Robertson and Christo Wilson, 'Misinformation in Action: Fake News Exposure Is Linked to Lower Trust in Media, Higher Trust in Government When Your Side Is in Power', *Harvard Kennedy School Misinformation Review* 1(4) (2020), https://doi.org /10.370916/mr-2020-024.

113 Diego Gambetta, 'Can We Trust Trust?' in D. Gambetta (ed.), *Trust: Making and Breaking Cooperative Relations* (Blackwell, 1988), 213–37, at 215.

114 Marvin Soroos, 'Global Change, Environmental Security, and the Prisoners' Dilemma', *Journal of Peace Research* 31(3) (1994): 317–32, at 327.

115 Ofcom, 'News Consumption in the UK: 2023 – Research Findings' (20 July 2023), https://ofcom.org.uk/__data/assets/pdf_file/0024/264651/news -consumption-2023.pdf; quote from Ruchira Sharma, '"People Get Bored Quickly": How UK Teens Turned to Social Media for Their News', *Guardian* (24 July 2022), https://www.theguardian.com/society/2022/jul/24/people-get -bored-quickly-how-uk-teens-turned-to-social-media-for-their-news.

116 For a useful review, see Cristina Criddle and Hannah Murphy, 'Social Media's Big Bet: The Shopping Revolution Will Be Livestreamed', *Financial Times* (11 August 2022), https://www.ft.com/content/3ad7595b-557d-4086-a01e -be5d54b28b45.

117 Symeon Browne, 'Hustle and Hype: The Truth About the Influencer Economy', *Guardian* (24 February 2022), https://www.theguardian.com/fashion/2022 /feb/24/hustle-and-hype-the-truth-about-the-influencer-economy#:~: text=There%20are%20some%20feigning%20their,and%20multimillion %2Ddollar%20Ponzi%20schemes; Miriam Rahali and Sonia Livingstone, '#SponsoredAds: Monitoring Influencer Marketing to Young Audiences', LSE Media Policy Brief 23 (2022), http://eprints.lse.ac.uk/113644/7/Sponsoredads _policy_brief.pdf.

118 Crystal Abidin, 'From "Networked Publics" to "Refracted Publics": A Companion Framework for Researching "Below the Radar" Studies', *Social Media & Society* 7(1) (2021), https://doi.org/10.1177/2056305120984458; Stuart Cunningham and David Craig, *Social Media Entertainment* (2019); Kelley Cotter, 'Playing the Visibility Game: How Digital Influencers and Algorithms Negotiate Influence on Instagram', *New Media & Society* 21(4) (2019): 895–913; Crystal Abidin, *Internet Celebrity* (Emerald, 2018), Chapter 4.

119 Abby Ohlheiser, 'How Aspiring Influencers Are Forced to Fight the Algorithm', *MIT Tech Review* (14 July 2022), https://www.technologyreview.com/2022 /07/14/1055906/tiktok-influencers-moderation-bias/. On social media and

micro-celebrity generally, see Alice Marwick, 'Instafame: Luxury Selfies in the Attention Economy', *Public Culture* 27(1) (2015): 137–59.

120 Ellie Violet Bramley, 'The Sudden Dawn of the De-influencer: Can Online Superstars Stop Us Shopping?', *Guardian* (22 February 2023), https://www.theguardian.com/lifeandstyle/2023/feb/22/the-sudden-dawn-of-the-deinfluencer-can-online-superstars-stop-us-shopping.

121 Daniel Boffey, 'Brand Management: How Online Soapbox Helped Build Conspiracy-fuelled Identity', *Guardian* (20 September 2023) (print edition); and the interview by Zoe Williams with Matt Shea, researcher on Andrew Tate, '"To His Followers, This Man Is a Messiah"', *Guardian* (28 August 2023), https://www.theguardian.com/news/2023/aug/28/to-his-followers-this-man-is-a-messiah-matt-shea-on-his-long-fight-to-expose-andrew-tate.

122 Sanna Malinen and Aki Koivula, 'Influencers and Targets on Social Media: Investigating the Impact of Network Homogeneity and Group Identification on Online Influence', *First Monday* 25(4) (2020), https://doi.org/10.5210/fm.v25i4.10453.

123 Rita Basilio Simoes, Agda Dias Baeta and Bruno Frutuoso Costa, 'Mapping Feminist Politics on TikTok during the COVID-19 Pandemic: A Content Analysis of the Hashtags #Feminismo and #Antifeminismo', *Journalism and Media* (2023) 4(1): 244–57; Gabriel Weimann and Natalie Asri, 'Research Note: Spreading Hate on TikTok', *Studies in Conflict & Terrorism* 46(5) (2020): 752–65.

124 For example, using humour to undermine spreading memes and more fact-source criticism: Joan Donovan, 'How Civil Society Can Combat Misinformation and Hate Speech Without Making It Worse', *Medium* (28 September 2020), https://medium.com/political-pandemonium-2020/how-civil-society-can-combat-misinformation-and-hate-speech-without-making-it-worse-887a16b8b9b6; Steensen, 'Journalism's Epistemic Crisis'. On so-called 'pre-bunking': Nico Grant and Tiffany Hau, 'Google Finds "Inoculating" People Against Misinformation Helps Blunt Its Power', *New York Times* (24 August 2022), https://www.nytimes.com/2022/08/24/technology/google-search-misinformation.html.

Chapter 5: Uncivil Societies

1 Zygmunt Bauman, *The Individualised Society* (Polity, 2001), 2, quoted in Sumiala, *Mediated Death*, 6.

2 Craig Timberg, Elizabeth Dwoskin and Reed Albergotti, 'Inside Facebook, Jan 6 Violence Fuelled Anger, Regret Over Missed Warning Signs', *Washington Post* (22 October 2021), https://www.washingtonpost.com/technology/2021/10/22/jan-6-capitol-riot-facebook/.

3 Annie Njanja, 'Facebook Risks Ban in Kenya for Failing to Stop Hate Speech', *TechCrunch* (29 July 2022), https://techcrunch.com/2022/07/29/facebook -risks-ban-in-kenya-for-failing-to-stop-hate-speech/.

4 Craig Silverman, Ryan Mac and Pranav Dixit, '"I Have Blood on My Hands": A Whistleblower Says Facebook Ignored Global Political Manipulation', *Buzzfeed News* (14 September 2020), https://www.buzzfeednews.com/article /craigsilverman/facebook-ignore-political-manipulation-whistleblower-memo (accessed 28 July 2023), citing memo published by Sophie Zhang. See also Nick Statt, 'Facebook Ignored Blatant Political Manipulation Around the World, Claims Former Data Scientist', *The Verge* (14 September 2020), https://www.theverge.com/2020/9/14/21436852/facebook-data-scientist -memo-political-manipulation.

5 UNESCO/Ipsos, 'Survey on the Impact of Online Disinformation'.

6 Pomerantsev, 'The Disinformation Age'.

7 Nick Couldry, 'The "Myth of Us": Digital Networks, Political Change and the Production of Collectivity', *Information Communication and Society*, 18(6) (2014): 608–26.

8 See on a recent craze for 'non-playable characters' (NPTs) on TikTok, Arwa Mahdawi, 'No, I Didn't Imagine It – the "NPC" Craze Really Offers Money for Robotic Gibberish', *Guardian* (21 July 2023), https://www.theguardian .com/commentisfree/2023/jul/21/npc-tiktok-robotic-make-money. Thanks to Louise Hurel for this reference.

9 See Yascha Mounk, *The People Versus Democracy* (Harvard University Press, 2018), 146, which argues that 'social media is not necessarily good or bad for liberal democracy. Nor is it that social media inherently strengthens or undermines tolerance. On the contrary, it is that social media closes the technological gap between insiders and outsiders'. But this analysis ignores almost entirely the evidence on which this book has drawn. Among empirical researchers who are sceptical of the connections between social media and polarisation, see Michael Beam, Myiah Hutchens and Jay Hmielowski, 'Facebook News and (De)polarisation: Reinforcing Spirals in the 2016 US Elections', *Information Communication & Society* 21(7) (2018): 940–58; Magdalena Wojcieszak et al. (five authors), 'No Polarisation from Partisan News: Over-Time Evidence from Trace Data', *The International Journal of Press/Politics* 28(3) (2021): 601–26.

10 Philipp Lorenz-Spreen, Lisa Oswald, Stephan Lewandowsky and Ralph Hertwig, 'Digital Media and Democracy: A Systematic Review of Causal and Correlational Evidence Worldwide', *Nature Human Behavior* 7 (2023): 74–101.

11 Ibid., 74.

12 Eli Pariser, *The Filter Bubble* (Viking/Penguin, 2011).

13 Axel Bruns, *Are Filter Bubbles Real?* (Polity, 2019), citing, for example, Mario Haim, Andreas Graefe and Hans-Bernd-Brosius, 'Burst of the Filter Bubble?', *Digital Journalism* 6(3) (2018): 330–43. See also Sebastian Meineck, 'Deshalb ist "Filterblase" die blödeste Metapher des Internets', *Vice* (18 March 2018), https://www.vice.com/de/article/pam5nz/deshalb-ist-filterblase-die-blodeste -metapher-des-internets.

14 Amy Ross Arguedas, Craig Robertson, Richard Fletcher and Rasmus Nielsen, 'Echo Chambers, Filter Bubbles and Polarisation: A Literature Review', Reuters Institute for the Study of Journalism (January 2022), https://reutersinstitute .politics.ox.ac.uk/echo-chambers-filter-bubbles-and-polarisation-literature -review.

15 Ibid., 18.

16 Ibid., 29.

17 Newman et al., *Reuters Institute Digital News Report 2021*.

18 Elizabeth Dubois and Grant Blank, 'The Echo Chamber Is Overstated: The Moderating Effect of Political Interest and Diverse Media', *Information, Communication & Society* 21(5) (2018): 729–45, at 729. For the history of the idea, see Kathleen Hall Jamieson and Joseph Cappella, *Echo Chamber: Rush Limbaugh and the Conservative Media Establishment* (Oxford University Press, 2008); Cass Sunstein, *Republic.com 2.0* (Princeton University Press, 2009).

19 Candace Rondeaux et al., 'Parler and the Road to the Capital Attack', New America Foundation (5 January 2022), https://www.newamerica.org/future -frontlines/reports/parler-and-the-road-to-the-capitol-attack/.

20 Hywel Williams, James McMurray, Tim Kurz and Hugo Lambert, 'Network Analysis Reveals Open Forums and Echo Chambers in Social Media Discussions of Climate Change', *Global Environmental Change* 32 (2015): 126–38.

21 Christian Vaccari, Augusto Valeriani, Paola Barbera, John Jost, Jonathan Nagler and Joshua Tucker, 'Of Echo Chambers and Contrarian Clubs: Exposure to Political Disagreement Among German and Italian Users of Twitter', *Social Media & Society* 2(3) (2016), https://doi.org/10.1177/2056305116664221.

22 Richard Fletcher, Craig Robertson and Rasmus Nielsen, 'How Many People Live in Politically Partisan Online News Echo Chambers in Different Countries?', *Journal of Quantitative Description: Digital Media* 1 (2021): 1–56.

23 Ibid. For the US only, see Tian Yang, Silvia Majo-Vasquez, Rasmus Neilsen and Sandra Gonzales-Bailón, 'Exposure to News Grows Less Fragmented With an Increase in Mobile Access', *PNAS* 117(46) (2020): 28678–83.

24 Pere Masip, Jaume Shau and Carlos Ruiz-Caballero, 'Incidental Exposure to Non-like-minded News Through Social Media: Opposing Voices in Echo-chambers' News Feeds', *Media and Communication* 8(4) (2020): 53–62; Vaccari et al., 'Of Echo Chambers'.

25 Paul Röttger and Balazs Vedres, 'The Information Environment and Its Effects on Individuals and Groups' (Oxford Internet Institute, 2022), https://royalsociety.org/-/media/policy/projects/online-information-environment/oie-the-information-environment.PDF; Brendan Nyhan et al. (twenty-nine authors), 'Like-minded Sources on Facebook are Prevalent but Not Polarizing', *Nature* 620 (2023) 137–44.

26 Quoted in Tom Scocca, 'How the Awful Stuff Won', *New York Review of Books* (5 November 2020), https://www.nybooks.com/articles/2020/11/05/how-the-awful-stuff-won/.

27 Dubois and Blank, 'The Echo Chamber Is Overstated', 737.

28 Andrew Chadwick, 'The New Crisis of Public Communication' (Online Civic Culture Centre, Loughborough University, 2021), https://repository.lboro.ac.uk/articles/report/The_new_crisis_of_public_communication_Challenges_and_opportunities_for_future_research_on_digital_media_and_politics/11378748, 10.

29 Chantal Mouffe, *The Democratic Paradox* (Verso, 2001).

30 Alexander Bor and Michael Bang Petersen, 'The Psychology of Online Political Hostility: A Comprehensive, Cross-National Test of the Mismatch Hypothesis', *American Political Science Review* 116 (2022): 1–18, especially 15.

31 Aaron Smith, Laura Silver, Courtney Johnson and Jingjing Jiang, 'Publics in Emerging Economies Worry Social Media Sow Division, Even as They Offer New Chances for Political Engagement', Pew Research Center (13 May 2019), https://www.pewresearch.org/internet/2019/05/13/publics-in-emerging-economies-worry-social-media-sow-division-even-as-they-offer-new-chances-for-political-engagement/. For a detailed study of Turkey (a country not included in the Pew study) and how its social media audiences are increasingly concerned about speaking up on politics, see Cigdem Bozdag, 'Managing Diverse Online Networks in the Context of Polarization: Understanding How We Grow Apart On and Through Social Media', *Social Media & Society* (October–December 2020), https://journals.sagepub.com/doi/full/10.1177/2056305120975713.

32 'An Update to Dislikes on YouTube' (YouTube, 10 November 2021), https://blog.youtube/news-and-events/update-to-youtube/ (accessed 26 July 2023).

33 Nicholas John and Noam Gal, '"He's Got His Own Sea": Political Facebook Unfriending in the Personal Public Sphere', *International Journal of Communication* 12 (2018): 2971–88; Nicholas John and Aysha Agbarya, 'Punching Up or Turning Away? Palestinians Unfriending Jewish Israelis on Facebook', *New Media & Society* 23(5) (2020): 1063–79. See also for Turkey, Bozdag, 'Managing Diverse Online Networks', 6–7.

34 See, e.g., Robert Reich, 'Supreme Court, Facebook, Fed: Three Horsemen

of Democracy's Apocalypse', *Guardian* (10 October 2021), https://www
.theguardian.com/commentisfree/2021/oct/10/facebook-fed-federal-reserve
-supreme-court-democracy-apocalypse; Dan Milmo, 'Democracy at Risk
if Facebook Doesn't Change', *Guardian* (3 November 2021), https://www
.theguardian.com/technology/2021/nov/03/democracy-at-risk-if-facebook
-does-not-change-says-former-zuckerberg-adviser.

35 Quotes from Jonathan Haidt, 'Yes, Social Media Really Is Undermining
Democracy', *The Atlantic* (20 July 2022), https://www.theatlantic.com/ideas
/archive/2022/07/social-media-harm-facebook-meta-response/670975/, 9,
referring to the earlier article, Haidt, 'Why the Past Ten Years'.

36 For example, Vaidhyanathan, *Anti-Social Media*; Whitney Phillips, *Why We
Can't Have Nice Things: Mapping the Relationship Between Online Trolling
and Mainstream Culture* (MIT Press, 2015); Jose Van Dijck, *The Culture of
Connectivity* (Oxford University Press, 2013).

37 Eytan Bakshy, Solomon Messing and Lada Adamic, 'Exposure to Ideologically
Diverse News and Opinion on Facebook', *Science* 348 (2015): 1130–32. This
short paper has now been cited over 3,000 times according to Google Scholar.

38 Levi Boxell, Matthew Gentzkow and Jesse Shapiro, 'Greater Internet Use
Is Not Associated With Faster Growth in Political Polarization Among US
Demographic Groups', *PNAS* 114(40) (2017): 10612–17. This paper was
cited approvingly in, for example, Bruns, *Are Filter Bubbles Real?*, 105,
Benkler et al., *Network Propaganda*, 339.

39 Hunt Allcott, Luca Braghieri, Sarah Eichmeyer and Matthew Gentzkow, 'The
Welfare Effects of Social Media', *American Economic Review* 110(3) (2020):
629–46.

40 Allcott et al., 'Welfare Effects', 672.

41 Karsten Müller and Carlo Schwarz, 'Fanning the Flames of Hate: Social
Media and Hate Crime', *Journal of the European Economic Association*, 19(4)
(2021): 2131–67, with quotation at 2149.

42 Shanto Iyengar, Gaurav Sood and Yphtach Lelkes, 'Affect, not Ideology: A
Social Identity Perspective on Polarization', *The Public Opinion Quarterly*
76(3) (2012): 405–31, quote at 428. See also Eli Finkel et al. (ten authors),
'Political Sectarianism in America', *Science* 370(6516) (2020).

43 Iyengar et al., 'Affect, Not Ideology'; Shanto Iyengar and Sean Westwood,
'Fear and Loathing Across Party Lines: New Evidence on Group Polarization',
American Journal of Political Science 59(3) (2015): 690–707.

44 Dan Kahan, 'Ideology, Motivated Reasoning, and Cognitive Reflection',
Judgement and Decision-Making 8(4) (2013): 407–24, 420. For the link
from affective to ideological polarisation, see also Matthew Levendusky,
'Partisan Media Exposure and Attitudes Towards the Opposition', *Political
Communication* 30 (2013): 565–81.

45 Kahan, 'Ideology', 420.

46 Iyengar and Westwood, 'Fear and Loathing', 705, mentioning social media as an exposure factor at 691. In a later article, the authors are cautious about offering any causal explanation of the rise in affective polarisation (isolating a factor like viewing of partisan media or social media will always be difficult), while mentioning social media in passing: Shanto Iyengar, Yphtach Lelkes, Matthew Levendusky, Neil Malhotra and Sean Westwood, 'The Origins and Consequences of Affective Polarization in the United States', *Annual Review of Political Science* 22(7) (2018): 1–18, especially 6–8.

47 Norbert Elias, *The Society of Individuals* (Continuum, 1991).

48 Henri Tajfel, M. Billig, R. Bundy and C. Flament, 'Social Categorization and Intergroup Behaviour', *European Journal of Social Psychology* 1(2) (1971): 149–78; Michael Billig and Henri Tajfel, 'Social Categorization and Similarity in Intergroup Behaviour', *European Journal of Social Psychology* 3(1) (1973): 27–52; Henri Tajfel and John Turner, 'The Social Identity Theory of Intergroup Behavior', in W. G. Austin and Stephen Worchel (eds.), *The Social Psychology of Intergroup Relations* (Brooks/Cole, 1979), 33–47.

49 John Turner and Penelope Oakes, 'The Significance of the Social Identity Concept for Social Psychology with reference to Individualism, Interactionism, and Social Influence', *British Journal of Social Psychology* 25 (1986): 237–52.

50 The technical term in Social Identity Theory for what marks out this representative person is 'perceived relative prototypicality': Turner and Oakes, 'The Significance', 247.

51 Ibid. 241.

52 Iyengar et al., 'Affect, Not Ideology', 408.

53 Even so, Social Identity Theory has been influential theory across economics, legal theory and elsewhere: George Akerlof and Rachel Kranton, 'Economics and Identity', *The Quarterly Journal of Economics* 115(3) (2000): 715–53; Cass Sunstein, 'The Law of Group Polarization', *The Journal of Political Philosophy* 10(2) (2002): 175–95, at 180–81.

54 As argued by Steven Brown and Peter Lunt, 'A Genealogy of the Social Identity Tradition: Deleuze and Guattari and Social Psychology', *British Journal of Social Psychology* 41 (2002): 1–23.

55 Kahan, 'Ideology', 419.

56 Zeynep Tufekci, 'How Social Media Took Us from Tahrir Square to Donald Trump', *MIT Tech Review* (14 August 2018), https://www.technologyreview.com/2018/08/14/240325/how-social-media-took-us-from-tahrir-square-to-donald-trump/, 13.

57 Emphasising polarisation does not, however, rule out other dynamics of social media, for example social stratification, on which see a recent study of

Instagram: John Boy and Justus Uitermark, *On Display: Instagram, the Self and the City* (Oxford University Press, 2024), 19–20.

58 In this sense, the current state of social media is even worse than its early critics such as Mark Andrejevic could have anticipated, but those critics deserve great credit for anticipating the direction of travel so clearly.

59 Anne Quito, 'Jack Dorsey Admits Twitter's "Like" Button Should Never Have Existed', *Quartz* (16 April 2019), https://qz.com/work/1597035/ted2019-jack-dorsey-rethinks-twitters-like-feature, added emphasis.

60 Chris Wetherell, quoted by Alex Kantrowitz, 'The Man Who Built the Retweet: "We Handed a Loaded Weapon to Four-year-olds"', *Buzzfeed News* (23 July 2019), https://www.buzzfeednews.com/article/alexkantrowitz/how-the-retweet-ruined-the-internet.

61 Narayanan, 'Understanding Social Media Recommendation Algorithms', 17.

62 Narayanan provides a useful general discussion here.

63 Jing Zeng and Bondy Valdovinos Kaye, 'From Content Moderation to Visibility Moderation: A Case Study of Platform Governance on TikTok', *Policy Internet* 14 (2022): 79–95, at 83; Boeker and Urman, 'An Empirical Investigation', 7; Ben Smith, 'How TikTok Reads Your Mind', *New York Times* (5 December 2021), https://www.nytimes.com/2021/12/05/business/media/tiktok-algorithm.html; 'Inside TikTok's Algorithm: An Investigation', *Wall Street Journal* (21 July 2021) (video), https://www.wsj.com/articles/tiktok-algorithm-video-investigation-11626877477. Note that YouTube also measures how long you watch a video: Christos Goodrow, 'On YouTube's Recommendation System', https://blog.youtube/inside-youtube/on-youtubes-recommendation-system/ (accessed 8 November 2023).

64 Zeng and Kaye, 'From Content Moderation', 80.

65 Kaitlyn Regehr, Caitlin Shaughnessy, Minzhu Zhao and Nicola Shaughnessy, *Safer Scrolling: How Algorithms Popularise and Gamify Online Hate and Misogyny for Young People* (University College London and University of Kent, February 2024), https://www.ascl.org.uk/ASCL/media/ASCL/Help%20and%20advice/Inclusion/Safer-scrolling.pdf.

66 Narayanan, 'Understanding Social Media Recommendation Algorithms', 15.

67 Arvind Narayanan, 'Twitter Showed Us Its Algorithm. What Does It Tell Us?', blog (10 April 2023), https://knightcolumbia.org/blog/twitter-showed-us-its-algorithm-what-does-it-tell-us (accessed 19 August 2023).

68 Tufekci, 'How Social Media'; Rogers Brubaker, 'Digital Hyperconnectivity and the Self', *Theory and Society* 49 (2020): 771–801.

69 Sandra Gonzalez-Bailon and Yphtach Lelkes, 'Do Social Media Undermine Social Cohesion? A Critical Review', *Social Issues and Policy Review* 17(1) (2022): 175–90.

70 Brubaker, 'Digital Hyperconnectivity', 775; Timothy Graham and Aleesha

Rodriguez, 'The Sociomateriality of Rating and Ranking Devices on Social Media: A Case Study of Reddit's Voting Practices', *Social Media & Society* 7(3) (2021), https://doi.org/10.1177/20563051211047667.

71 Andrew Chadwick and James Stanyer, 'Deception as a Bridging Concept in the Study of Disinformation, Misinformation, and Misperceptions: Towards a Holistic Framework', *Communication Theory* 32 (2022): 1–24.

72 Timur Kuran and Cass Sunstein, 'Availability Cascades and Risk Regulation', *Stanford Law Review* 51(4) (1999): 683–768.

73 Scocca, 'How the Awful Stuff Won'.

74 Alice Wanless and Michael Berk, 'The Audience Is the Amplifier: Participatory Propaganda', in P. Baines, N. O'Shaughnessy and N. Snow, (eds.) *The Sage Handbook of Propaganda* (Sage, 2019), 85–104.

75 Davey Alba, Ella Koeze and Jacob Silver, 'What Happened When Trump Was Banned on Social Media', *New York Times* (7 June 2021), https://www.nytimes.com/interactive/2021/06/07/technology/trump-social-media-ban.html.

76 Wendy Chun, *Discriminating Data* (MIT Press, 2021); Boutylin and Willer, 'Social Structure of Echo Chambers'.

77 Jonas Kaiser and Adrian Rauchfleisch, 'Birds of a Feather Get Recommended Together: Algorithmic Homophily in YouTube's Channel Recommendations in the United States and Germany', *Social Media & Society* (2020), https://doi.org/10.1177/2056305120969914, especially 5, 8.

78 Annie Chen, Brendan Nyhan, Jason Reifler, Ronald Robertson and Christo Wilson, 'Subscriptions and External Links Help Drive Resentful Users to Alternative and Extremist YouTube Channels', *Science Advances* 9(35) (2023), https://doi.org/10.1126/sciadv.add8080.

79 Ressa, *How to Stand Up to a Dictator*, 140.

80 William Brady, Julian Wills, John Jost, Joshua Tucker and Jay Van Bavel, 'Emotion Shapes the Diffusion of Moralized Content in Social Networks', *PNAS* 114(28) (2017): 7313–18; J. Berger and K. Milkman, 'Social Transmission, Emotion and the Virality of Online Content', Wharton research paper, available from https://faculty.wharton.upenn.edu/wp-content/uploads/2011/11/Virality.pdf.

81 Kiran Garimella, Gianmarco de Francisci Morales, Aristides Gionis and Michael Mathioudakis, 'Political Discourse on Social Media: Echo Chambers, Gatekeepers, and the Price of Bipartisanship', *WWW 2018: the 2018 Web Conference* (April 2018), https://doi.org/10.1145/3178876.3186139. Although this paper was harshly criticised by Bruns (*Are Filter Bubbles Real?*, 44–5), this side-finding remains suggestive.

82 Daniel Kilvington, 'The Virtual Stages of Hate: Using Goffman's Work to Conceptualise the Motivations for Online Hate', *Media Culture & Society* 43(2) (2021): 256–72, especially 268 on 'backstage mimicry'.

83 Matthew Levendusky and Neil Malhotra, 'Does Media Coverage of Partisan Polarization Affect Political Attitudes?', *Political Communication* 33 (2016): 283–301.

84 Ov Christian Norocel and Dirk Lewandowski, 'Google, Data Voids and the Dynamics of the Politics of Exclusion', *Big Data & Society* (2023), https://doi.org/10.1177/20539517221149099. In addition, because sources for less mainstream queries are likely to be much sparser, they are more open to manipulation by search-engine optimisation techniques: Michael Golebiewski and danah boyd, *Data Voids: Where Missing Data Can Easily Be Exploited* (Data & Society, November 2019), https://datasociety.net/wp-content/uploads/2019/11/Data-Voids-2.0-Final.pdf.

85 Philip Howard, *Lie Machines* (Yale University Press, 2020).

86 Lewis Friedland, 'Communication, Community and Democracy', *Communication Research* 28(4) (2001): 358–91.

87 Scott Aikin and Robert Talisse, *Political Argument in a Polarized Age* (Polity 2020), 37.

88 https://www.businessofapps.com/data/tik-tok-statistics/#:~:text=TikTok%20reached%201.7%20billion%20users,increase%20on%20the%20previous%20year (accessed 2 October 2023).

89 Shanto Iyengar and Kyu Hahn, 'Red Media, Blue Media: Evidence of Ideological Selectivity in Media Use', *Journal of Communication* 59 (2009): 19–39; Ulrike Klinger and Jakob Svensson, 'The Emergence of Network Media Logic in Political Communication: A Theoretical Approach', *New Media & Society* 17(8) (2015): 1241–57.

90 Ro'ee Levy, 'Social Media, News Consumption, and Polarization: Evidence from a Field Experiment', *American Economic Review* 111(3) (2021): 831–70.

91 Jieun Shin and Kjerstin Thorson, 'Partisan Selective Sharing: The Biased Diffusion of Fact-checking Messages on Social Media', *Journal of Communication* 67 (2017): 233–55.

92 Shin and Thorson, 'Partisan Selective Sharing', 237.

93 Ibid.; compare Chung-hong Chan and King-wa Fu, 'The Relationship Between Cyberbalkanization and Opinion Polarization: Time Series Analysis on Facebook Pages and Opinion Polls during the Hong Kong Occupy Movement and the Associated Debate on Political Reform', *Journal of Computer-mediated Communication* 22 (2017): 266–83.

94 Mohammad Atari et al. (six others), 'Morally Homogeneous Networks and Radicalism', *Social Psychological and Personality Science* 13(6) (2022): 999–1009. On radicalisation generally, see Kevin McDonald, *Radicalization* (Polity 2018).

95 Ibid., 20.

96 Ibid., 5, 15.

97 Dan Kahan, 'Why We Are Poles Apart on Climate Change', *Nature* 488 (August 2012): 255.

98 Matthew Hornsey, Emily Harris, Paul Bain and Kelly Fielding, 'Meta-analyses of the Determinants and Outcomes of Belief in Climate Change', *Nature Climate Change* 6 (2016): 622–6. For a European study with similar findings, see Joakim Kulin, Ingemar Johansson Sevä and Riley Dunlap, 'Nationalist Ideology, Right-Wing Populism and Public Views About Climate Change in Europe', *Environmental Politics* 30(7) (2021): 1111–34.

99 Kerrie Unsworth and Kelly Fielding, 'It's Political: How the Salience of One's Political Identity Changes Climate Change Beliefs and Policy Support', *Global Environmental Change* 27 (2014): 131–7; Jay Hmielowski, Lauren Feldman, Teresa Myers, Anthony Leiserowitz and Edward Maibach, 'An Attack on Science? Media Use, Trust in Scientists and Perceptions of Global Warming', *Public Understanding of Science* 23(7) (2014): 866–83.

100 See the important meta-study by Aaron McWright, Sandra Marquatt-Pyatt, Rachael Shwom, Steven Brechin, Summer Allen, 'Ideology, Capitalism and Climate: Explaining Public Views About Climate Change in the United States', *Energy Research & Social Science* 21 (2016): 180–89, at 186.

101 R. E. Dunlap and A. C. McCright, 'A Widening Gap: Republican and Democratic Views on Climate Change', *Environment* 50(5) (2008): 26–36, https://www.sciencedirect.com/science/article/abs/pii/S2214629616301864. See also William Eveland and Kathryn Cooper, 'An Integrated Model of Communication Influence on Beliefs', *PNAS* 110 (2013): 14088–95.

102 Hank Jenkins-Smith et al. (six others), 'Partisan Asymmetry in Temporal Stability of Climate Change Beliefs', *Nature Climate Change* 10 (2020): 322–8.

103 Williams et al., 'Network Analysis Reveals Open Forums'.

104 McWright et al., 'Ideology, Capitalism and Climate', 186.

105 Shakuntala Banaji and Ramnath Bhat, *Social Media and Hate* (Routledge, 2022); Arlie Hochschild, *Strangers in Their Own Land* (New Press, 2018); Khiara Bridges, 'Language on the Move: "Cancel Culture", "Critical Race Theory", and the Digital Public Sphere', *Yale Law Journal* 131 (2021–2), https://www.yalelawjournal.org/forum/language-on-the-move.

106 Phillips, *This Is Why We Can't Have Nice Things*.

107 Donovan et al., *Meme Wars*. See also David Newert, *Alt-america* (Verso, 2017); Andrew Marantz, *Anti-Social: Online Extremists, Techno-Utopians, and the Hijacking of the American Conversation* (Viking, 2019). On the importance of memes more generally, see Beck, *Metamorphosis*, 138.

108 Donovan et al., *Meme Wars*, 41.

109 Ibid., 329. Compare Phillips, *This is Why We Can't Have Nice Things*, 8, on the wider impact of marketing culture on social media.

110 Donovan et al., *Meme Wars*, 328.

111 Michał Krzyanowski, Mattias Ekman, Per-Erik Nilsson, Mattias Gardell, and Christian Christensen, 'Uncivility, Racism and Populism: Discourses and Interactive Practices in Anti- and Post-democratic Communication', *Nordicom Review* 42(S1) (2021): 3–15.

112 Diana Mutz, *In-Your-Face Politics: The Consequences of Uncivil Media* (Princeton University Press, 2015).

113 See, for example, Paddy Bullard (ed.), *The Oxford Handbook of British Satire* (Oxford University Press, 2019); Andrew DelBanco, *The War Before the War* (Penguin, 2018).

114 Spyros Kosmidis and Yannis Theocharis, 'Can Social Media Incivility Induce Enthusiasm? Evidence from Survey Experiments', *Public Opinion Quarterly* 84 (2020): 284–308; Gina Chen, Ashley Muddiman, and Natalie Stroud, 'We Should Not Get Rid of Incivility Online', *Social Media & Society*, 5(3) (2019), https://doi.org/10.1177/2056305119862641.

115 Chung-hong Chan, Cassius Chow and King-wa Fu, 'Echoslamming: How Incivility Interacts With Cyberbalkanization on the Social Media in Hong Kong', *Asian Journal of Communication* 2(4) (2019): 307–27.

116 Respectively, Matthew Weaver, 'Eight Met Officers Guilty of Misconduct Over Discriminatory WhatsApp Messages', *Guardian* (4 April 2023), https://www.theguardian.com/uk-news/2023/apr/13/eight-met-officers-guilty-of-misconduct-over-discriminatory-whatsapp-messages; 'Understanding Antisemitism on Twitter After Musk', Institute for Strategic Dialogue (30 March 2023), https://www.isdglobal.org/digital_dispatches/understanding-antisemitism-on-twitter-after-musk/; Jason Okundaye, 'Why It's Time to Stop Filming Strangers in Public for Social Media Thrills', *Guardian* (25 January 2023), https://www.theguardian.com/commentisfree/2023/jan/25/filming-strangers-public-social-media.

117 Sahana Udupa and Matti Pohjonen, 'Extreme Speech: Extreme Speech and Global Digital Cultures – Introduction', *International Journal of Communication* 13 (2019): 3049–67; Banet-Weiser, *Empowered*; Laura Bates, *Men Who Hate Women* (Simon and Schuster, 2021).

118 Ashley Muddiman and Natalie Jomini Stroud, 'News Values, Cognitive Biases, and Partisan Incivility in Comment Sections', *Journal of Communication* 67 (2017): 586–607; Silvia Majo-Vasquez, Rasmus Neilsen, Joan Verdu, Nandan Rao, Manlio De Domenico and Omiros Papaspiliopoulos, 'Volume and Patterns of Toxicity in Social Media Conversations During the COVID-19 Pandemic', Reuters Institute for the Study of Journalism (July 2020), https://reutersinstitute.politics.ox.ac.uk/volume-and-patterns-toxicity-social-media-conversations-during-covid-19-pandemic.

119 Gabriele de Seta, 'Wenming Bu Wenming: The Socialization of Incivility

in Postdigital China', *International Journal of Communication* 12 (2018): 2010–30.

120 Quoted Debbie Ging and James O'Higgins Norman, 'Cyberbullying, Conflict Management or Just Messing? Teenage Girls' Understandings and Experiences of Gender Friendship, and Conflict on Facebook in an Irish Second-level School', *Feminist Media Studies* 16(5) (2016): 805–21, at 814.

121 Jin Woo Kim, Andrew Guess, Brendan Nyhan, Jason Reifler, 'The Distorting Prism of Social Media: How Self-Selection and Exposure to Incivility Fuel Online Comment Toxicity', *Journal of Communication* 71(6) (2021): 922–46.

122 Quoted Debbie Ging and Eugenia Siapera, 'Special Issue on Online Misogyny', *Feminist Media Studies* 18(4) (2018): 515–24, at 520.

123 Angelo Antoci, Laura Bonelli, Fabio Paglieri, Tommaso Reggiani and Fabio Sabatini, 'Civility and Trust in Social Media', *Journal of Economic Behavior and Organization* 160 (2019): 83–99.

124 Maeve Duggan and Aaron Smith, 'The Political Environment on Social Media', Pew Research Center (October 2018), https://www.pewresearch.org /internet/2016/10/25/the-political-environment-on-social-media/, 2.

125 Ibid., 4.

126 Ashley Anderson, Dominique Brossard, Dietram Scheufele, Michael Xenos and Peter Ladwig, 'The "Nasty Effect": Online Incivility and Risk Perceptions of Emerging Technologies', *Journal of Computer-Mediated Communication* 19 (2014): 373–87.

127 Yannis Theocharis, Pablo Barbera, and Sebastian Popa, 'The Dynamics of Political Incivility on Twitter', *Sage OPEN* 10(2) (2020), https://doi.org/10 .1177/2158244020919447.

128 Yannis Theocharis, Pablo Barbera, Zoltan Fazekas, Sebastian Popa and Olivier Parnet, 'A Bad Workman Blames His Tweets: The Consequences of Citizens' Uncivil Twitter Use When Interacting With Party Candidates', *Journal of Communication* 66 (2016): 1007–31.

129 Ludovic Rhenault, Erica Rayment and Andreea Musulan, 'Politicians in the Line of Fire: Incivility and the Treatment of Women on Social Media', *Research and Politics* 6(1) (2019), https://doi.org/10.1177/2053168018816228; Tess McClure, 'Jacinda Ardern: Political Figures Believe Abuse and Threats Contributed to Ardern's Resignation', *Guardian* (20 January 2023), https:// www.theguardian.com/world/2023/jan/20/jacinda-ardern-speculation-that -abuse-and-threats-contributed-to-resignation.

130 Luciano di Meco, 'Monetizing Misogyny: Gendered Disinformation and the Undermining of Women's Rights and Democracy Globally', #ShePersisted (February 2023), https://she-persisted.org/wp-content/uploads/2023/02 /ShePersisted_MonetizingMisogyny.pdf.

131 Ashifa Kassam, 'Online Vitriol Could Undo Decades of Political Progress,

Says Dutch Deputy PM', *Guardian* (4 November 2023), https://www
.theguardian.com/world/2023/nov/03/online-vitriol-could-undo-decades
-political-progress-dutch-deputy-pm/.

132 Jeffrey Berry and Sarah Sobieraj, *The Outrage Industry* (Oxford University
Press, 2014).

133 Aaron Smith, Laura Silver, Courtney Johnson and Jingjing Jiang, 'Publics in
Emerging Economies Worry Social Media Sow Division' Pew Research Center
(13 May 2019), https://www.pewresearch.org/internet/2019/05/13/publics
-in-emerging-economies-worry-social-media-sow-division-even-as-they-offer
-new-chances-for-political-engagement/. Digital access is defined there as
access to 'mobile phones, internet and social media'; the only countries of the
eleven surveyed going the other way were India and Vietnam.

134 Smith et al., 'Publics in Emerging Economies'. Only adults in Mexico felt in
the majority that it wasn't.

135 Robert Esposito, Riannon Noel Welch, Vanessa Lemm, *Terms of the Political:
Community, Immunity, Biopolitics* (Fordham University Press, 2012), 43.

Chapter 6: Can Solidarity Survive?

1 UN Secretary General, *Our Common Agenda: Report of the Secretary-General*
(United Nations, September 2021), https://www.un.org/en/content/common
-agenda-report/assets/pdf/Common_Agenda_Report_English.pdf#page=11, 3.

2 On the renewed importance of solidarity and organisation across difference,
see Astra Taylor and Leah Hunt-Hendrix, *Solidarity: The Past, Present and
Future of a World Changing Idea* (Pantheon Books, 2024).

3 Details at https://www.nationaltheatre.org.uk/whats-on/all-of-us/ (accessed
26 March 2024).

4 Thomas Piketty, *Capital in the 21st Century* (Harvard University Press, 2013);
Mike Savage, *The Return of Inequality* (Harvard University Press, 2021).

5 Trust in government in the US was 58 per cent in 1970, but had fallen
to 20 per cent in 2022 (https://ourworldindata.org/grapher/public-trust-in
-government), against an OECD average in 2022 of 42 per cent (https://
ourworldindata.org/grapher/oecd-average-trust-in-governments). The belief
that 'most people can be trusted' fell 46 per cent to 32 per cent between
1972 and 2018 according to the 2022 US General Social Survey (https://
gssdataexplorer.norc.org/variables/441/vshow). On the increasingly unequal
nature of US society, see Anne Case and Angus Deaton, *Deaths of Despair and
the Future of Capitalism* (Princeton University Press, 2020).

6 See Ipsos, *Interpersonal Trust Across the World* (March 2022), which reported
five Latin American countries (in a thirty-country study) where less than 25
per cent of people said 'most people can be trusted' (Brazil, Chile, Colombia,

Mexico, Peru) against a global average of 30 per cent, available from https://www.ipsos.com/sites/default/files/ct/news/documents/2022-03/node-880851-887091.zip, 2-3. In the same survey, the US is shown at slightly above the median (at 33 per cent).

7 Aidan Connaughton, 'Social Trust in Advanced Economies Is Lower Among Young People and Those With Less Education', Pew Research Center (3 December 2020), https://www.pewresearch.org/fact-tank/2020/12/03/social-trust-in-advanced-economies-is-lower-among-young-people-and-those-with-less-education/.

8 Amitav Ghosh, *The Great Derangement* (Chicago University Press, 2015), 87, 146; compare Purdy, *After Nature*, 46.

9 Daniel Kreiss and Shannon McGregor, 'A Review and Provocation: On Polarization and Platforms', *New Media & Society* (2023), https://journals.sagepub.com/doi/10.1177/14614448231161880.

10 Purdy, *After Nature*, 5.

11 Aaron McCright, Sandra Marquart-Pyatt, Rachael Shwom, Steven Brechin and Summer Allen, 'Ideology, Capitalism, and Climate: Explaining Public Views About Climate Change in the United States', *Energy Research & Social Science* 21 (2016): 180–89, especially 184.

12 Michael Sandel, *The Tyranny of Merit* (Penguin, 2021), 221.

13 Phrase quoted from Rowan Williams, 'Remember the Tenacity of 400,000 Welsh Women Today: Then Use Your Power to Shape Events Today', *Guardian* (30 December 2023), https://www.theguardian.com/commentisfree/2023/dec/30/welsh-women-wales-peace-petition.

14 Tarnoff, *Internet for the People*, 177.

15 Homero Gil de Zúñiga, Logan Molyneux and Pei Zheng, 'Social Media, Political Expression, and Political Participation: Panel Analysis of Lagged and Concurrent Relationships', *Journal of Communication* 64 (2014): 612–34.

16 Hyehyun Yong and Yeuseung Kim, 'What Makes People Engage in Civic Activism on Social Media?', *Online Information Review*, 45(3) (2021): 562–76. For older research on lack of opportunities to express political opinions, see Nina Eliasoph, *Avoiding Politics* (Cambridge University Press, 2004).

17 Denise Wilkins, Andrew Livingstone and Mark Levine, 'All Click, No Action? Online Action, Efficacy Perceptions and Prior Experience Combine to Affect Future Collective Action', *Computers in Human Behavior* 91 (2019): 97–105.

18 Ying Xoing, Moonhee Cho and Brandon Boatwright, 'Hashtag Activism and Message Frames Among Social Movement Organizations: Semantic Network Analysis and Thematic Analysis of Twitter During the #Metoo Movement', *Public Relations Review* 45 (2019): 10–23; Sarah Jackson, Moya Bailey and Brooke Foucault Welles, *#Hashtag Activism: Networks of Race and Gender Justice* (MIT Press, 2020).

19 Shelley Boulianne, Mireille Lalancette and David Ilkiw, '"School Strike 4 Climate": Social Media and the International Youth Protest on Climate Change', *Media and Communication* 8(2) (2020): 208–18.

20 Roula Khalaf, 'Daring Saudi Tweets Fuel Political Debate', *Financial Times* (16 March 2012), https://www.ft.com/content/1749888e-6f5e-11e1-b368 -00144feab49a; Haining Liu, 'China's Social Media Explosion Has Shattered the Official Silence', *Financial Times* (17 August 2015), https://www.ft.com /content/637a0e0e-44cb-11e5-af2f-4d6e0e5eda22.

21 Anastasia Kavada, 'Social Movements and Political Agency in the Digital Age: A Communication Approach', *Media and Communication* 4(4) (2016): 8–12.

22 Dave Cullen, *Parkland: Birth of a Movement* (Riverrun, 2019), 37, 43.

23 Srinivasan, *Beyond the Valley,* 120; https://www.ushahidi.com.

24 Johanna Sumiala and Minttu Tikka, 'Reality on Circulation – School Shootings, Ritualised Communication and the Dark Side of the Sacred', *ESSACHESS Journal for Communication Studies,* 4(2) (2011): 145–59, at 153.

25 Maya Oppenheim, 'Sexually Explicit Images of Women Being Traded by Men on Reddit', *Independent* (22 August 2022), https://www.independent .co.uk/news/uk/home-news/sexually-explicit-images-reddit-collector-culture -b2150223.html.

26 Sukrita Baruah, 'Before Manipur Sexual Assault Video Went Viral, a Bid to Get the Clip Deleted from Phones', *Indian Express* (4 August 2023), https:// indianexpress.com/article/india/before-video-went-viral-manipur-outfit -made-an-attempt-to-bury-it-8875530/.

27 Dante Donate, Victor Orozco and Nandan Rao, 'Combating Regressive Gender Norms and Violence Against Women Through Social Media Edutainment Campaigns – Lessons from India' (World Bank, 23 November 2022), https://blogs.worldbank.org/developmenttalk/combating-regressive-gender-norms-and-violence-against-women-through-social-media (accessed 24 October 2023).

28 Jeremy Gilbert, 'Platforms and Potency: Democracy and Collective Agency in the Age of Social Media', *Open Cultural Studies* 9 (2020): 154–68, at 159, 163.

29 Ellen E. Jones, 'Opal Tometi, Co-founder of Black Lives Matter : "I do it because we deserve to live"' (interview), *Guardian* (24 September 2020), https://www.theguardian.com/society/2020/sep/24/opal-tometi-co-founder -of-black-lives-matter-i-do-this-because-we-deserve-to-live.

30 For example, the early days of the Egyptian uprising in January 2011, described in Gal Beckerman, *The Quiet Before* (Penguin, 2022), 168–72.

31 Ibid., 199, cf. Mounk, *The People Versus Democracy.*

32 Robert Gehl, *Reverse Engineering Social Media* (Temple University Press, 2014), 142.

33 Catherine Knight Steele, *Digital Black Feminism* (New York University Press, 2021), 132, 139.

34 Jackson et al., *#Hashtag Activism*, 230.

35 André Brock, *Distributed Blackness: African American Cybercultures* (New York University Press, 2020), 1, 20.

36 Sarah Florini, *Beyond Hashtags: Racial Politics and Black Digital Networks* (New York University Press, 2019), 23, 185. For the Black social media public as a 'public sphere' see also Brock, *Distributed Blackness*, 86.

37 Keeanga Yamatta-Taylor, *From #BlackLivesMatter to Black Liberation* (Haymarket Books, 2016), 174.

38 Meredith D. Clark, 'Elon Musk's Purchase Is Not Black Twitter's Problem', *The Grio* (3 November 2022), https://thegrio.com/2022/11/03/elon-musks-purchase-is-not-black-twitters-problem/#:~:text=OPINION%3A%20The%20actions%20of%20one,be%20brought%20down%20by%20it.

39 Christopher Lebron, *The Making of Black Lives Matter* (Oxford University Press, 2017), 148.

40 For discussion of this problem, see Lawrence Wilde, 'The Concept of Solidarity: Emerging From the Theoretical Shadows?', *British Journal of Politics and International Relations* 9(1) (2007): 171–81.

41 Lance Bennett and Alexandra Segerberg, *The Logic of Connective Action* (Cambridge University Press, 2013); and see Maria Bakardjeva, 'Do Clouds Have Politics? Collective Actors in Social Media Land', *Information Communication & Society* 18(8) (2015): 983–90 for sympathetic critical discussion.

42 Bakardjeva, 'Do Clouds Have Politics?', 985.

43 Shelley Boulianne and Yannis Theocharis, 'Young People, Digital Media and Engagement: A Meta-analysis of Research', *Social Science Computer Review* 38(2) (2020): 111–27.

44 Ibid., 121–2.

45 Ibid., 123.

46 Quotations from Stephanie Kirchgaessner, 'Saudis Accused of Using Snapchat to Promote Crown Prince and Silence Critics', *Guardian* (18 July 2023), https://www.theguardian.com/technology/2023/jul/18/snapchat-saudi-arabia-ties.

47 Mentioned by Opal Tometi in the interview cited in note 29 above.

48 Cheryll Soriano and Jason Cabanes, 'Entrepreneurial Solidarities: Social Media Collectives and Filipino Digital Platform Workers', *Social Media & Society* (2020), https://doi.org/10.1177/2056305120926484.

49 Zeynep Tufekci, *Twitter and Teargas: The Power and Fragility of Networked Protest*, (Yale University Press, 2017), 21.

50 Soriano and Cabanes, 'Entrepreneurial Solidarities', 9.

51 Tufekci, *Twitter and Teargas*; Paolo Gerbaudo, *The Mask and the Flag* (Hurst, 2017), especially 234, 243.

52 Quotes from Beckerman, *The Quiet Before*, 185, 179. For the broader point on social media, see Nick Couldry, *Media Society World* (Polity, 2012), 126, 128; Pierre Rosanvallon, *Counter-Democracy* (Cambridge University Press, 2008).

53 Kaarina Nikunen, 'From Irony to Solidarity: Affective Practice and Social Media Activism', *STSS: Studies of Transition States and Societies* 10(2) (2018), 10–21, available from https://www.ssoar.info/ssoar/handle/document/62611; compare Veronica Barassi, *Activism on the Web* (Routledge, 2015).

54 Pope Francis, *Fratelli Tutti* (March 2020), https://www.vatican.va/content /francesco/en/encyclicals/documents/papa-francesco_20201003_enciclica -fratelli-tutti.html. For commentary, see Vincent Miller, 'Solidarity on Social Media? A View from Pope Francis and Fratelli Tutti' (Berkeley Center for Religion, Peace and World Affairs, Georgetown University, November 2021), https://berkleycenter.georgetown.edu/responses/solidarity-on-social-media -a-view-from-pope-francis-and-fratelli-tutti (accessed 10 August 2023).

55 Hyunjin Seo, *Networked Collective Actions: The Making of an Impeachment* (Oxford University Press 2022), especially 133–9.

56 Judith Butler, *Notes Toward a Performative Theory of Assembly* (Harvard University Press, 2015), 23.

57 Verónica Gago, *Feminist International: How to Change Everything* (Verso, 2020), 23.

58 Gilbert, 'Platforms and Potency'; Raphael Minder and Barbara Erling, '"A Sense of Solidarity": How Poles Mobilised in Historic Vote', *Financial Times* (17 October 2023), https://www.ft.com/content/70c1a6f8-fff7-4f70-ace2 -98eb9173dc05.

59 Beckerman, *The Quiet Before*, 40.

60 Bennett and Segerberg, *Logic of Connective Action*, 210.

61 Wendy Brown, *Undoing the Demos* (Zone books, 2015); Will Davies, *The Limits of Neoliberalism* (Sage, 2017).

62 Lilie Chouliaraki, *The Ironic Spectator* (Polity, 2013).

63 Kathleen Lynch and Manolis Kalaitzake, 'Affective and Calculative Solidarity: The Impact of Individualism and Neoliberal Capitalism', *European Journal of Social Theory* 23(2) (2020): 238–57. On 'affective solidarity', see also Claire Hemmings, 'Affective Solidarity: Feminist Reflexivity and Political Transformation', *Feminist Theory* 13(2) (2012): 147–61.

64 Lynch et al., 'Affective and Calculative Solidarity', 239.

65 See for helpful review Lawrence Wilde, 'A "Radical Humanist" Approach to the Concept of Solidarity', *Political Studies* 52 (2004): 162–78.

66 Craig Calhoun, 'Nationalism, Political Community and the Representation

of Society: Or, Why Feeling at Home is Not a Substitute for Public Space', *European Journal of Social Theory* 2(2) (1999): 217–31, 228.

67 Michael Walzer, 'Pluralism and Social Democracy', *Dissent* (Winter 1998), 48–53, at 51.

68 Theda Skocpol, *Diminished Democracy: From Membership to Management in American Civic Life* (University of Oklahoma Press, 2003).

69 Gambetta, 'Can We Trust Trust?'

70 Pope Francis, *Fratelli Tutti*, 31.

71 Alexander Stewart, Mohsen Mosleh, Marina Dakonova, Antonio Arechar, David Rand and Joshua Plotkin, 'Information Gerrymandering and Undemocratic Decisions', *Nature* 573 (2019): 117–21, at 117, 120.

72 Stewart et al., 'Information Gerrymandering'.

73 Robert Jervis, 'Realism, Game Theory and Cooperation', *World Politics* 40(3) (1988): 317–49, at 327.

74 Jervis, 'Realism', 327.

75 Klein, *Doppelganger,* 328.

76 Leo Hickman, 'James Lovelock on the Value of Sceptics and Why Copenhagen Was Doomed', *Guardian* (29 March 2010), https://www.theguardian.com /environment/blog/2010/mar/29/james-lovelock.

77 Gaia Vince, *Nomad Century: How to Survive the Climate Upheaval* (Allen Lane, 2022).

78 Daniel Trilling, 'How to Survive the Climate Upheaval – Humanity on the Move', Review, *Guardian* (20 August 2022), https://www.theguardian.com /books/2022/aug/19/nomad-century-how-to-survive-the-climate-upheaval -review-humanity-on-the-move.

79 Rebecca Wills, 'Is Democracy Up to the Task of Climate Change?', *Guardian* (30 October 2021), https://www.theguardian.com/books/2021/nov/01/the -big-idea-is-democracy-up-to-the-task-of-climate-change.

80 Purdy, *After Nature*, 48–9.

81 Richard Schiffman, 'Climate Deniers Shift Tactics to "Inactivism"', *Scientific American* (11 January 2021), https://www.scientificamerican.com /article/climate-deniers-shift-tactics-to-inactivism/; Jack Shenker, 'Meet the "Inactivists": Tangling Up the Climate Crisis in Culture Wars', *Guardian* (11 November 2021).

82 Alec Tyson, Cary Funk and Brian Kennedy, 'What the Data Says About Americans' Views About Climate Change', Pew Research Center (9 August 2023), https://www.pewresearch.org/short-reads/2023/08/09/what-the-data -says-about-americans-views-of-climate-change/.

83 Gillian Tett, 'How Do You Persuade Republicans to Save the Planet', *Financial Times* (29 June 2022), https://www.ft.com/content/0becfebb-a15c-435f-86a5 -64178884efb9.

84 Alberto Melucci, *Nomads of the Present* (Temple University Press, 1989), 30, cited by Bakardjeva, 'Do Clouds Have Politics?', 983–4.

85 Mark Coeckelbergh, *The Political Philosophy of AI* (Polity, 2022), 153–4.

86 Tarleton Gillespie, 'Content Moderation, AI and the Question of Scale', *Big Data & Society* 7(2) (2020), https://doi.org/10.1177/2053951720943234, 4.

Chapter 7: Rebuilding Social Media

1 Terry Winograd and Fernando Flores, *Understanding Computers and Cognition* (Sage, 1986), xi.

2 Berjon, 'The Internet Transition', 7, original emphasis.

3 Compare on the need for 'ecological literacy' in relation to digital media, Whitney Phillips and Ryan Milner, *You Are Here: A Field Guide for Navigating Polarized Speech, Conspiracy Theories and Our Polluted Media Landscape* (MIT, 2021), 13.

4 Global Voices, 'Officials Blame WhatsApp for Spike in Mob Killings, but Indians Say Vicious Party Politics Are at Fault' (2 August 2018), https://globalvoices.org/2018/08/02/officials-blame-whatsapp-for-spike-in-mob-killings-but-indians-say-vicious-party-politics-are-at-fault/; Aria Thaker, 'WhatsApp Is Going Global With a Restriction Used to Fight Fake News in India', *Quartz India* (22 January 2019), https://qz.com/india/1529461/whatsapp=indian=step-against-fake-news-has-gone-global/.

5 The maximum size of a WhatsApp group was originally 100, increased to 256 in 2016, to 512 mid-2022 and to 1,024 at end of 2022: Stan Schneider, 'WhatsApp Increases Group Size to 1024 People' (10 October 2022), https://mashable.com/article/whatsapp-group-1000; WhatsApp, 'About Forwarding Limits', https://faq.whatsapp.com/1053543185312573 (accessed 11 October 2023). Meanwhile the forwarding limit turned out to be a limit on forwarding to five *recipients*, which could include group chats. Take advantage of this and, although you aren't allowed to share something already forwarded to you to more than one group chat, a chain of others can repeat this: it needn't take long to reach the same 5,000 people that you could, if you initiated a new chain of forwarded content.

6 For *colonialism*'s relations to capitalism, considering which may open up new fronts of resistance, see Ulises Mejias and Nick Couldry, *Data Grab: The New Colonialism of Big Tech and How to Fight It* (WH Allen, 2024).

7 Ivan Illich, *Tools for Conviviality* (Fontana, 1975), 11.

8 Ibid., 33.

9 Gehl, *Reverse Engineering*, 142.

10 Compare Ben Tarnoff, 'The Technologies of All Dead Generations', blog

at Metal Machine Music (9 April 2023), https://bentarnoff.substack.com/ (accessed 24 September 2023).

11 Milton Friedman, *Capitalism and Freedom*, 2nd edition (Chicago University Press, 1982), ix.

12 Aaron Smith, 'Public Attitudes Toward Technology Companies', Pew Research Center (28 June 2018), https://www.pewresearch.org/internet/2018/06/28 /public-attitudes-toward-technology-companies/.

13 Robert Frank, 'The Economic Case for Regulating Social Media', *New York Times* (11 February 2021), https://www.nytimes.com/2021/02/11/business /social-media-facebook-regulation.html.

14 Ezra Klein, 'I Didn't Want It to be True, but the Medium Really Is the Message', *New York Times* (7 August 2022), https://www.nytimes.com/2022 /08/07/opinion/media-message-twitter-instagram.html.

15 Lauren Goode, 'Social Media Has Run Out of Ideas', *Wired* (24 July 2023), https://wired.me/business/social-media-has-run-out-of-fresh-ideas/; Edward Onweso Jr, 'Super Apps Are Terrible for People – and Good for Companies', *Wired* (10 September 2023), https://www.wired.com/story/super-app-musk -x-wechat-regulation/; Cory Doctorow, '"Enshittification" Is Coming for Absolutely Everything', *Financial Times* (8 February 2024), https://www.ft .com/content/6fb1602d-a08b-4a8c-bac0-047b7d64aba5.

16 Joe Biden, 'Republicans and Democrats, Unite Against Big Tech Abuses', *Wall Street Journal* (11 January 2023), https://www.wsj.com/articles/unite -against-big-tech-abuses-social-media-privacy-competition-antitrust-children -algorithm-11673439411; Tess McClure, 'Jacinda Ardern to Tackle Online Extremism in New Role as Special Envoy for Christchurch Call', *Guardian* (5 April 2023), https://www.theguardian.com/world/2023/apr/04 /jacinda-ardern-to-tackle-online-extremism-in-new-role-as-special-envoy-for -christchurch-call.

17 This call was first made by Esther Ghey, mother of murdered trans teenager Brianna Ghey: see Heather Stewart, '"Our Kids Are Suffering": Calls for Ban on Social Media to Protect Under-16s', *Guardian* (11 February 2024), https://www.theguardian.com/media/2024/feb/11/our-kids-are-suffering -calls-for-ban-on-social-media-to-protect-under-16s. The calls were picked up by other parents: Mabel Banfield-Nwachi, '"It Went Nuts": Thousands Join UK Parents Calling for Smartphone-free Childhood', *Guardian* (17 February 2024), https://www.theguardian.com/technology/2024/feb/17/thousands -join-uk-parents-calling-for-smartphone-free-childhood.

18 Mark Zuckerberg, 'A Blueprint for Content Governance and Enforcement', Facebook (last edited 5 May 2021), https://www.facebook.com/notes /751449002072082/ (accessed 11 October 2023).

19 Peter Guest, 'I'm Reddit's CEO and I Think Regulating Social Media

Is Tyranny. AITA?', *Wired* (17 April 2023), https://www.wired.com/story/reddit-ceo-steve-huffman-social-media-regulation/?utm_source=flipboard&utm_content=user%2FWIRED.

20 Advertisement in hard copy version of *Guardian* (15 December 2023).

21 Bryan Harris, 'Bolsonaro Crafts New Social Media Strategy Ahead of Brazil Election', *Financial Times* (12 January 2022), https://www.ft.com/content/6804e103-c8b5-45b2-8be5-24b610330888.

22 Ashley Boyd, 'TikTok, YouTube and Facebook Want to Appear Trustworthy. Don't Be Fooled', *New York Times* (8 August 2021), https://www.nytimes.com/2021/08/08/opinion/tiktok-facebook-youtube-transparency.html; Deepa Seetharaman, Jeff Horwitz and Justin Scheck, 'Facebook Says AI Will Clean Up the Platform. Its Own Engineers Have Doubts', *Wall Street Journal* (17 October 2021), https://www.wsj.com/articles/facebook-ai-enforce-rules-engineers-doubtful-artificial-intelligence-11634338184.

23 Miranda Bryant, 'Leading Adviser Quits over Instagram's Failure to Remove Self-harm Content', *Observer* (16 March 2024), https://www.theguardian.com/technology/2024/mar/16/instagram-meta-lotte-rubaek-adviser-quits-failure-to-remove-self-harm-content-#:~:text=In%20her%20resignation%20letter%2C%20she,young%20people%20on%20your%20platforms.%E2%80%9D; Alex Hern, 'Violent Content Online "Unavoidable" for UK Children, Ofcom Finds', *Guardian* (15 March 2024), https://www.theguardian.com/technology/2024/mar/15/violent-online-content-unavoidable-for-uk-children-ofcom-finds.

24 Charlotte Chang, Nikhil Desmukh, Paul Armsworth and Yuta Masuda, 'Environmental Users Abandoned Twitter After Musk Takeover', *Trends in Ecology & Evolution* 38(10) (2023): P893–5.

25 David Gilbert, 'Elon Musk Is Shitposting His Way Through the Israel-Hamas War', *Wired,* (10 October 2023), https://www.wired.com/story/elon-musk-israel-hamas-war-disinformation-x/; Marina Hyde, 'Look at the Horror of the Israel-Hamas War, Then at Elon Musk's X Site. It's Clear He's Not Fit to Run It', *Guardian* (11 October 2023), https://www.theguardian.com/commentisfree/2023/oct/10/horror-israel-hamas-war-elon-musk-x-twitter-not-fit-to-run-it. Eliot Higgins, founder of investigative report website Bellingcat, tweeted that 'Musk has created a fundamental issue with Twitter's credibility in moments of crisis': https://twitter.com/EliotHiggins/status/1711613868634505382 (11 October 2023).

26 Gehl, *Reverse Engineering*, 141ff; Benjamin Kunkel, 'Socialize Social Media!', *nplusone* (8 November 2013), https://www.nplusonemag.com/online-only/online-only/socialize-social-media/.

27 Anna Lowenhaupt Tsing, 'On NonScalability: The Living World Is Not Amenable to Precision-nested Scales', *Common Knowledge* 18(3) (2012): 505–24.

28 Caroline Gerlitz and Anne Helmond, 'The Like Economy: Social Buttons and the Data-intensive Web', *New Media & Society* 15(8) (2013): 1348–65.

29 Abidin, *Internet Celebrity*, 81.

30 Compare Robert Gehl, 'The Case for Alternative Social Media', *Social Media & Society* (2015), https://doi.org/10.1177/2056305115604338, 6.

31 See, for example, 'Party at My House: Darius Kazemi on Human-scaled Social Media', *Logic(s)* (4 May 2020), https://logicmag.io/security/party-at -my-house-darius-kazemi-on-human-scaled-social-media/; the published principles of the Decentralized Web collective, started in 2014, available from https://getdweb.net /; and Michael Kwet, 'Fixing Social Media: Towards a Democratic Digital Commons', *Markets, Globalization & Development Review* 5(1) (2020), DOI: 10.23860/MGDR-2020-05-01-04.

32 Cory Doctorow, *The Internet Con* (Verso, 2023).

33 As proposed by Mark Zuckerberg, 'A Privacy Focussed Vision for Social Networking', Facebook (6 March 2019), https://about.fb.com/news/2019/03 /vision-for-social-networking/.

34 https://www.inrupt.com/solid.

35 Cory Doctorow, 'alt.interoperability.adversarial', Electronic Frontier Foundation blog (November 2019), https://www.eff.org/deeplinks/2019/10 /adversarial-interoperability; compare James Muldoon, *Platform Socialism* (Pluto, 2022), 134.

36 Transferability of contacts and data doesn't require a commodity price to be put on people's data (*contra* the Data Dignity proposal of Jaron Lanier and Glen Weyl: 'A Blueprint for a Better Digital Society', *Harvard Business Review* (26 September 2018), https://hbr.org/2018/09/a-blueprint-for-a- better-digital-society).

37 As emphasised by Eugen Rochko, CEO of Mastodon, quoted in Nilay Patel, 'Can Mastodon Seize the Moment from Twitter?', *The Verge* (28 March 2023), https://www.theverge.com/23658648/mastodon-ceo-twitter-interview-elon -musk-twitter, 13.

38 Gehl, *Reverse Engineering*, 147.

39 Amy Hasinoff and Nathan Schneider, 'From Scalability to Subsidiarity in Addressing Online Harm', *Social Media & Society* (2022), https://doi.org/10 .1177/20563051221126041.

40 Meredith Whittaker, 'Standing Firm Against Threats to Private and Safe Communication', blog (9 March 2023), https://signal.org/blog/uk-online -safety-bill/.

41 https://tella-app.org/; https://wearehorizontal.org/index.

42 On limiting virality, see Ellen Goodman, 'Digital Fidelity and Friction', *Nevada Law Journal* 21 (2021): 623–53, especially 648–52.

43 Ben Brubaker, 'How the Physics of Resonance Shapes Reality', *Quanta*

(26 January 2022), https://www.quantamagazine.org/how-the-physics-of
-resonance-shapes-reality-20220126/, gives an explanation for a lay audience.

44 https://en.wikipedia.org/wiki/Acoustic_resonance.

45 I began developing this idea in late 2022. In October 2023 I was delighted to
find that resonance has been discussed by the feminist and queer Systerserver
collective (https://systerserver.net) as a form of connecting without scalability, particularly around federated platforms: nate wessalowski and Mar
Karagianni, 'From Feminist Servers to Feminist Federation', *APRJA* 12(1)
(2023): 192–208, https://aprja.net/article/view/140450#From_Feminist
_Servers_to_Feminist_Federation, especially 203. Thanks to Rob Gehl for
helping me make this link.

46 Niklas Tesla once performed experiments to exploit this resonance frequency
(thanks to Deb Roy for this point).

47 Alison Powell, *Undoing Optimisation* (Yale University Press, 2021).

48 Berjon, 'The Internet Transition', 9. Compare Mary Anne Franks, 'Beyond
the Public Square: Imagining Digital Democracy', *Yale Law Journal* 131
(November 2021), https://www.yalelawjournal.org/forum/beyond-the-public
-square-imagining-digital-democracy; Niloufar Salehi, 'Do No Harm', *Logic*
11 (31 August 2020), https://logicmag.io/care/do-no-harm/.

49 Thanks to Joshua Fairfield for suggesting 'resonance chambers', as a development of the principle of 'resonance', in a conversation in December
2023.

50 Michael Savage '"Toxic" Online Culture Fuelling Rise in Sexual Assaults on
Children by Other Children, Police Warn', *Guardian* (17 February 2024),
https://www.theguardian.com/society/2024/feb/17/toxic-online-culture
-fuelling-rise-in-sexual-assualts-on-children-by-other-children-police-warn.

51 Ofcom, *Online Nation* (2022).

52 Maanvi Singh, 'Utah Bans Under-18s From Using Social Media Unless
Parents Consent', *Guardian* (24 March 2023), https://www.theguardian.com
/us-news/2023/mar/23/utah-social-media-access-law-minors#:~:text=The
%20new%20law%20prohibiting%20minors,unless%20parents%20modify
%20the%20settings.

53 Muldoon, *Platform Socialism*, 132–6.

54 Robert Gehl and Diana Zulli, 'The Digital Covenant: Non-centralized
Platform Governance on the Mastodon Social Network', *Information
Communication & Society* (2022), https://doi.org/10.1080/1369118X.2022
.2147400, 8.

55 Tarnoff, *Internet for the People*, 159.

56 Eugen Rochko, 'Gab Switches to Mastodon's Code', blog (4 July 2019),
https://blog.joinmastodon.org/2019/07/statement-on-gabs-fork-of
-mastodon/#:~:text=After%20crowdfunding%20millions%20of%20dollars

,API%20would%20allow%20any%20existing (accessed 30 October 2023); Adi Robertson, 'How the Biggest Decentralized Social Network Is Dealing with its Nazi Problem', *The Verge* (12 July 2019), https://www.theverge .com/2019/7/12/20691957/mastodon-decentralized-social-network-gab -migration-fediverse-app-blocking; José van Dijck, Tim de Winkel and Mirko Tobias Schäfer, 'Deplatformization and the Governance of the Platform Ecosystem', *New Media & Society* 25(12) (2023): 3438–54, at 3446–8; Derek Caelin, 'Decentralized Networks Versus the Trolls'. In H. Mahmoudi, M. Allen and K. Seaman (eds.), *Fundamental Challenges to Global Peace and Security* (Springer, 2022), pp. 143–68, https://doi.org/10.1007/978-3-030 -79072-1_8.

57 Richard Rogers, 'Deplatforming: Following Extreme Internet Celebrities to Telegram and Alternative Social Media', *European Journal of Communication* 35(3) (2020): 213–29.

58 Moderation need not be done by individuals: on distributed moderation, see Donath, *Social Machine*, 177.

59 Compare Beckerman, *The Quiet Before*, 10.

60 Nathan Schneider and Amy Hasinoff, 'Mastodon Isn't Just a Replacement for Twitter', *Noema* (29 November 2022), https://www.noemamag.com /mastodon-isnt-just-a-replacement-for-twitter/.

61 https://pixelfed.org/; https://joinpeertube.org/; https://join-lemmy.org/. There are useful Wikipedia articles about each of them: https://en.wikipedia.org /wiki/Pixelfed; https://en.wikipedia.org/wiki/PeerTube; https://en.wikipedia. org/wiki/Lemmy_(social_network).

62 Detailed statistics for the Fediverse and Mastodon at https://the-federation. info and https://joinmastodon.org/servers respectively.

63 For the ActivityPub protocol, see https://www.w3.org/TR/activitypub/. See also https://en.wikipedia.org/wiki/ActivityPub.

64 Paul Sawers, 'Standard Protocol: In a Post-Twitter World, Mastodon and Bluesky Need to Get on the Same Page', *TechCrunch* (6 July 2023), https://techcrunch. com/2023/07/06/mastodon-bluesky-protocol-twitter-elon-musk/.

65 Ian Johnston, 'Twitter Rival Mastodon Rejects Funding to Protect Non-Profit Status', *Financial Times* (28 December 2022), https://www.ft.com/content/ de808736-2e05-4c3b-a53c-55b170ae9efd; Patel, 'Can Mastodon Seize the Moment from Twitter?', 5–6, 9–10.

66 Gehl and Zulli, 'The Digital Covenant'.

67 Sarah Perez, 'Mastodon Tackles the Problem of "Reply Group" With Its Latest Feature', *TechCrunch* (22 November 2023), https://techcrunch.com/2023/11 /22/mastodon-tackles-the-problem-of-reply-guys-with-its-latest-feature/.

68 See discussion in Chapter 2.

69 https://pol.is/home, implemented in Taiwan as https://vtaiwan.tw/.

70 Sarah Perez, 'As Threads Soars, Twitter Rival Bluesky Adopts a New Personalized, Algorithmic Feed', *TechCrunch* (28 July 2023), https://techcrunch.com/2023/07/28/as-threads-soars-twitter-rival-bluesky-adopts-a-new-personalized-algorithmic-feed/; Sawers, 'Standard Protocol'.

71 For an early Mastodon study, see Lucio La Cava and Andrea Tagarelli, 'Information Consumption and Boundary Spanning in Decentralized Online Social Networks: The Case of Mastodon Users', *Online Social Networks and Media* 30 (2022): 100220, available from https://doi.org/10.48550/arXiv.2203.15752.

72 Cindy Cohn and Rory Mir, 'The Fediverse Could Be Awesome (If We Don't Screw It Up)', Electronic Frontier Foundation blog (16 November 2022), https://www.eff.org/deeplinks/2022/11/fediverse-could-be-awesome-if-we-dont-screw-it (accessed 23 October 2023).

73 Bill Budington, 'Is Mastodon Private and Secure? Let's Take a Look', Electronic Frontier foundation blog (16 November 2022), https://www.eff.org/deeplinks/2022/11/mastodon-private-and-secure-lets-take-look (accessed 23 October 2023).

74 Darius Kazemi, quoted 'Party at My House', 4.

75 Nathan Edwards, 'Mastodon Gets Better Search, Onboarding and Cross-server Interactions', *The Verge* (21 September 2023), https://www.theverge.com/2023/9/21/23884312/mastodon-search-onboarding-cross-server-interactions-4-2; Sarah Perez, 'Mastodon's Latest Release Makes the Open Source Twitter Alternative Easier to Use', *TechCrunch* (21 September 2023), https://techcrunch.com/2023/09/21/mastodons-latest-release-makes-the-open-source-twitter-alternative-easier-to-use/.

76 As I write, extensive regulatory codes are being developed by Ofcom on important issues such as age verification and pornography. Their long-term effectiveness is, at this stage, entirely uncertain.

77 See, for example, Natasha Lomas, 'Meta Faces More Questions in Europe About Child Safety Risks on Instagram', *TechCrunch* (1 December 2023), https://techcrunch.com/2023/12/01/meta-dsa-rfi-2-child-safety/.

78 Dan Milmo, 'EU opens Investigation into Tiktok Over Online Content and Child Safeguarding', *Guardian* (19 February 2023), https://www.theguardian.com/technology/2024/feb/19/eu-investigation-tiktok-online-content-child-safeguarding.

79 Zuckerberg, 'A Privacy-focussed Vision'; Hannah Murphy, 'Meta's Revenue Growth Boots Shares as It Touts AI Progress', *Financial Times* (27 April 2023), https://www.ft.com/content/3cccff6e-7589-4db0-9cfc-637fc3dd682c; and most recently, Natasha Lomas, 'Meta to Offer Ad-Free Subscription in Europe in Bid to Keep Tracking Users', *TechCrunch* (30 October 2023), https://techcrunch.com/2023/10/30/meta-ad-free-sub-eu/.

80 Devin Coldewey, 'There Is No "Next Twitter", and That's OK', *TechCrunch* (27 December 2022), https://techcrunch.com/2022/12/27/there-is-no-next-twitter-and-thats-ok/.

81 Johnathan Flowers, 'The Whiteness of Mastodon' (interview with Justin Hendrix), *Tech Policy Press* (23 November 2022), https://techpolicy.press/the-whiteness-of-mastodon/.

82 I say 'most of us' because, in countries with great poverty, devices may need to be shared.

83 Compare Ghosh, *The Great Derangement*, 135, on the 'individualising imaginary'.

84 Gordon Gow, 'Alternative Social Media for Outreach and Engagement: Considering Technology Stewardship as a Pathway to Adoption', in Marco Adria (ed.), *Using New Media for Citizen Engagement and Participation* (IGI Global, 2019), 160–80. Compare the work done in feminist communities in Barcelona and Berlin by Systserver (wessalowski and Karagianni, 'From Feminist Servers') and, on the 'radical democratic pedagogy' alternative social media needs, see Gehl, *Reverse Engineering*, 148.

85 https://dynamicland.org/.

86 https://sursiendo.org/.

87 'Community Defense: Sarah T. Hamid on Abolishing Carceral Technologies', *Logic(s)* 11 (31 August 2020), https://logicmag.io/care/community-defense-sarah-t-hamid-on-abolishing-carceral-technologies/.

88 Flowers, 'Whiteness of Mastodon'.

89 McIlwain, *Black Software*.

90 See Mastodon Server Covenant, https://joinmastodon.org/covenant (accessed 25 October 2023).

91 https://nively.org/docs/papers/fsep/ (accessed 27 October 2023). Thanks to Rob Gehl for alerting me to this.

92 On the feminist ethics of care, see, for example, Virginia Held, *The Ethics of Care: Personal, Political, and Global* (Oxford University Press, 2006); Carol Gilligan, *Joining the Resistance* (Polity, 2011).

93 Flowers, 'Whiteness of Mastodon'; Gehl and Zulli, 'Digital Covenant'.

94 Gehl, *Reverse Engineering*, 149. Compare Sasha Costanza Chock, *Design Justice* (MIT Press, 2020).

95 https://dynamicland.org/; Joy Buolamwini, *Unmasking AI* (Random House, 2023).

96 Claudia Chwalisz, 'Moving Beyond the Paradigm of "Democracy": 12 Questions' (March 2024), 3, https://ash.harvard.edu/sites/hwpi.harvard.edu/files/ash/files/chwalisz_iword_essay.pdf?m=1709741292.

97 Compare Driscoll, *Modem World*, 199.

98 Piketty, *Capital in the 21st Century*. And see, for the rise in inequality across all developed countries between 1985 and 2013, the summary

table in Martin Wolf, 'The Long and Painful Journey to World Disorder', *Financial Times* (5 January 2017), https://www.ft.com/content/ef13e61a-ccec-11e6-b8ce-b9c03770f8b1.

99 For the prehistory of how climate and capitalism/colonialism interact, see Mike Davis, *Late Victorian Holocausts* (Verso, 2001).

100 Levendowsky, 'Partisan Political Media'.

101 Pickard, *Democracy Without Journalism?*; Nielsen and Ganter, *The Power of Platforms*.

102 See for the US, Pickard, *Democracy Without Journalism?*; and for the UK, Media Reform Coalition, *Who Owns the UK Media?* (October 2023), https://www.mediareform.org.uk/wp-content/uploads/2023/10/Who-Owns-the-UK-Media-2023.pdf, 6, 16–18.

103 Media Reform Coalition, *Who Owns the UK Media?*, table 1, drawing on Ipsos/MORI/Ofcom, *Media Plurality and Online News* (Ofcom, November 2022), https://www.ofcom.org.uk/__data/assets/pdf_file/0030/247548/discussion-media-plurality.pdf.

104 Daniel Thomas, 'Mirror and Express Publisher Hit by Advertising Drop and Meta's Shift', *Financial Times* (5 March 2024), https://www.ft.com/content/93efa90e-128c-4885-a7b8-4d0ea5f17d52.

105 Morgan Meaker, 'Australia's Standoff Against Google and Facebook Worked – Sort Of', *Wired* (22 February 2022), https://www.wired.co.uk/article/australia-media-code-facebook-google.

106 Tracey Lindemann, '"Disaster": Warning for Democracy as Experts Condemn Meta Over Canada News Ban', *Guardian* (5 August 2023), https://www.theguardian.com/world/2023/aug/04/canada-meta-news-ban-facebook-fake; Katie Paul and Steve Scherer, 'Exclusive: Meta's News Ban Fails to Dent Facebook Usage', *Reuters* (29 August 2023), https://www.reuters.com/technology/metas-canada-news-ban-fails-dent-facebook-usage-2023-08-29/.

107 Pickard, *Democracy Without Journalism?*, 156.

108 Schneider and Hasinoff, 'Mastodon Isn't Just a Replacement'.

109 On requiring commitment to public values in return for public financial support, see Geert-Jan Bogaerts, Jose van Dijck and Ethan Zuckerman, 'Creating PublicSpaces: Centering Public Values in Digital Infrastructures', *Digital Government: Research and Practice* 4(2) (2023), 1–13, at 8.

110 See Newman et al., *Reuters Institute Digital News Report 2023*, chapters 2–4.

111 Wendy Brown, *In the Ruins of Neoliberalism* (Columbia University Press, 2019); Anna Lowenhaupt Tsing, *The Mushroom at the End of the World: On the Possibility of Life in Capitalist Ruins* (Princeton University Press, 2015).

112 91.58 per cent: https://gs.stacounter.com/search-engine-market-share (accessed 18 October 2023). Curiously Baidu is the dominant search engine in China (72 per cent of market share and over half a billion monthly users

by 2020: Shobith Seth, 'Baidu vs Google: What's the Difference?', https:// www.investopedia.com/articles/investing/051215/baidu-vs-google-how-are-they-different.asp), but registers in global statistics as having only 1 per cent of the global market.

113 Vaidhyanathan, *The Googlization of Everything*. For a useful recent summary, see Astrid Mager, Ov Cristian Norocel and Richard Rogers, 'Advancing Search Engine Studies: The Evolution of Google Critique and Intervention', *Big Data & Society* (2023), https://doi.org/10.1177/20539517231191528.

114 Bernhard Rieder, 'What Is in PageRank? A Historical and Conceptual Investigation of a Recursive Status Index', *Computational Culture* 2 (2012), http://computationalculture.net/what_is_in_pagerank/; Noble, *Algorithms of Oppression*.

115 Norocel and Levandowsky, 'Google, Data Voids'.

116 Jutta Haider and Malte Rödl, 'Google Search and the Creation of Ignorance: The Case of the Climate Crisis', *Big Data & Society* (2023), https://doi.org /10.1177/20539517231158997, quotation at 10, and see especially 7–8.

117 Benjamin Toff, Ruth Palmer and Rasmus Kleis Nielsen, *Avoiding News: Reluctant Audiences for Journalism* (Columbia University Press, 2023), 138.

118 For more detail, see the appendix published by the UK Competition and Markets Authority on 'search quality and economies of scale' for its 2020 report on Online Platforms and Digital Marketing: https://assets.publishing. service.gov.uk/media/5fe4957c8fa8f56aeff87c12/Appendix_I_-_search_ quality_v.3_WEB_.pdf, 24; wider report at https://www.gov.uk/cma-cases/ online-platforms-and-digital-advertising-market-study#final-report.

119 https://gs.stacounter.com/search-engine-market-share (accessed 18 October 2023).

120 https://en.wikipedia.org/wiki/DuckDuckGo (accessed 18 October 2023).

121 https://www.mojeek.com; https://www.qwant.com.

122 Tom Dotan, 'Even AI Hasn't Helped Microsoft's Bing Chip Away at Google's Search Dominance', *Wall Street Journal* (17 August 2023), https://www.wsj .com/tech/ai/microsoft-bing-search-artificial-intelligence-google-competition -6e51ec04.

123 Google's payment to Apple was revealed only recently; its amount has never been disclosed. A recent estimate put it at US$16–17 billion a year: Dan Gallagher, 'Apple's Easy Google Money May Get Harder to Keep', *Wall Street Journal* (9 October 2023), https://www.wsj.com/tech/ apples-easy-google-money-may-get-harder-to-keep-7fe55409.

124 https://opensearchfoundation.org/en/.

125 Dirk Lewandowski, 'Why We Need an Independent Index of the Web', in R. König and M. Rasch (eds.), *Society of the Query Reader* (Institute of Network Cultures, 2014), 50–58.

126 Developer for Open Web Index, quoted Astrid Mager, 'European Search? How to Counter-Imagine and Counteract Hegemonic Search With European Search Engine Projects', *Big Data & Society* (2023), https://doi.org/10.1177/20539517231163173, 6.

127 https://signal.org/; https://proton.me/mail; https://frontporchforum.com/.

128 https://discord.com/. And see https://en.wikipedia.org/wiki/Discord.

129 For the internet as surveillance space, see Philip Agre, '"Surveillance and Capture": Two Models of Privacy', *The Information Society* 10(2) (1994): 101–27; Paul Schwartz, 'Internet Privacy and the State', *Connecticut Law Review* 32 (1999): 815–59.

130 Sandel, *What Money Can't Buy*.

131 Robert Wuthnow, *Communities of Discourse* (Harvard University Press, 1989), 9, 17, 548, 552.

132 On public values and platforms, see van Dijck et al., *The Platform Society*.

133 Lauren Berlant, 'The Commons: Infrastructures for Troubling Times', *Environment and Planning D: Society and Space* 34(3) (2016): 393–419; K. Sabeel Rahman, 'Infrastructure Regulation and the New Utilities', *Yale Journal on Regulation* 35 (2018): 911–39.

134 Ethan Zuckerman and Chand Rajendra-Nicolucci (2023), 'From Community Governance to Customer Service and Back Again: Re-examining Pre-Web Models of Online Governance to Address Platforms' Crisis of Legitimacy', *Social Media & Society* (2023), https://doi.org/10.1177/20563051231196864. See also Gowden, *The New Leviathan*.

135 Ethan Zuckerman, *What Is Digital Public Infrastructure?*, Center for Journalism and Liberty (November 2020), https://www.journalismliberty.org/publications/what-is-digital-public-infrastructure, 8.

136 https://newpublic.org/; https://www.humanetech.com/.

137 https://publicspaces.net/, https://pubhubs.net/en/. And see PublicSpaces' manifesto at https://publicspaces.net/english-section/manifesto/.

138 See response on PubHubs' website to the FAQ 'How Does PubHubs Compare to Decentralized Platforms Such as Mastodon?'

139 Zuckerman, *What Is Digital Public Infrastructure?*, 10, 14.

140 https://publicspaces.net/english-section/ (accessed 19 October 2023).

141 https://mayfirst.coop/en/.

142 Paul Romer, 'A Tax That Could Fix Big Tech', *New York Times* (6 May 2019), https://www.nytimes.com/2019/05/06/opinion/tax-facebook-google.html#:~:text=Putting%20a%20levy%20on%20targeted,change%20their%20dangerous%20business%20models.&text=Mr.,Nobel%20in%20economics%20in%202018.

143 Zuckerman, *What Is Digital Public Infrastructure?*, 10.

144 Myria Georgiou and Koen Leurs, 'Smartphones as Personal Digital Archives?

Recentring Migrant Authority as Curating and Storytelling Subjects', *Journalism* 23(3) (2022): 668–89; Arjun Appadurai, 'Traumatic Exit, Identity Narratives, and the Ethics of Hospitality', *Television & New Media* 20(6) (2019): 558–65. But mobile phone and social media also operate as surveillance systems for authorities: Lilie Chouliaraki and Myria Georgiou, 'The Digital Border: Mobility Beyond Territorial and Symbolic Divides', *European Journal of Communication* 34(6) (2019): 594–605.

145 Trebor Scholz and Nathan Schneider (eds.), *Ours to Hack and Own* (OR Books, 2017). For quotation, see in that book Trebor Scholz, 'How Platform Cooperativism Can Unleash the Network', 20–6, at 23.

146 Yochai Benkler, 'The Realism of Cooperativism', in Scholz and Schneider, *Ours to Hack*, 91–5.

147 Rankin, *A People's History of Computing*.

148 Van Dijck et al., 'Deplatformization', 3448–52.

149 On the potential role of local communities in the management of the underlying infrastructure of the digital world, such as data centres, see Julia Rone, 'The Shape of the Cloud: Contesting Data Centres' Construction in North Holland', *New Media & Society* (2023), https://doi.org/10.1177/14614448221145928.

150 Gehl and Zulli, 'Digital Covenant'.

151 Daniel Heslep and PS Berge, 'Mapping Discord's Darkside: Distributed Hate Networks on Disboard', *New Media & Society* (2021), https://doi.org/10.1177/14614448211062548.

152 Heslep and Berge, 'Mapping Discord's Darkside', 16. Mastodon encountered a variation of this problem, when Gab, after adopting Mastodon's code, started to rely on third-party apps listed on Mastodon's central pages to gain visibility on the platform, but it appears that most, if not all, those apps decided to block this, so sealing off this alternative entry-point: Robertson, 'How the Biggest Decentralized Network'.

153 Peter Kollock and Marc Smith, 'Managing the Virtual Commons: Cooperation and Conflict in Computer Communities', in Susan Herring (ed.), *Computer-Mediated Communication* (John Benjamins, 1996), pp. 109–28, at 115, summarising Elinor Ostrom, *Governing the Commons* (Cambridge University Press, 1990).

154 Sasha Costanza Chock, *Design Justice: Community-Led Practices to Build the Worlds We Need* (MIT Press, 2020); Arturo Escobar, *Designing for the Pluriverse* (Duke University Press, 2018).

155 *The Nation* (14 April 2022), https://www.thenation.com/article/society/elon-musk-twitter-board/. Compare Pickard, *Democracy Without Journalism?*.

156 Taylor Hatmaker, 'Jack Dorsey Says His Biggest Regret Is That Twitter Was a Company At All', *TechCrunch* (26 August 2022), https://techcrunch.com/2022/08/26/jack-dorsey-biggest-regret/.

157 Nick Srnicek, 'We Need to Nationalise Google, Facebook and Amazon. Here's Why', *Guardian* (30 August 2017), https://www.theguardian.com/commentisfree/2017/aug/30/nationalise-google-facebook-amazon-data-monopoly-platform-public-interest; Evgeny Morozov, 'Socialize the Data Centres', *New Left Review* 91 (2015): 45–66; Jeremy Gilbert and Alex Williams, *Hegemony Now: How Big Tech and Wall Steet Won the World (and How to Win It Back* (Verso, 2022), 242.

158 Tarnoff, *Internet for the People*, 154–5. Even Ethan Zuckerman, an advocate of more community control on commercial platforms, notes its limits (Zuckerman and Rajendra-Nicolucci, 'From Community Governance to Customer Service', 10). The limits of public deliberation's role around corporate platforms also affects the reform proposals of Jamie Susskind, *The Digital Republic* (Bloomsbury, 2022).

159 https://small-tech.org/ (accessed 27 October 2023). Compare the IndieWeb project's vision of reorganising the internet on a 'people-focused' basis: https://indieweb.org/.

160 Jeremy Gilbert, *Twenty First Century Socialism* (Polity, 2020), 31–2.

161 Ibid., 69.

162 Ibid., 46.

163 'There are ideas, and ways of thinking, with the seeds of life in them, and there are others, perhaps deep in our minds, with the seeds of a general death' (Raymond Williams, *Culture and Society* [Penguin, 1958], 323).

Index

Page numbers in *italics* refer to a figure

263